DIGITAL TEXTILE DESIGN

LAURENCE KING

First published in Great Britain in 2009.
Second edition published in 2012 by
Laurence King Publishing in association
with Central Saint Martins College of
Art & Design

This book has been produced by
Central Saint Martins Book Creation,
Southampton Row, London,
WC1B 4AP, United Kingdom

Laurence King Publishing,
361-373 City Road, London,
EC1V 1LR, United Kingdom
T +44 20 7841 6900
F +44 20 7841 6910
enquiries@laurenceking.com
www.laurenceking.com

ISBN: 978 1 78067 002 7
A catalog record for this book is
available from the British Library.

Text by Melanie Bowles
and Ceri Isaac
Additional text for chapter 6
by Amanda Briggs-Goode
Tutorial 20 by Kenny Taylor

Design by Eleanor Ridsdale Design

Cover: Deja Abati, www.dejaabati.com

Melanie Bowles dedicates this book to
Eve, Maya, and Ben

Printed in China

LAURENCE KING PUBLISHING

DIGITAL TEXTILE DESIGN

SECOND EDITION

MELANIE BOWLES AND CERI ISAAC

CONTENTS:

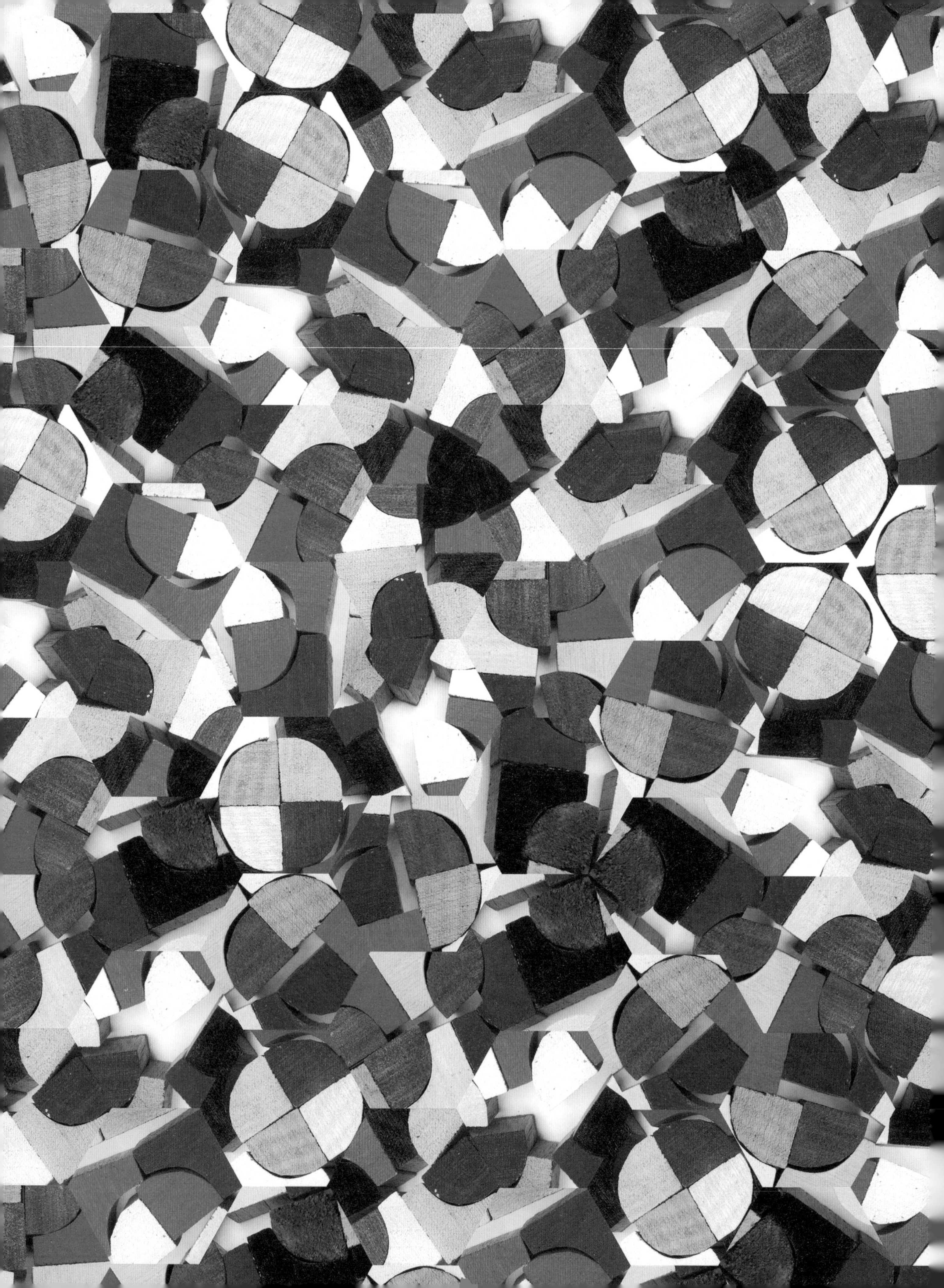

INTRODUCTION

Digital technology is changing the face of textile design, from methods of creating and presenting designs to the ways in which they are realized. Working in a digital environment, designers are afforded more time to experiment, explore, and create, while manufacturing technologies offer innovative new printing solutions. This practical and inspirational book examines a new era of textile design and features clear tutorials and case studies revealing how digital techniques are being employed in the fashion, interior design, and home furnishings industries.

The development of digital printing onto fabric is changing printing methods and removing the restrictions that textile designers have traditionally faced: freed from concerns about repeat patterns and color separation that are key considerations in screen and roller printing, designers are able to work with thousands of colors and create designs with a high level of detail. There is also greater freedom for experimentation, as one-off production is now possible as well as small print runs and prints engineered specifically to fit within a garment.

Software programs such as Adobe Photoshop and Illustrator present the perfect platform for textile design. These have become the industry standard tools for textile designers, offering them the freedom to work with both bitmap and vector-based imagery, manipulate drawings and photography, and create accurate details and graphic effects.

While digital printing allows a rich mix of layered imagery, the surface and tactile qualities associated with some methods of traditional printing can be lost: as a result designers are finding ways to put these qualities back into the fabric using techniques such as overprinting and embellishment, and this combination of digital and handcrafted techniques has even created a new hybrid craft.

Whatever your interest in textiles—whether you are a student or professional, designer or producer—you will find this to be an essential and comprehensive guide to an exciting new field that is pushing the boundaries of textile design.

1
TEXTILE DESIGN AND PRINT IN THE DIGITAL AGE

NEW DIRECTIONS IN TEXTILE DESIGN

As the most significant advance in fabric-printing technology since the invention of the silk screen, digital textile printing is bringing about a revolution in textile design. Designers are seeking inspiration from previously unexplored sources, and a new visual language for surface design is starting to evolve.

The cross-disciplinary use of graphics software, digital photography, video, and special effects by a hybrid generation of young designers is creating a new look for printed fabrics. Fashion designers such as Issey Miyake, Hussein Chalayan, and Comme des Garçons have continued to utilize and adapt digital design and production technologies and are breaking new ground with the creation and use of highly innovative prints that make little reference to traditional patterns: florals have been reinvented through the use of photography, and geometric designs as the focal point of a garment have been given a futuristic edge by designers such as Jonathan Saunders. The process is now widely used in runway fashion collections today, through the use of large engineered or placement prints where the artwork is tailored to fit the structure of the garment. Designers working in other areas such as costume, theater, interior, and product design are also finding it easier to involve themselves in the creation of surface designs for their work. The accessibility of this technology through the use of service bureaus also makes it possible for artists and designers who do not have specialist knowledge of textile printing to design and produce their own fabrics and decorative surfaces.

The use of digital print has rapidly established itself within fashion and textile design, although, due to its high production costs, the major creative developments are to be found in the mid- to high end of the fashion and textile design industry (as demonstrated by the range of examples shown in this chapter). But already it is drawing together disciplines such as textiles, fashion, and interior design, changing the way that designers work. Increasingly, the integration of print is becoming as vital to the designer's vision as the form of the garment or product itself, due to the immediacy and spontaneity of digital tools.

This chapter looks at the impact of this new technology on textile design and explores the work of both well-known and emerging designers who are using computer-aided design and digital print to their full potential throughout a wide range of applications.

From top to bottom:
Danish designer Dorte Agergaard places everyday objects in unusual contexts for her furnishing range.

Mark Van Gennip, "Ink Storm" (2008): In this experimental work, the post-print process was interrupted to create an organic digital print.

The design on Trust Fun's "Glory Scarf Money Bag" was created using fractal software. Each design is a mathematically valid fractal based on a unique equation and cannot be replicated.

Clockwise from top:
Alexander McQueen, F/W 10: Skulls and bones are the basis for these technically brilliant digital prints, which cover the entire garment.

Basso & Brooke, "Madame Brun," F/W 09: Digital design creates a new contour for the figure.

Mary Katrantzou's S/S 11 trompe l'oeil print collection "This Is Not a Room" creates a three-dimensional interior view with garment shapes inspired by lampshades and fringing.

Jonathan Saunders's F/W 11 collection, inspired by 1940s art deco design, features an elegant and sophisticated use of digital design and print.

DIGITAL TEXTILE PRINTING

The digital printing of textiles grew out of reprographic technologies originally developed for paper and signage printing, and it now offers the same advantages to the textile industry that digital production affords the paper- and banner-printing businesses. For individual designers and hobbyists it is analogous to the rise of desktop publishing, albeit more costly. Technology was slower to emerge in the textile industry because of the need to develop suitable inks and large-format printers specifically designed to accommodate woven as well as stretchable cloth. With the emergence of large-format digital textile printers, such as the Mimaki in 1998, and then the release of industrial-scale printers in 2003 by companies such as Konica, Minolta, Reggiani, Robustelli, and Dupont, there is now the potential for major changes in the textile and fashion industries in terms of increased speed and long run capability. The introduction of the Isis printer by Osiris in 2008 means that the speed of inkjet printing machines may begin to rival that of traditional rotary screen printing.

Digital printing has perhaps four main advantages over traditional printing: speed of translation of the design onto the fabric; the ability to print intricate details and millions of colors; the possibility of producing very large-scale images; lessened impact on the environment. Traditional methods of printing based on processes similar to stenciling—including silk screen, woodblock, and gravure—first require that a separate template for each color be made, and for the image to then be built up in stages as each color must be laid down separately. The more colors, the more expensive and time consuming the process, so the number of colors is limited by practical considerations, often placing considerable restraints upon the designer. Repeated patterns are the norm in industrialized traditional textile printing, and very large-scale images are also impractical as the size of the design is constrained to the exact measurements of the template.

Digital printing means that there is virtually no limit to the kinds of images that may accurately be reproduced using inkjet technology. It is this exciting advantage that has paved the way for the new styles of design that are explored in this chapter.

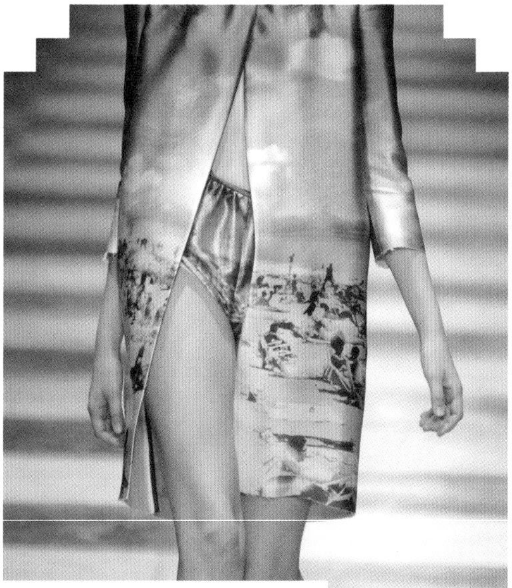

From top to bottom:
Prada's S/S 10 ready-to-wear collection featuring faded postcard beach scenes evoked the nostalgia of summer holidays.

Hussein Chalayan's S/S 09 collection was based on crushed cars, meticulously painted and then digitally printed to retain the painted detail.

Christopher Kane's 2011 Resort collection takes to the skies with this "Galaxy" print dress.

A NEW VISUAL LANGUAGE

Historically, the introduction of new technology does not usually result in an immediate change in design styles. Initially, design for any industrial application continues to follow the style associated with the preceding technology; the first automobiles, for example, were designed to resemble horse-drawn carriages. Change only begins to occur once practitioners come to understand the potential of a new technology and are comfortable with it.

Heat-transfer printing aside, the introduction of inkjet printing for textiles has meant that textile designers are now able to catch up with graphic designers by exploring the possibilities of computer-aided design (CAD). The early design styles that resulted from the introduction of digital imaging were often obviously computer-generated; the focus was on displaying technology for its own sake rather than using CAD as a tool for achieving a more sophisticated visual effect. A more mature style of digital textile design is now evolving due to increased experimentation by designers, who are creating designs based on scanned or digitally photographed subjects, facilitating effects such as trompe l'oeil as well as graphic and illustrative styles that are only possible using computerized drawing and manipulation tools. Designers are also beginning to combine digital print with traditional techniques to create a new digital craft, which is explored in Chapter Five.

Couture designer Ralph Rucci used dramatically large scale in his F/W 09 collection.

DIGITAL SURFACE DESIGN AND PHOTOGRAPHY

The use of photography first became noticeable in textile design in the 1960s and 1970s, when dye-sublimation (or heat-transfer) printing onto synthetic high-polymer content fabrics such as polyester first became prevalent. As software packages that could manipulate imagery, such as Adobe Photoshop, were not yet available, designs tended to be based on photomontage or collage, such as the ubiquitous "disco" shirts of the 1970s.

Being able to manipulate and transform an image digitally means that incorporating photography into textile design is now much more sympathetic to the nature of cloth as a material. Cloth comes to life in a way that paper does not: it moves, reflects light, and is often transparent or highly textured. Photographs formatted as if for printing onto paper can make a stark and incongruous statement when translated onto fabric. Designing a textile often involves a very different sensibility from that inherent in pure photography. On paper, photographs are usually intended as narrative documents, whereas the hybrid use of photography in textile design has begun to create a very different style in which the image is subtle or abstracted.

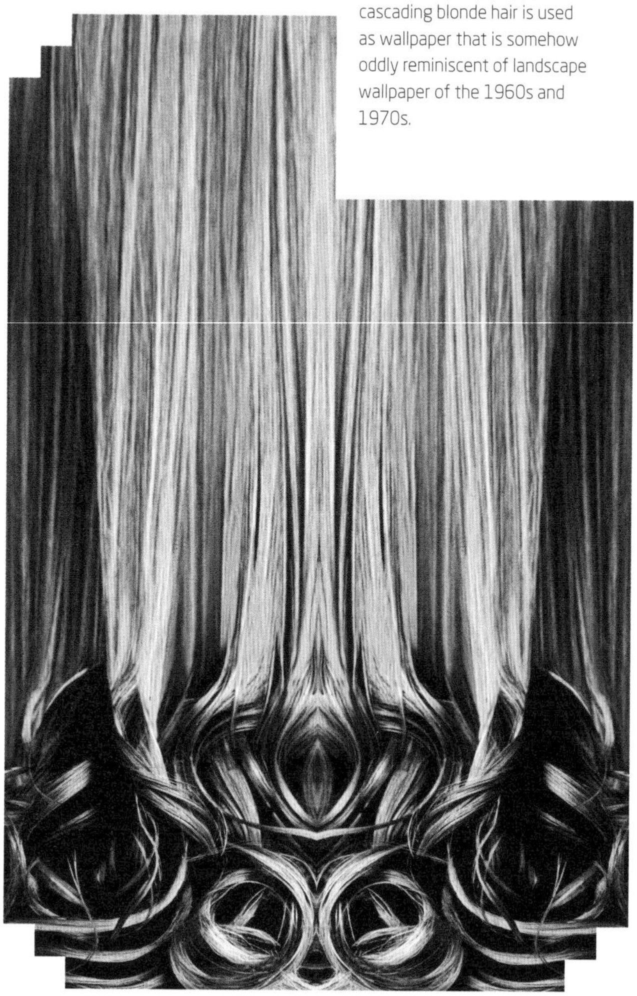

Nicolette Brunklaus is a Dutch designer who makes very clever use of digital print in her line of home furnishings. This hugely enlarged photograph of cascading blonde hair is used as wallpaper that is somehow oddly reminiscent of landscape wallpaper of the 1960s and 1970s.

Paul Smith is a pioneer of digital surface design, using inkjet prints in both his menswear and womenswear collections. The majority of his digital textile designs are photographic in style, such as this daffodil-print dress.

Showroom Dummies, a group of British designers headed by Abigail Lane, use digital imaging as the focal point for their work. This British company produces an eclectic range of products that spans home furnishings and clothing. Their signature print, shown here, of clouds and flies against a blue sky is both surreal and humorous.

Above: This design is a collaboration between Ceri Isaac and Hitoshi Ujiie. An object was specially created and photographed, and then the motif was isolated, abstracted, and layered transparently to form the design.

Left: Ceri Isaac's work uses photographs or textures that are reminiscent of traditional patterns and are not too obviously computer generated. This pattern of birds in flight was made by taking motion stills from video footage by Martin Stumph and collaging selected areas together in Photoshop. The colors were also enhanced in Photoshop.

GRAPHIC AND ILLUSTRATIVE STYLES

As the generation that has come of age in the digital era, many young and emerging textile designers have begun to use digital prints in their collections. For some it provides a natural foundation for the conceptualization of their work, and they seamlessly integrate their other design skills as graphic and illustrative artists into the creation of each piece of work.

Mary Katrantzou's F/W 11 collection features opulent prints of birds, florals, and mosaic formations. The print dictates the shape of the garment, giving a new silhouette.

Katie Eary used digital printing in her powerful and striking F/W 10 menswear collection.

Stefan Sagmeister's "Darwin Chair" (2009/10) utilizes a free, swinging structure that includes about 200 sheets of attached prints. As the top sheet gets dirty, the user simply rips it off, thereby transforming the chair's appearance.

Lucinda Abell's talent as an illustrator is apparent in the beautifully drafted fairytale images and intricate floral designs she created for her graduation fashion collection.

TROMPE L'OEIL

Trompe l'oeil, a French expression that translates as "trick of the eye," is used to describe extremely realistic imagery created to give the illusion that the depicted objects really exist, instead of being what they really are—a two-dimensional image. This is a style that lends itself especially well to digital design.

For this "hair cut" shirt, created for her MA collection, London College of Fashion graduate Jula Reindell plays with our perception of a two-dimensional surface.

Danish designer Dorte Agergaard recreates everyday objects in interior spaces using trompe l'oeil.

Imogen Houldsworth's "Private View" collection features a subtle illusion of cracked paint.

DESIGN ADVANTAGES

As we have already touched upon, digital textile printing has some major advantages over traditional printing methods in design terms. These are: immediacy; the ability to print intricate details and millions of colors as well the possibility of printing images on a much larger scale; being able to create customized products and engineered designs.

The immediacy of digital tools in the rapid transformation of ideas into finished garments is crucial in the high-speed world of fashion. Experimentation and the evolution of a concept through a process of trial and error is an essential part of the creative process, and digital print is the perfect tool to facilitate this.

Prior to the introduction of inkjet textile printing, with the exception of heat-transfer printing onto polyester-based fabrics, it was not possible to translate the millions of colors required to reproduce all the nuances of images such as oil paintings, watercolors, or photographs onto natural-fiber fabrics. Printers such as the Mimaki TX2 are capable of printing much finer lines than is possible using traditional rotary screens (see Chapter Six), and millions of colors may be used in a single image.

In addition to the design advantages offered by digital printing, inkjet textile printing is significantly more eco-friendly than traditional rotary and flatbed silk-screen methods. According to some estimates, digital printers consume 50 percent less energy than traditional rotary screen-printing machines. There is also less wastage of materials as less dye or pigment is used in laying down the image than in traditional industrial methods, and water is saved as there are no screens to wash.

LARGE-SCALE PRINTS

With traditional printing techniques, repeats were constrained to the size of the pattern block, the size of the screen, or the circumference of the roller, thus limiting the scale of the pattern. By eliminating the screen, digital print has transformed textile design, and the designer's decision to use a repeated pattern is an aesthetic choice rather than a technical necessity.

The use of digital tools such as Photoshop and Illustrator in conjunction with the ability to print on a larger scale makes it easier to create designs that fit the pattern piece for a garment exactly. Such designs are known as "engineered" or "placement" prints. All the pattern pieces containing the print may then be grouped together as "a lay plan" that is ready to cut and sew. This technique can also be taken one step further—into the realm of custom design.

Joan Truckenbrod is an artist at the Art Institute of Chicago who has been creating computer-generated images since the 1970s. She was among the first artists to explore digital fabric printing as a fine art form. Her digitally printed image of swimming fish was floated in Brush Creek, Kansas City.

Michael Angove's exquisite bespoke Chinoiserie wallpapers are printed digitally. "Dill" is a non-repeating panorama printed in England on traditional wallpaper. The design was built from specialized 3-D scans of plants.

LAY PLANS

In his F/W 07/08 collection, Hussein Chalayan experimented with scanning and digitally manipulating the fabrics used in his ready-to-wear collection, creating a trompe l'oeil effect that captured the textures of the weave. Once these textures and patterns were digitized, they were overlaid as transparent layers and laid out as geometric shapes within the engineered pattern pieces, creating an unusual harmony.

Chalayan's prints are emblematic of his overall ability to fascinate by removing what has inspired him from its original context and then reconstructing something new. Below is the lay plan containing the printed pattern pieces used to create the garments; below at right are the garments as seen on the runway.

ENGINEERED PRINTS

An "engineered" or "placement" print is designed to fit the pattern pieces of a garment exactly. When the pattern pieces are assembled, the image or repeated design flows continuously around the form of the garment without being broken by the seams. These digitally tailored garments are perceived as being more luxurious because of the high levels of cost and time spent in producing them. Designers such as Tristan Webber, Hussein Chalayan, Jonathan Saunders, Basso & Brooke, and Alexander McQueen have all applied engineered print techniques using digital textile printing.

The fact that digital tools make it easier to create an engineered print is a very exciting prospect for fashion and textile designers alike, as both digital print and digitally fitted garments can be brought together. Designers may use geometric designs that follow the form of the body to enhance the sculptural effects of a garment's cut. Engineered prints may also be used more subtly to highlight elements such as cuffs, collars, and bodices.

Alexander McQueen's spectacular S/S 10 collection pushed the boundaries of what digital print can offer, with beautiful snake and reptile prints cleverly engineered to create amazing garments.

LARGE- AND SMALL-SCALE CUSTOMIZATION

Digital printing is ideally suited to the creation of limited-edition designs that are customized to suit the tastes of an individual client. The addition of body scanning, as well as the introduction of software that automatically generates pattern pieces based on the scanned data, streamlines the process of placing a printed design exactly within a garment.

A body scanner digitally captures measurements to create a virtual three-dimensional model of an individual's body. This means that not only is a tape measure no longer necessary when fitting a client, but also that many more measurements are taken than would be practical when performing a fitting by hand. Department stores such as Selfridges and Harrods in London and Bloomingdale's in Los Angeles now provide this service.

While digital printing can be used to make one-off fitted designs, the technology can also be used for mass customization. Companies such as Nike use the Internet as a vehicle for mass customization, providing customers with the ability to individualize and "build" a product by allowing them to choose certain options. If the choices are limited to certain colors and design elements, however, then the result will not be unique. Other companies such as Cloth construct one-of-a-kind pieces of upholstered furniture by digitally printing an image sent to them by the client.

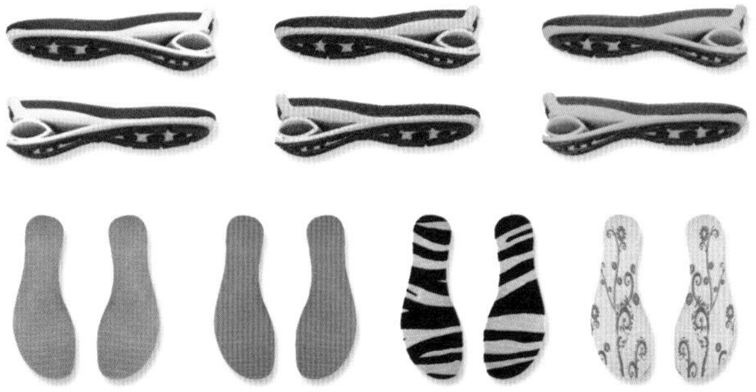

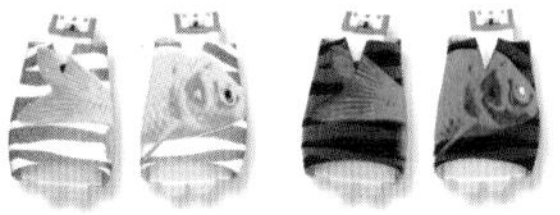

Austrian company Wexla have a modular shoe system that allows for both mass customization and a personalized product. Customers choose from a variety of shoe bases and uppers and may even upload their own image to be printed.

This footstool by Cloth has been personalized with the customer's own photographs.

CUSTOMIZED JEANS

For its centenary celebration in 2006/7, researchers at the London College of Fashion collaborated to explore how state-of-the-art technology could be used to create a one-of-a-kind garment. The idea was to design one-off fitted and digitally printed jeans, and the project integrated 3-D body scanning, automatic pattern generation, digital printing, and digital embroidery. The project explored how the technology could be used to streamline the process of engineering the print onto the garment, as well as testing the accuracy of matching an image across the seams.

Above: Image of the Manhattan skyline by Ceri Isaac printed onto jeans.

Right: The lay plan showing the pattern pieces.

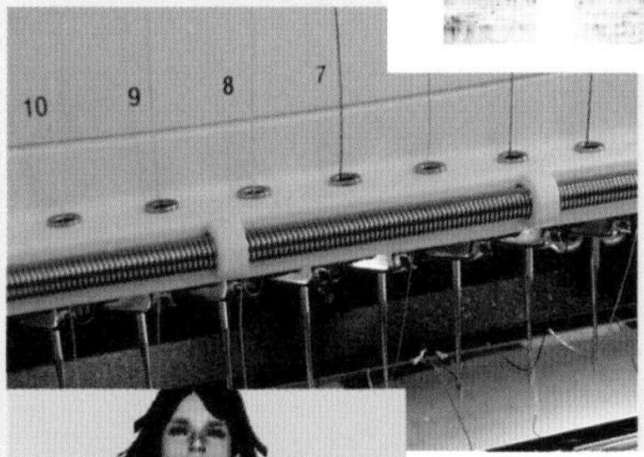

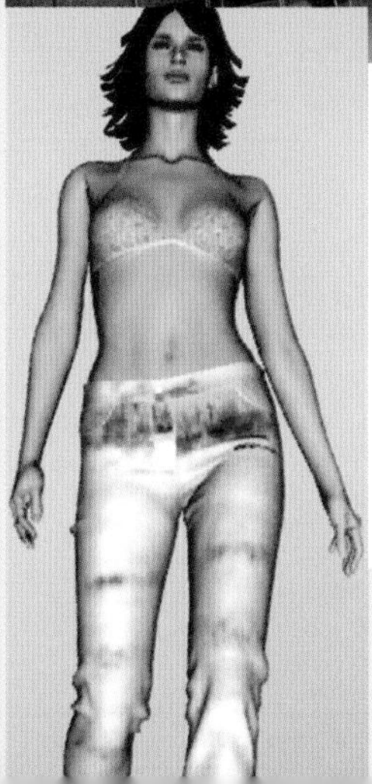

Above: Specialist software enables the embroidered areas to match up with the printed design.

Left: Still from an animated virtual runway. This digital "try-on" software meant that the concept for the jeans could be tested on an avatar before the design was finalized.

FASTER PRINT TIMESCALES

The fashion world moves at an extremely fast pace, and designers such as Paul Smith now have the added pressure of creating two collections for every season. Originality is crucial and it is hardly surprising that top designers are increasingly attracted to the possibilities that new technology has to offer in generating ideas for their collections. Digital design and printing are the perfect tools for high-speed fashion, as it is possible to deliver ready-to-wear fabric the same day, depending on the quantity required.

The speed with which fabric may be produced, together with the accessibility of design technology, is closing the gap between the textile design industry and its clients—the fashion and interior designers. In the West, the making of most printed and decorative textiles was historically the domain of specialist master craftsmen, their expertise acquired through many years of practice and apprenticeship. The textile and tailoring trades, although entirely dependent upon each other, were seen as separate professions. In catering for their wealthier clients, some designers would have commissioned special fabrics to suit their whims, but, for the most part, printed fabrics were bought from merchants stocking standard types of cloth. Digital print technology is changing this.

LOOKING TO THE FUTURE

A degree of separation between textile design and fashion is still the norm today. The current system of textile production supports the mass consumption of cheap goods and so reinforces the distance between the fashion and textile designer. Also, as fashion designers generally have higher profiles than textile designers, textile designers are sadly rarely credited alongside the name of the fashion designer who has used their design.

At the mid- to high end of the market, digital design and printing is rapidly closing the gap between textiles and fashion. Digital textile printing technology is advancing rapidly and has the potential to aid the creation of higher-quality goods. It may be hoped that, as digital design blurs the boundaries between professions such as fashion, textiles, and interior design, the consumer will come to value quality rather than quantity, and so move away from throwaway fashion and its harmful effect on the environment.

SPONTANEOUS FASHION

British designer Hussein Chalayan has used digital print to great effect in many of his collections. Since his graduate collection, when he began to experiment with garments that move independently of the body, his name has become synonymous with digital print technology.

The print for this dress from his S/S 07 "1011" collection is not quite what it first appears. The design evolved from a photograph that one of Chalayan's assistants took of the mannequin and muslin for the dress while documenting the design process. Chalayan and his team saw the potential to create a print from the slightly surreal imagery.

The figure in the photograph was isolated from its background, subtly recolored in Photoshop, then put into repeat, before being digitally printed. Viewed from a distance, the print resembles a traditional floral design, but when viewed closer up it reveals itself to be an entirely different motif. This is an excellent example of the immediacy that digital printing affords.

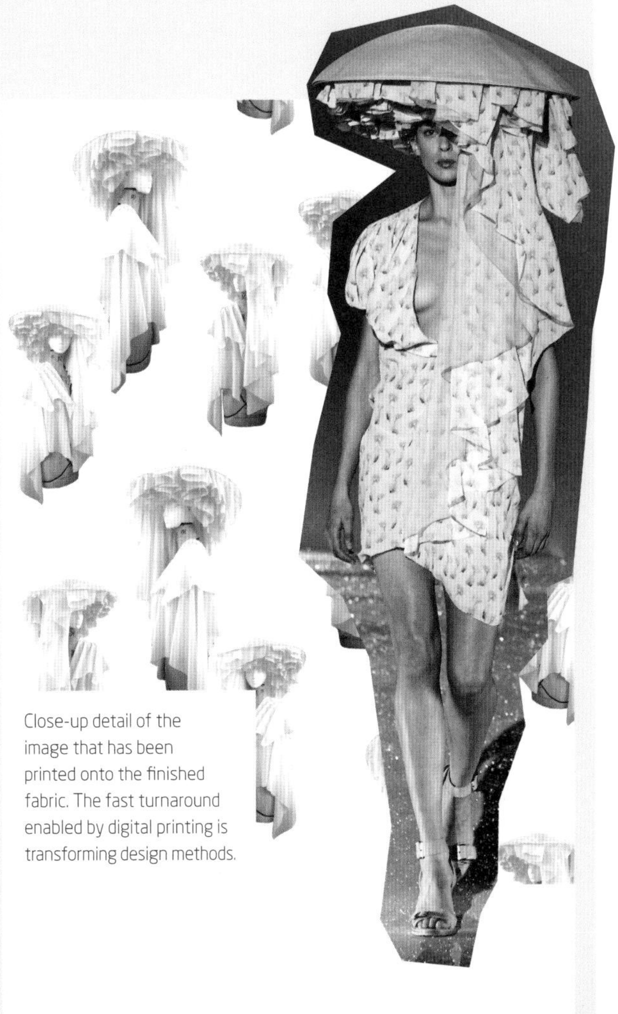

Close-up detail of the image that has been printed onto the finished fabric. The fast turnaround enabled by digital printing is transforming design methods.

2
DIGITAL DESIGN TUTORIALS

INTRODUCTION

Adobe Photoshop and Illustrator together offer a perfect platform for textile design. While the bitmap-based Photoshop gives you the freedom to edit and manipulate drawings and photographs, the vector-based Illustrator enables the creation of accurate graphic drawings and effects, such as streamlined shapes and sharp geometrics. Photoshop is programmed in such a way that an image is made up of a mosaic of individual colored pixels; the software itself does not automatically recognize shapes unless they have been separated out by the user. Motifs that are significantly enlarged, for example, will eventually lose their integrity and become "pixelated" so that fine lines appear jagged. The total number of pixels over an area is called the resolution, and this determines the quality of the image.

Illustrator creates a graphic image from a series of points, lines, curves, and shapes. Sophisticated and high-quality artwork and graphics can be created with the wide range of drawing tools on offer. Once an image is created it can be scaled indefinitely without degradation. It is possible to design solely using either Photoshop or Illustrator, or to work between the two—either way, they offer a perfect toolkit for textile design. The introduction of the digital stylus pen has also given fluidity to the action of drawing with the computer so that it is now more akin to drawing by hand.

Originally designed for the graphics industry, these tools are now leading textile designers along different avenues of creativity and extending the range of design possibilities available to them. Previously, designers were required to hand render their ideas and designs, which was often a time-consuming process, but working within a digital environment has speeded up this task. This allows more time for experimentation and exploration, thus freeing up the designer's imagination. Because these programs are now recognized as standard tools for textile designers, it is essential to acquire the skills to use them with confidence. With perseverance, designers will learn to use them intuitively, making them just as important as paint and brushes have always been. This chapter offers inspiration by demonstrating the wealth of possibilities that these programs give to the textile designer. With a series of step-by-step tutorials focusing on particular techniques that are relevant to textile design, amply illustrated with work by both students and established designers, this chapter is aimed at students who have already acquired a basic knowledge of Photoshop and Illustrator. It begins by looking at the skills and tools that underlie all good digital textile design, including research and drawing, the use of the scanner, the digital stylus pen, and the incorporation of photography.

Jemima Gregson's design "New York, New York" was created in Photoshop and digitally printed onto cotton canvas.

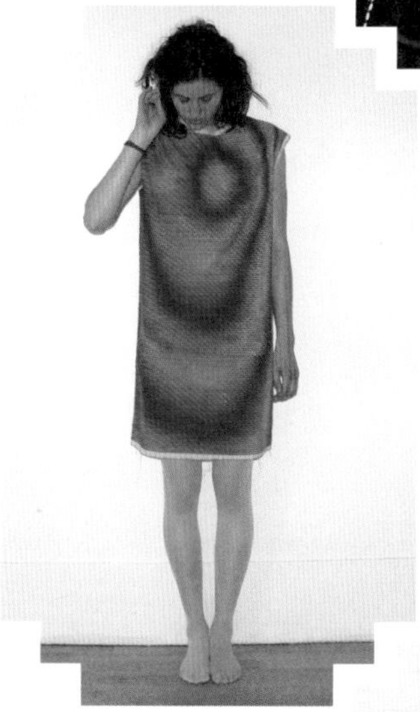

Marie O'Connor achieves a moiré effect through digital manipulation.

Rowenna Wilcox has fun with this paper-chain shirt from her collection "Lilian."

Claire Thorpe designed her fashion collection "Ballet Mécanique" entirely in Illustrator. Her inspiration came from the mechanical patterns found in Meccano toys and also in the work of Eduardo Paolozzi, which she then translated into graphic patterns. Thorpe's designs illustrate the crisp, clean lines that can be achieved using this vector-based program.

GETTING STARTED

When working digitally, the designer is faced with a vast array of options and it is all too easy to get carried away choosing between the technical effects and filters that are available at the click of a button. Consequently, it is vitally important to develop and explore ideas thoroughly before starting to work on the computer.

The starting point for a design can come from one of many sources. It might be a highly personal thought or experience that you want to express visually, or it might come from a commercial brief. Wherever it comes from, thorough research of the subject is essential, and the process can take you on an exciting and stimulating journey; one that may lead you to explore historical periods, other cultures from around the world, or contemporary design trends. You may even find inspiration in other creative disciplines such as fine art, literature, science, and music. Once a theme is established, the next stage is to gather material to help get the design underway. This can be anything from photographs, sketches, and drawings to found objects. It is important not to underestimate the amount of material needed; design work has now become a very sophisticated mix of graphic imagery, drawing, photography, pattern, texture, and motif. The more research, the greater the wealth of material you will have to work with, allowing your ideas and concept to develop fully. Explore ideas around the theme and collect anything that relates to it, gathering the material in a sketchbook to track the development of ideas and primary research. This sketchbook can then be referenced throughout the design process, and it can also act as a basis for discussion with your peers.

While you are researching your theme, you also need to keep the context for your design in mind and research the market. Historically, textile design has always had a very close relationship with fashion, whether for clothing or interiors, and so an awareness of contemporary trends is crucial. In our consumer society, buyers are constantly seeking the next new look. As a textile designer you need market awareness to stay on top of the game in this competitive field.

Kitty Joseph's collection "Color Immersion" was inspired by the play of light on the Thames River in London.

Beatrice Moys created designs for her "Building Blocks" collection by constructing wooden patterns.

Anjali D'Souza's travels to Egypt were the inspiration for her "Futuristic Traveller" collection.

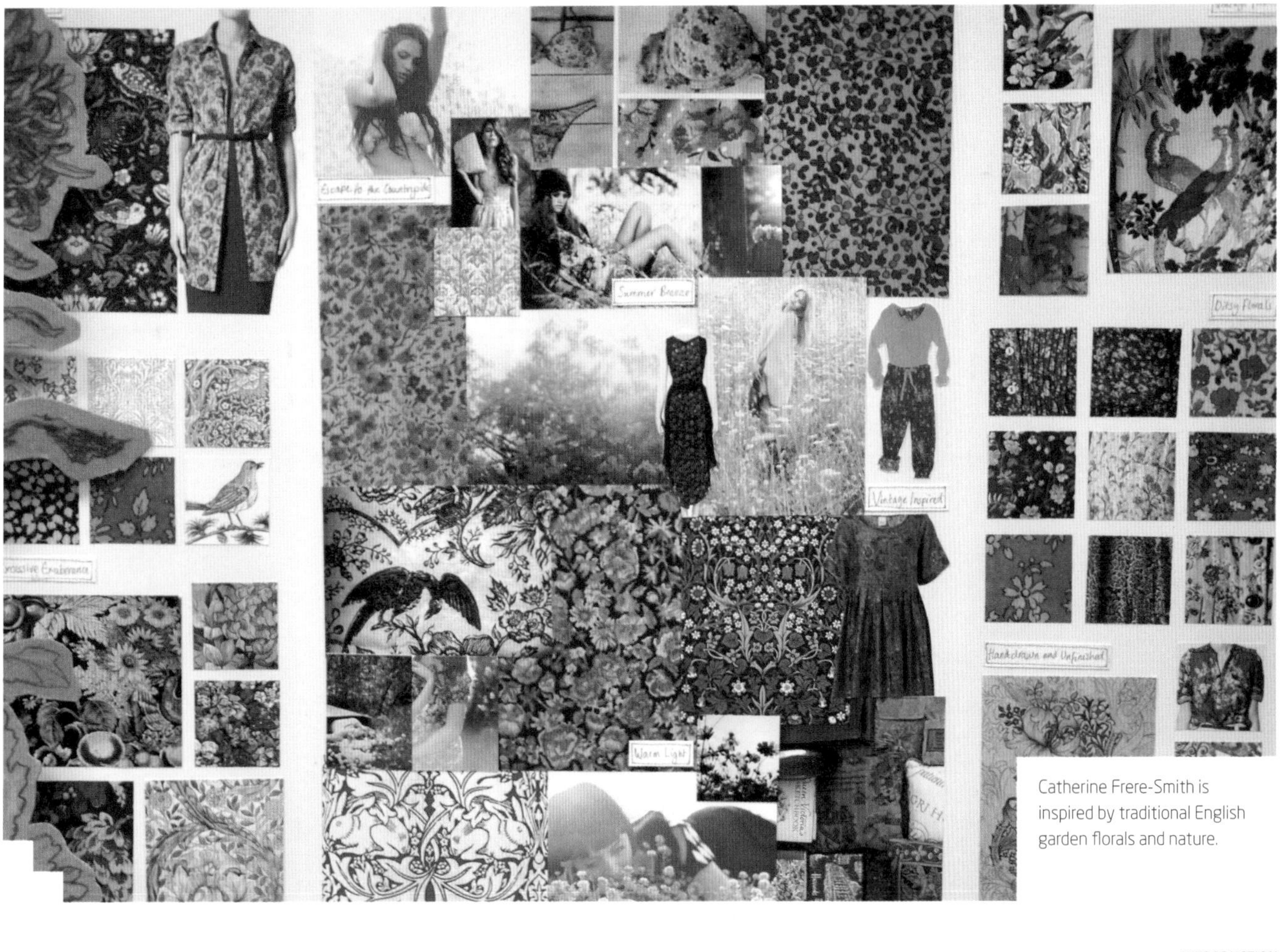

Catherine Frere-Smith is inspired by traditional English garden florals and nature.

SCANNING

Once you have gathered together all your material, you then need to assemble it into a form that you can work with digitally. Many of your items will be in two-dimensional form—such as drawings and photographs; others may be three-dimensional—such as buttons, textured fabrics, and trimmings. All of these elements can be scanned.

The scanner is an exciting tool for textile designers and has opened up a wide range of options for assembling imagery, allowing nondigital elements into the digital workspace. Designers, who are often magpies by nature, are able to experiment with real objects and imagery that they have collected, collaging them into designs that have a tactile quality and can also be highly personal, humorous, charming, and quirky.

Before you start scanning, it is important to know the final print output in dots per inch (dpi), as this determines the resolution required. Ideally, you should scan at the same dpi as the final output, and at the same dimensions as you wish to use the scan in your design. For a textile designer, the final output will usually be a collection of designs that are printed onto fabric or paper—usually 11 x 17 (tabloid) to 17 x 22 inches in size. To guarantee a high-quality image at this size, it is best to scan your raw materials at 300 dpi.

If you are outputting the design onto a length of fabric, you need to take more care. Textile designers often work on a large scale and may unwittingly create complex documents with file sizes that are too large to manage. One way to overcome this, if you are working in repeat, is to just give the printer the repeat unit. The printer will then use a specialist repeat program to fill the unit across whatever length of fabric that you require. Giving the repeat unit alone to the printer means that the document size is likely to be manageable, especially as the printer will usually request artwork at between 200 and 300 dpi.

When working with a large-scale placement or engineered design for fabric, you need to take extra care to maintain a balance between a high-enough resolution and a manageable document size. If you find your final artwork document becomes too large for your computer to manage, you will have to lower the resolution of the image gradually, while assessing the quality of the output.

File sizes generally become large when you scan in objects that are subsequently enlarged by a significant amount. In order to maintain the best photographic quality, scan objects at high resolution, so that when the object is reproduced at 100 percent in your design it is output at the required dpi. The box opposite provides the general rules that will allow you to reproduce good-quality imagery for print.

If your artwork is too large for the scanner, you may need to take it to a specialist bureau. A more complicated, but less expensive, alternative is to scan the work in sections and piece them together in Photoshop.

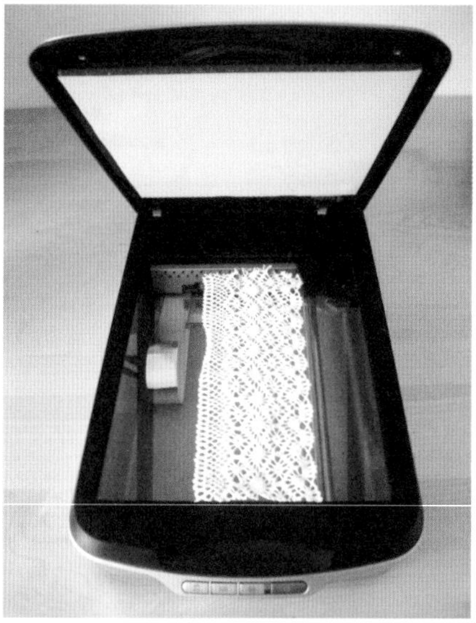

SCANNING QUALITY

From 8.5 x 11 to 17 x 22 inches:
Scan your work at 850 dpi;
your 17 x 22 inch artwork will be 300 dpi.

From 8.5 x 11 to 22 x 34 inches:
Scan your work at 600 dpi;
your 22 x 34 inch artwork will be 300 dpi.

From 8.5 x 11 to 34 x 44 inches:
Scan your work at 1300 dpi;
your 34 x 44 inch artwork will be 300 dpi.

NOTE ON COPYRIGHT

When scanning imagery for use in your designs, it is essential to be aware of copyright issues. Copyright is a form of intellectual property protection. It applies to artists' original work such as paintings, illustrations, photographs, maps, and any other work of craftsmanship. Scanning opens up a wide range of design opportunities and can sometimes be used as a quick design tool for copying and editing your work, but you must be aware that you should not scan other people's artwork as it may be copyright protected. Either use your own material to avoid infringing on copyright or be sure to use copyright-free imagery.

Kitty Joseph needs time and patience to create her intricate and complex collages from hand-colored paper. Once she has scanned her collages, however, she uses the speed of the computer to manipulate, compose, color, and edit her artwork further. The ability to preserve her images, once saved, gives her the freedom to experiment with color and layout without destroying her original artwork.

DRAWING

Drawing, sketching, and mark-making have always been solid starting points for design work. They are even more important in the digital age, in ensuring that work is original and that the designer's unique "handwriting" is not lost, but instead is enhanced, by the computer.

By starting with a beautiful set of drawings, you can scale, compose, and arrange them into a design collection using the basic transform tools in Photoshop. There is still skill involved in editing and assembling the drawings and merging them sensitively so that they do not simply look pasted together. Having a thorough understanding of the tools in Photoshop will allow you to choose the best method of selecting a drawing or motif and thereby retaining the feeling of fluid and sensitive artwork. Tools range from the Magic Wand tool (used to select flat colors) to more advanced tools, such as the Mask tool (used to select photography) or the Pen tool (used to draw accurately around an area and cut it out).

The detail and tone of Hana Kitazaki's beautifully fine hand-rendered drawings are captured perfectly by digital printing in her collection "The Magic Flute."

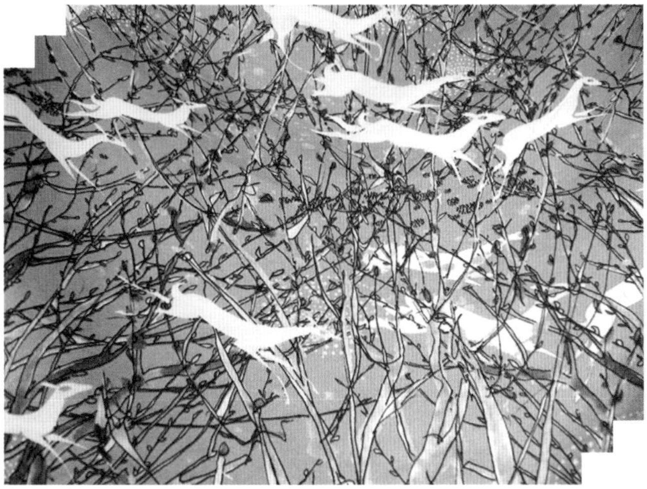

To replicate the softness and sensuality of the originals, Rosie MacCurrach uses the Quick Mask tool to select her drawings; she also feathers the edges so that the images blend softly together. Finally, she prints her designs onto silk, a fabric that allows her to maintain the delicate marks and blends present in her original drawings.

The computer allows Victoria Purver the freedom to translate her paintings onto fabric without losing any of the beautiful qualities achieved with her brush marks and drawing. She does not have to make color separations to screen-print them; instead she translates them directly onto fabric through digital printing. Her aim is to keep the sensual feel of the paintings when they are transferred onto cloth.

Deborah Vesey combines hand painting with a conceptual approach to maintain a spontaneous look for her digital collection.

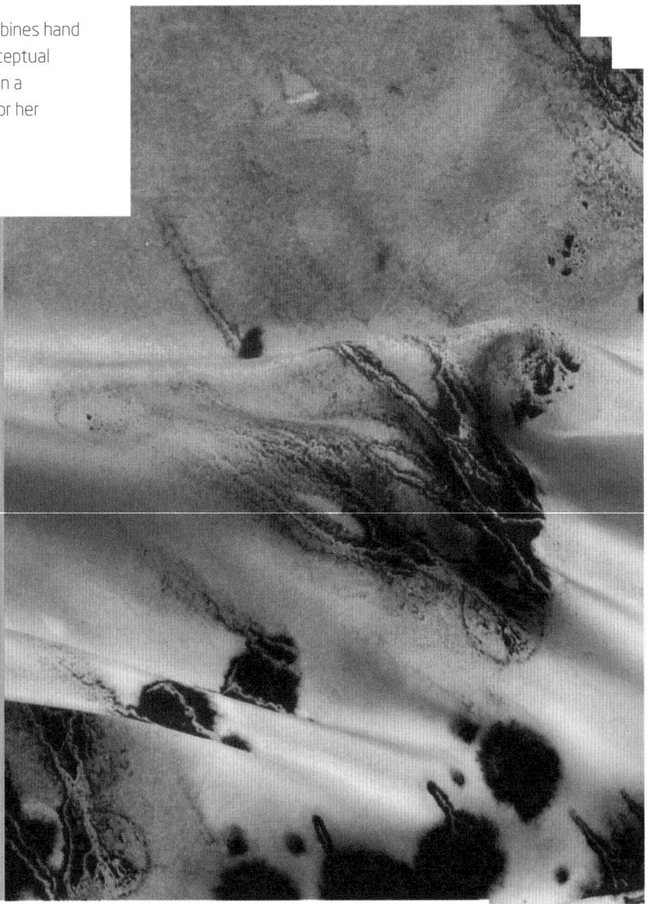

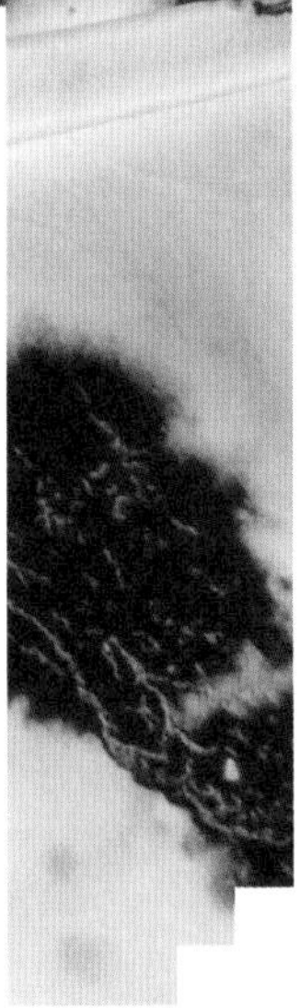

Rowenna Wilcox's collection "Lillian" is based on her grandmother's favorite ornaments.

Brian Barrett's inspiration for his "Classical/Contemporary Romantic" textile collection derives from vintage objects and antiques, including taxidermy. He looks at how collecting objects can harbor memories of the past and create new emotional attachments. Barrett created his own take on a traditional floral repeat that, on first viewing, is timeless and familiar. But by subtly weaving unconventional imagery into a traditional layout, the design took on a new meaning and narrative. The result is an intriguing mix of the bizarre and the familiar that creates a new look for textiles by mixing old and new methods in the design and print process.

Henry Muller created a woven effect for his menswear collection "The Outer Face," digitally printed onto heavy canvas.

THE DIGITAL STYLUS PEN

The introduction of the digital stylus pen has given artists the freedom to draw, paint, and sketch with a computer, in much the same way as if using traditional materials. You can draw directly onto a graphics tablet with the pen, or trace over an image, or even draw on the screen. Once mastered, the pen becomes an intuitive drawing tool, allowing the same freedom of movement and sensitivity as a traditional pen or brush. For the textile designer, the pen allows a sensitive and sensual approach to design and is a worthwhile investment. A pressure-sensitive stylus pen can also give depth to your lines, for a more natural way of drawing and rendering. In Photoshop you can even "harness" the numerous paintbrushes to it, allowing you to create effects ranging from subtle watercolors to bold line drawings. In Illustrator, the pen allows a high degree of dexterity and control when drawing.

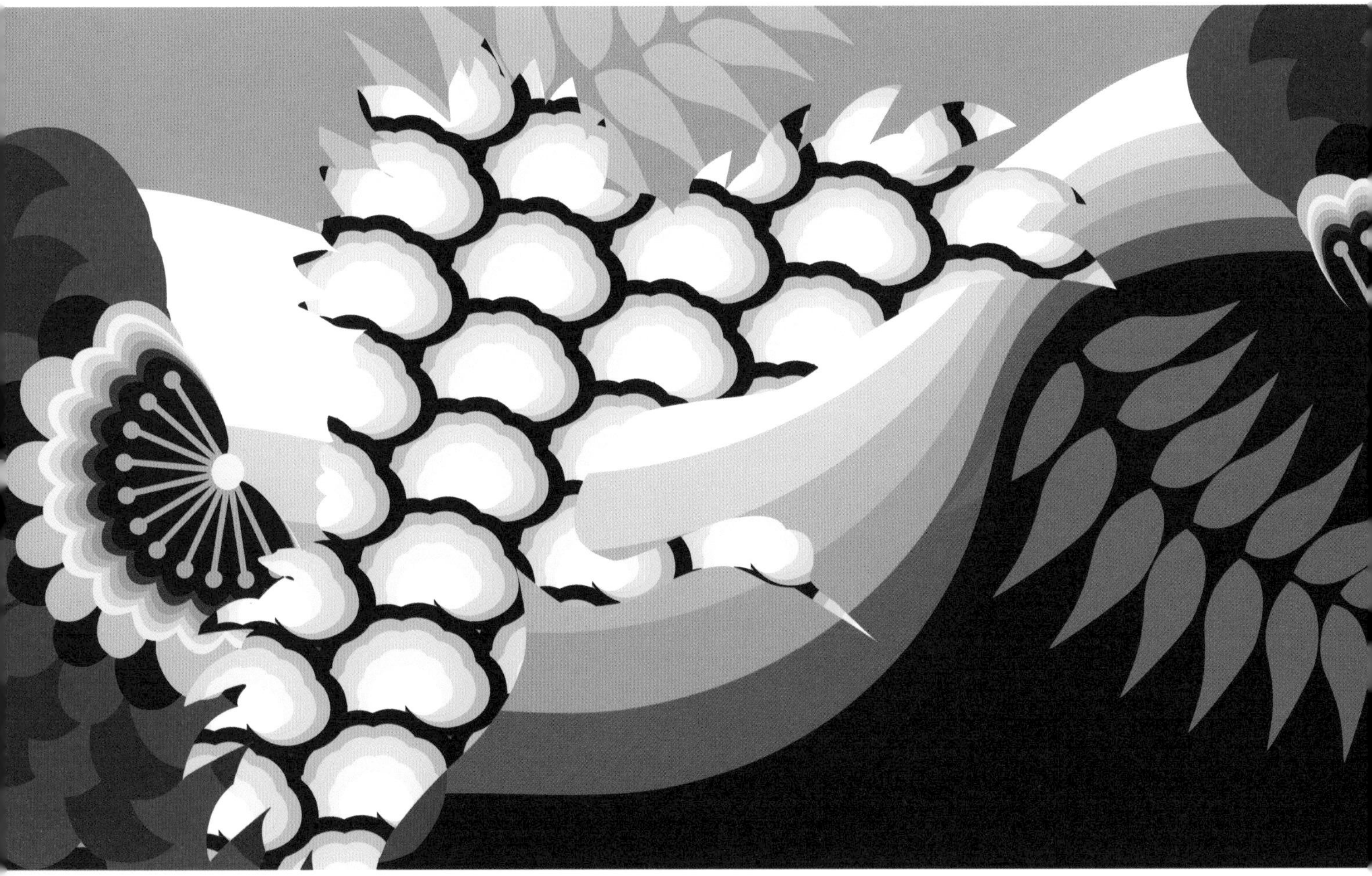

Melanie Bowles finds that using the stylus pen gives her the precision she needs to design in Illustrator. Her background in embroidered textiles influences not only her design aesthetic, but also how she uses the computer as a design tool. Bowles finds she can achieve the same dexterity with the stylus pen as with the embroiderer's needle, replicating the intricacies of fine stitchwork found in historical embroideries. Bowles uses the pen to draw streamlined shapes, build up motifs, and create subtle blends. She is able to create elegant, graphic designs by directly tracing from found or drawn imagery onto the screen with the pen. When printed onto silks, these designs become fluid and sensual.

PHOTOGRAPHY

Textile designers often make good photographers, having an eye for detail, texture, and color. It is no surprise, therefore, that with the ability to print high-quality photographic detail digitally, many students are now integrating photography into design.

Photography is an immensely useful medium for the textile designer, whether used directly in the design work or as a means of researching and collecting reference material. It can also be useful to draw and trace over photographs in Photoshop or Illustrator as a quick way of achieving an image outline.

The compact size of digital cameras means that many artists and designers use their cameras like sketchbooks or diaries, and are able to build up archives of imagery that they can access when needed. This approach is preferable to downloading images from the Internet because it avoids running into any copyright issues and, of course, the work is unique and personal.

Once you have imported your images into Photoshop you will find a huge number of options to help you adapt your photographs.

Melanie Bowles and Kathryn Round gave a vintage dress a second life by photographing it and digitally printing it on silk crêpe de Chine.

Alexa Ball's womenswear collection "Holiday Memories" incorporates childhood vacation photographs in complex pattern formations to achieve a quirky, nostalgic design.

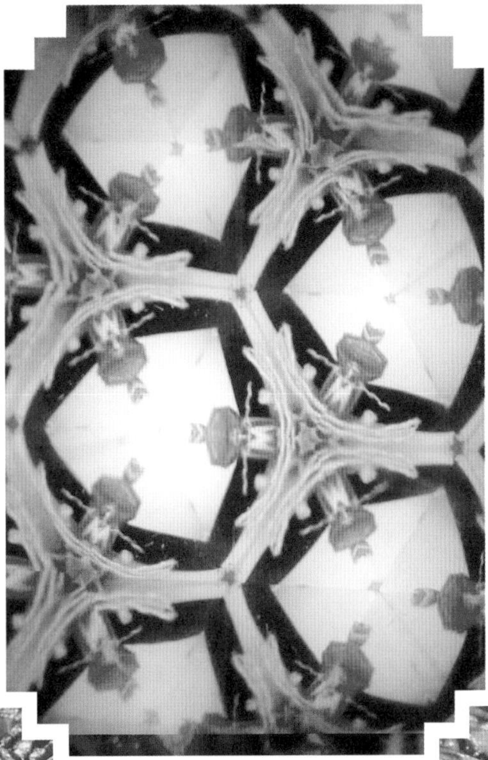

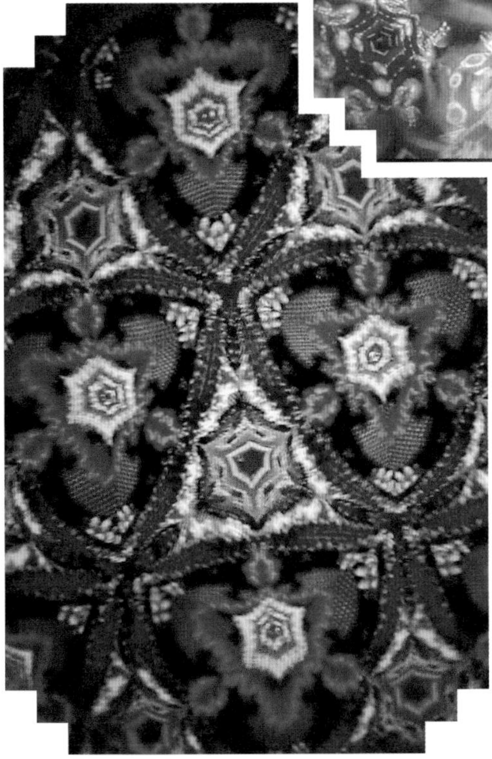

Croatian-born Nada Herceg demonstrates the creative use of photography in her textile collection "Kaleidoscope." Here, she arranged everyday objects and then photographed them through a kaleidoscope, creating these amazing pattern formations. She edited them further by putting them into repeat and printing them digitally onto silk, allowing her to maintain their rich, photographic qualities.

Emma Stone uses a complex combination of photography, scanning, drawing, and collage techniques to create elaborate and personal textiles.

Working digitally opened up a whole new world for illustrator and designer Emma Stone. It has allowed her to engage with a world of fantasy and surrealism. Her textile collection "Recollection" is based on sentimental objects, memories, and collections from her family history and aims to reinvent forgotten pieces.

Temitope Tijani plays with caricatures of family members in Photoshop, demonstrating how much fun it can be to integrate photography into design.

Inspired by the Aurora Borealis, designer Deja Abati digitally creates stunning light effects. He adds pleating to give more movement to the fabric.

Jemima Gregson exploits her love of fashion, photographing treasured pieces and placing them back onto a garment. She enhances her photographs digitally and places them carefully onto specific areas of clothing. The result is witty, glamorous, and sexy.

TUTORIAL 1

USING FILTERS IN PHOTOSHOP

There are numerous filters in Photoshop and the choice can seem overwhelming. Filters come in and out of fashion and can make your work look obviously "Photoshopped" and too familiar. But, if they are carefully integrated into your design work, they can add some amazing and subtle effects. Overuse of filters can confuse a design, so be clear from the start about what you want to achieve. You can apply a filter to the whole image or to a selected area. On these pages are just a few examples of favorite filters. Use RGB images, as some filters do not work with CMYK.

Melanie Bowles's design "The Brockwell Rose" is created from photographs of the rose garden in her local park; the design is put into a half-drop repeat. You can apply filters to a repeat unit to break up the traditional look of a design.

COLLAGE

Here the Cutout filter is used to add a collage effect to the original photographs. When you choose a filter, a dialog box will open, giving you several options. Experiment by moving the sliders to get your desired effect. In the bottom left corner of the image window, you can zoom in and out of the design.

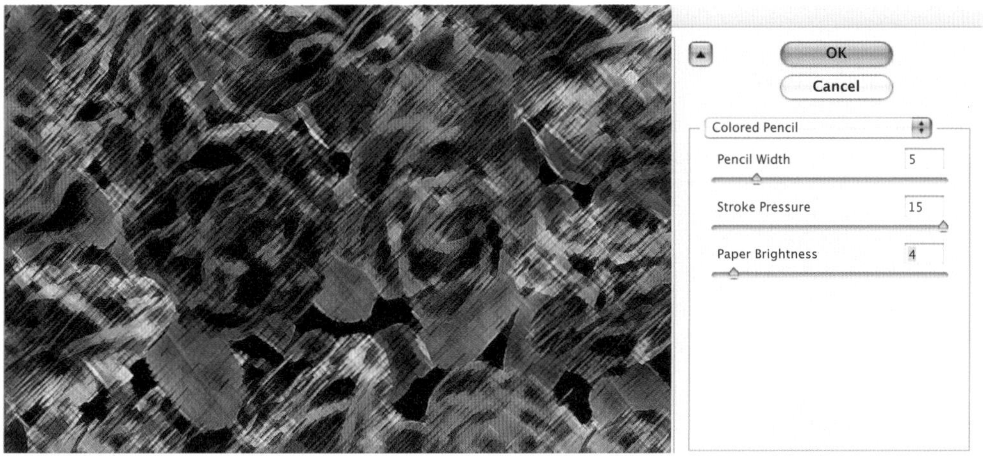

COLORED PENCIL

The Colored Pencil filter in Artistic filters was applied to give a bold, vibrant drawn effect. Altering Pencil Width, Stroke Pressure, and Paper Brightness gives a batik effect.

SOFT

With the Blur filter, you can soften the edges of a design.

VINTAGE

To create a vintage effect, try adding a Grain texture (**Filter > Texture > Grain**). Select Grain Type: Horizontal.

POP ART

The Color Halftone filter is found in Pixelate filters and simulates the effect of using a halftone screen on each channel of the image. For each channel, the filter divides the image into rectangles and replaces each rectangle with a dot.

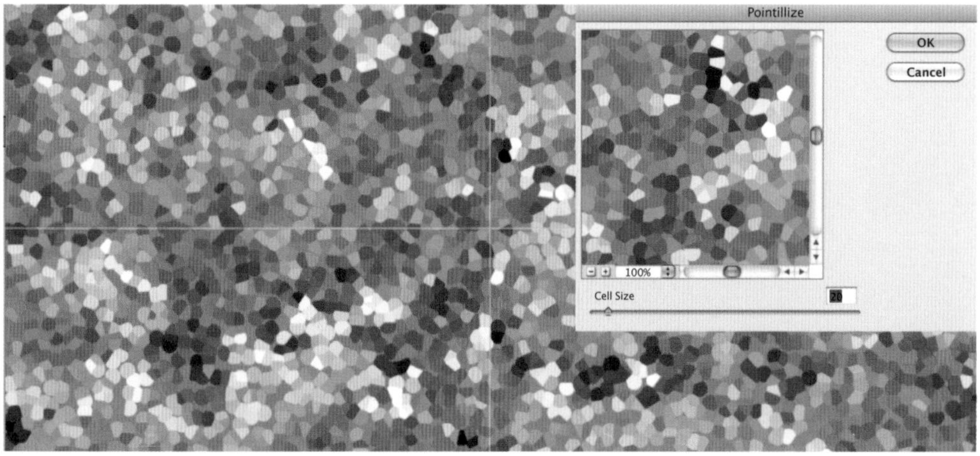

PIXELATE

To pixelate the image and break it up further, go to the Pixelate filter and select Pointillize.

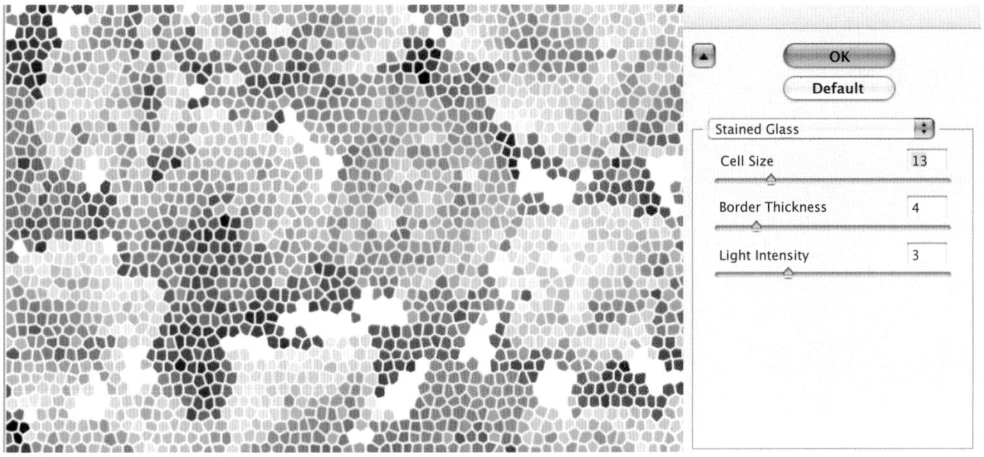

EMBROIDERED EFFECTS

The Stained Glass filter is in Texture filters and will transform an image into cells to give a stitched effect.

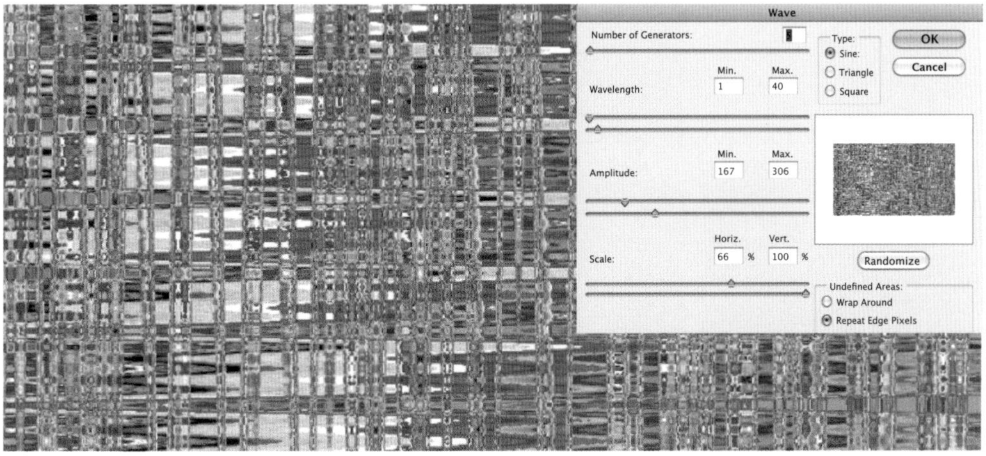

ABSTRACT DISTORTION

The Wave filter is found in Distort filters. This, along with other Distort filters, will give you numerous options with which to abstract and distort a photograph or image into an instant textile design that has fluidity and movement.

SILK-SCREEN EFFECT

Using the Posterize command (**Image > Adjustments > Posterize**) will give a photograph an instant silk-screen effect.

TUTORIAL 2

CREATING COMPLEX COLOR BLENDS

Emamoke Ukeleghe's collection "My Family Album" captures the essence of her ethnic background. Her inspiration comes from the journey her family made from Nigeria to England in the mid-1980s. Based on this childhood experience, she has created a collection of digital prints for scarfs and panels that showcases a new contemporary ethnicity.

Ukeleghe replaces the traditional techniques of hand-dyed batik used in African textiles with digital media. Working in Illustrator, she recreates simple geometrics and blends them to give them a rich and exotic feel. Her designs are dynamic, exciting, and reminiscent of ethnic textiles, retaining the luminosity of batik printing but with a contemporary twist.

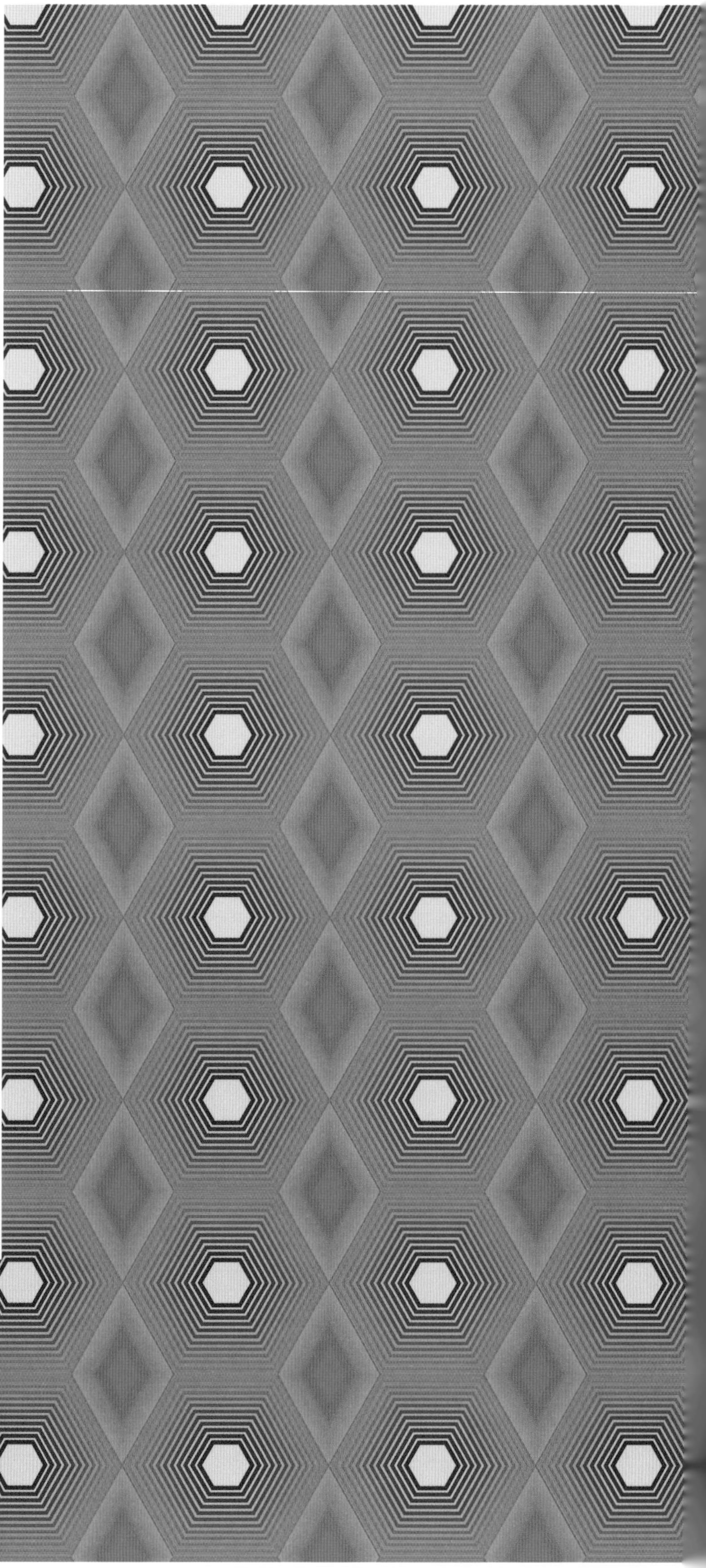

STEP 1

In Illustrator, select the Polygon tool from the Tool panel. Holding down the Shift key, click and drag to create a polygon.

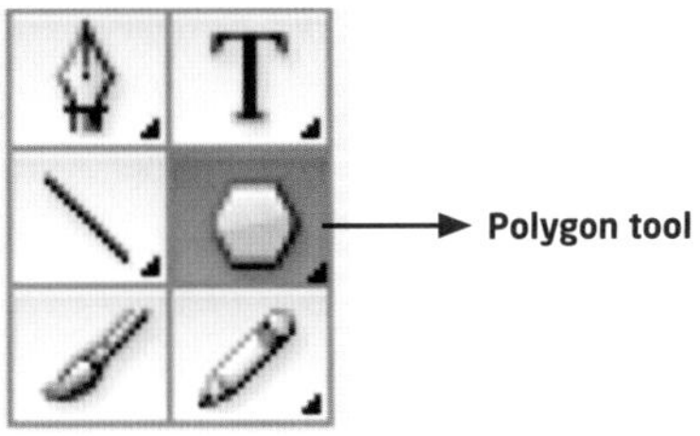

STEP 2

Window > Stroke.
Apply a stroke (Weight: 2 pt) in a contrasting color.

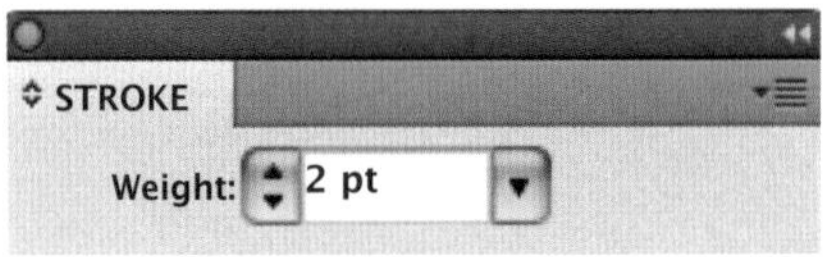

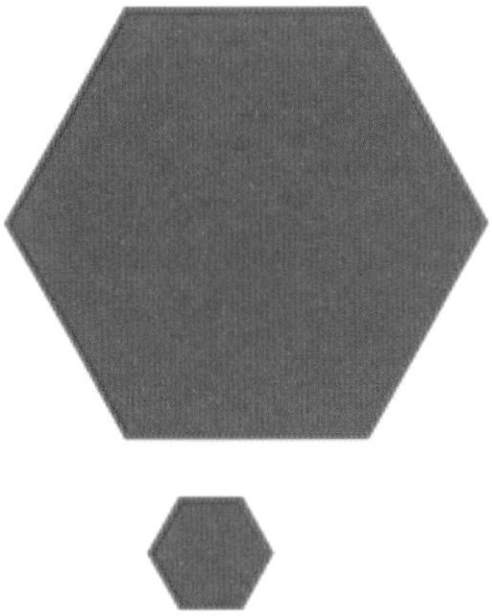

STEP 3

Copy and paste the polygon, and change the scale of the copied polygon to 25 percent.
Object > Transform > Scale.
Select both polygons.

STEP 4

Window > Align.
The Align panel will appear.

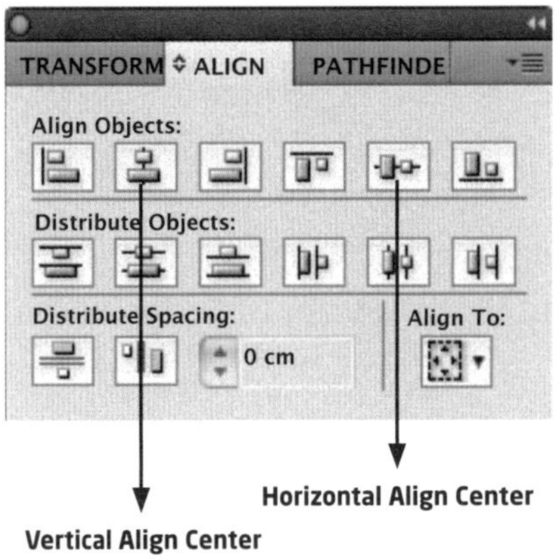

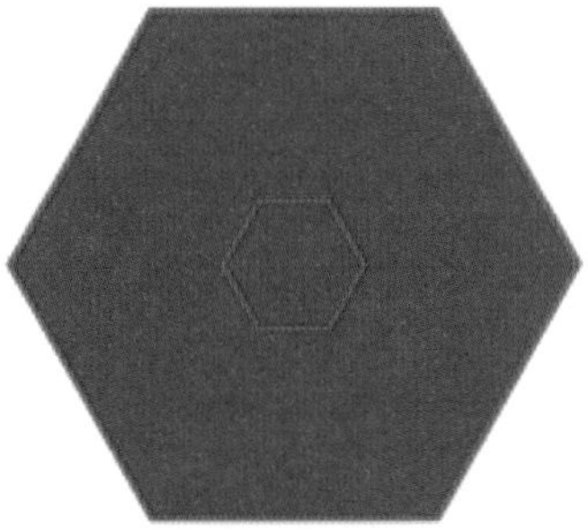

STEP 5

Select Vertical Align Center and Horizontal Align Center to centralize the polygons.

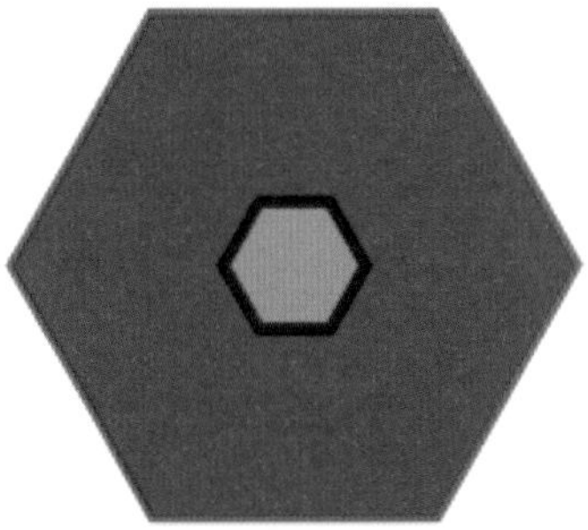

STEP 6

Apply a new Fill and Stroke color to the central polygon.

STEP 7

Select the Blend tool in the toolbar. Double-click it to reveal the Blend Options dialog box. Choose Specified Steps and enter “10.”

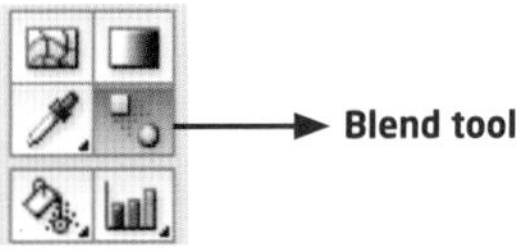

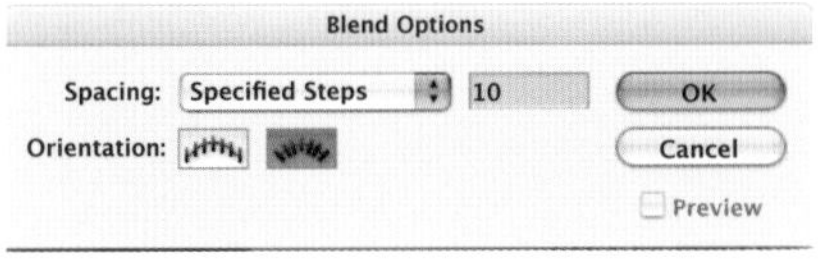

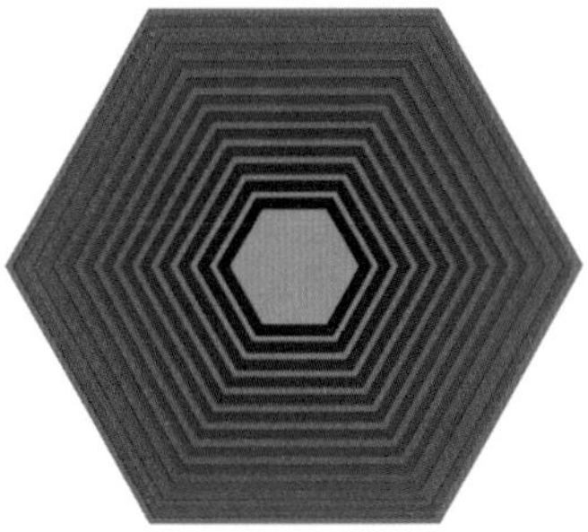

STEP 8

Place the Blend tool in the middle of the polygon; drag it to the outer edge and your blend will appear. It’s worth experimenting with the options the Blend tool offers to get different effects.

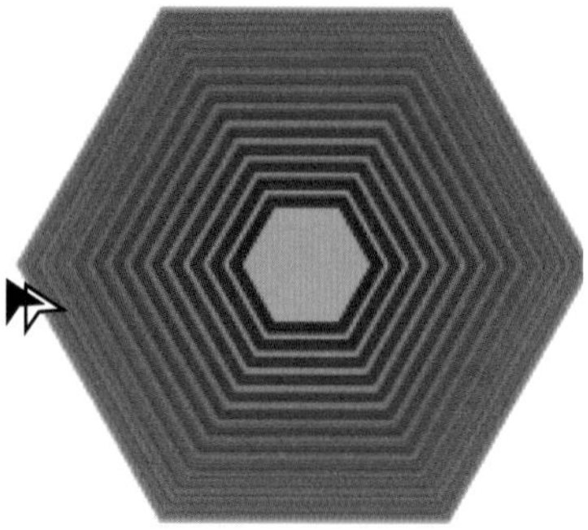

STEP 9

Now create a tile with the polygon. To position it accurately, go to the View menu and select Snap to Point and Smart Guides. Position the pointer on the left-hand anchor point and drag it to the right.

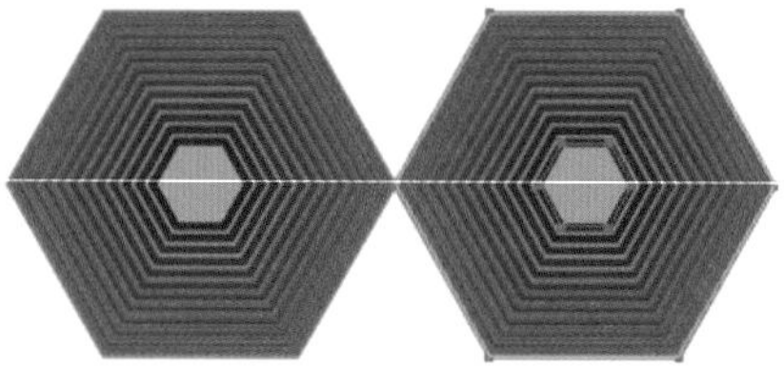

STEP 10

Holding down the Shift and Option/Alt keys, drag the tile across until it snaps into place and leaves a copy. The cursor will turn white when it has snapped to point.

STEP 11

Repeat this action to tile four polygons.

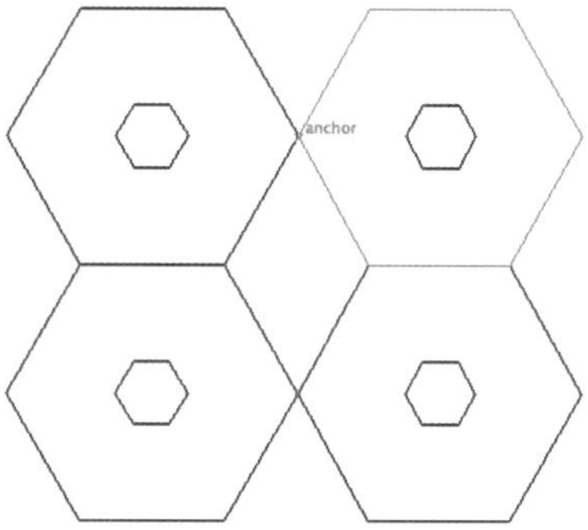

STEP 12

View > Outline.

With the Pen tool, draw a central diamond, clicking on the anchor points as a guide.

STEP 13

Window > Attributes.

A dialog box will appear. With your diamond selected, select the Show Center icon. This will show the center of the diamond.

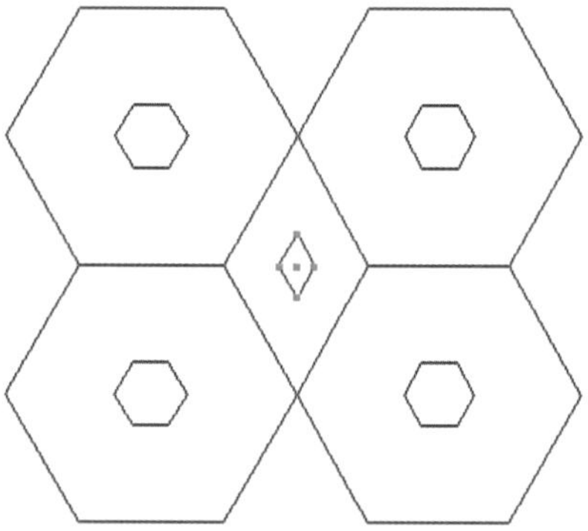

STEP 14

View > Outline.

Make a copy of your diamond, change its scale, and place it in the center of the first diamond.

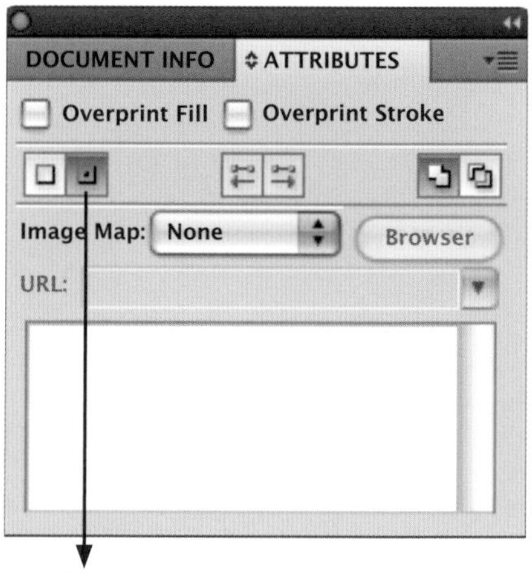

Show Center icon

STEP 15
Fill and Stroke both diamonds with contrast colors.

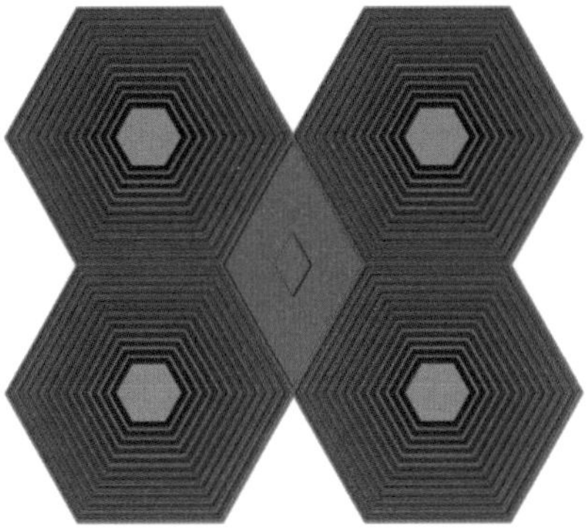

STEP 16
Now apply a blend to the diamond.

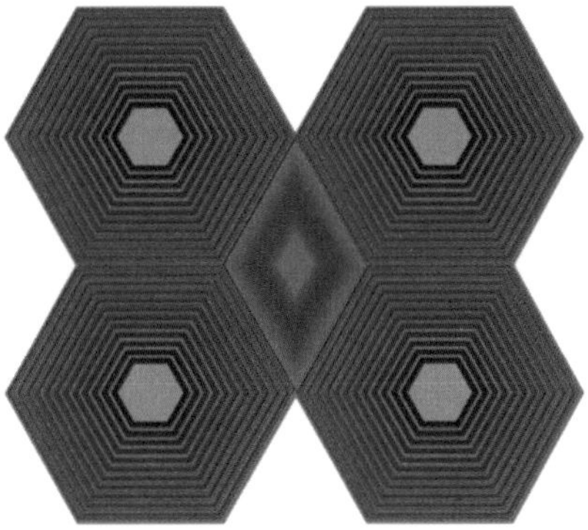

STEP 17
Now to put the design unit into repeat in Photoshop:
Select the design unit in Illustrator.
Edit > Copy.
Create a new document in Photoshop.
Edit > Paste.

STEP 18
A dialog box will appear. Select the Paste As Pixels option, and click OK.

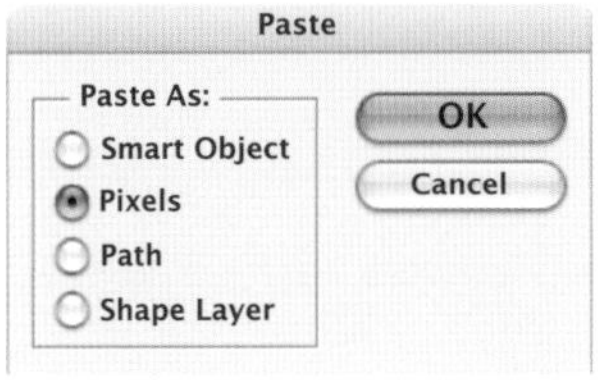

STEP 19
Another dialog box will appear.
Click Place.

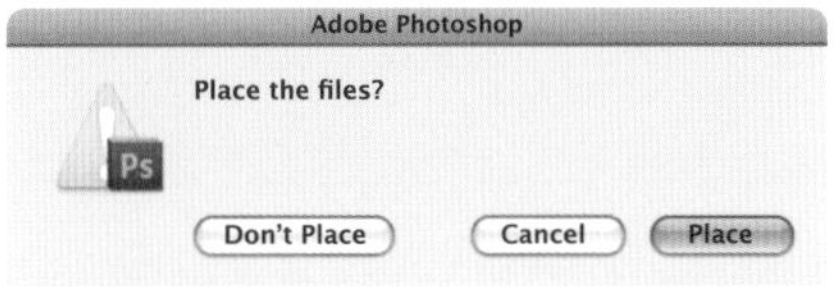

STEP 20
View > Rulers > Show Rulers.
View > Guides > Show Guides.

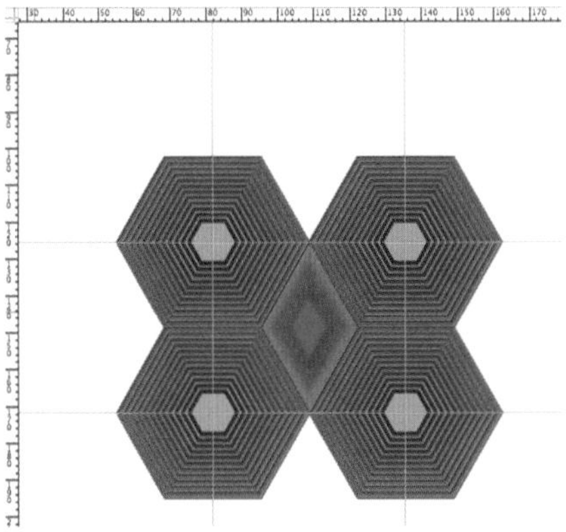

STEP 21
Bring down horizontal and vertical guides to the center points of all four polygons.

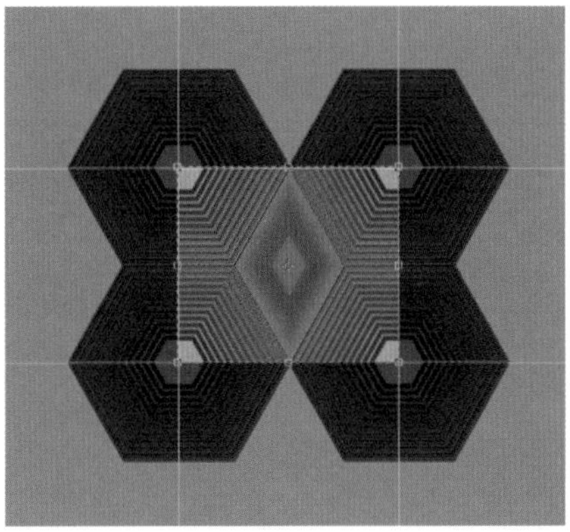

STEP 22
Select the Crop tool from the Tool panel and, using the guides, crop the unit.

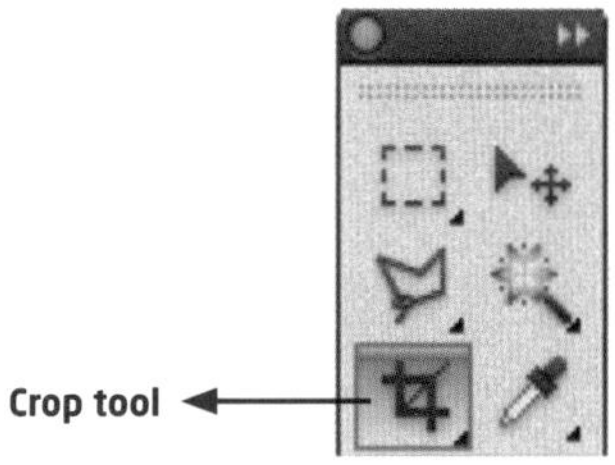

STEP 23
Select > All.

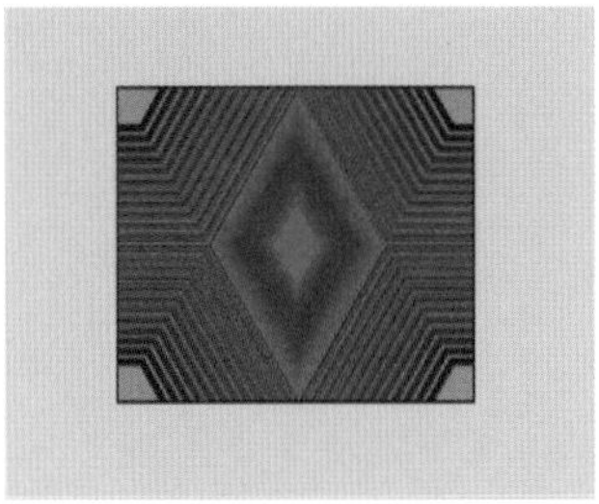

STEP 24
Edit > Define Pattern.
Name the pattern and press OK.

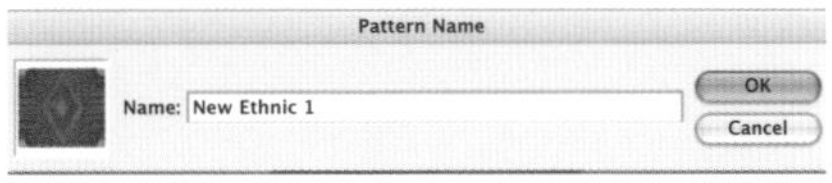

STEP 25
Create a new document.
Edit > Fill > Pattern.

TUTORIAL 3

BUILDING FLORAL MOTIFS

"Making Flowers" is a collection of digital prints created by Melanie Bowles. With Illustrator she creates clean, graphic florals that give her work a striking, contemporary look.

This tutorial shows you the principles of creating flowers in Illustrator by making a basic petal, and then duplicating and rotating it to build up a complex flower. You can build up ornate patterns from the basic design. The possibilities are endless for the textile designer who wishes create a fresh, bold floral look.

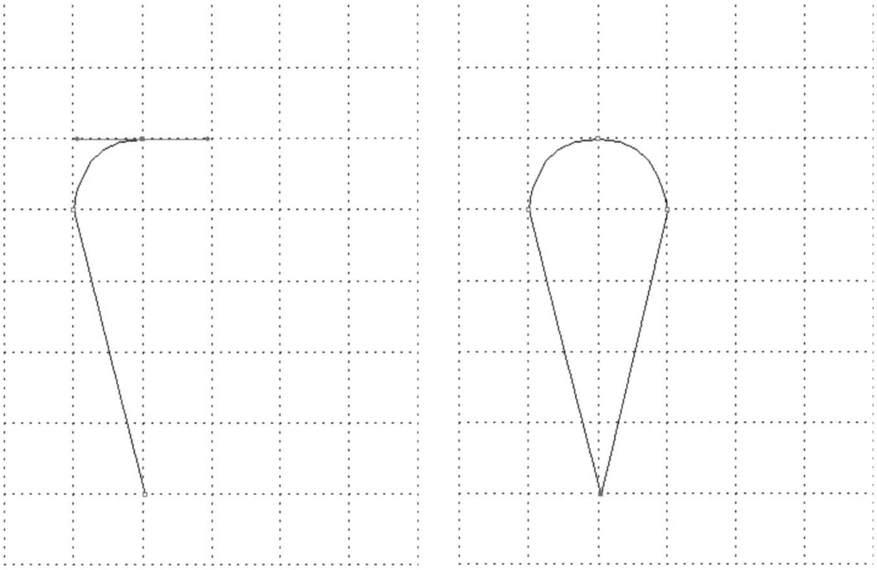

STEP 1

Reveal a grid on your Illustrator document page to help you create the basic petal shapes.
View > Show Grid.
Work in the Outline mode to create petals.
View > Outline.
Now use the Pen tool to create your petal shapes.

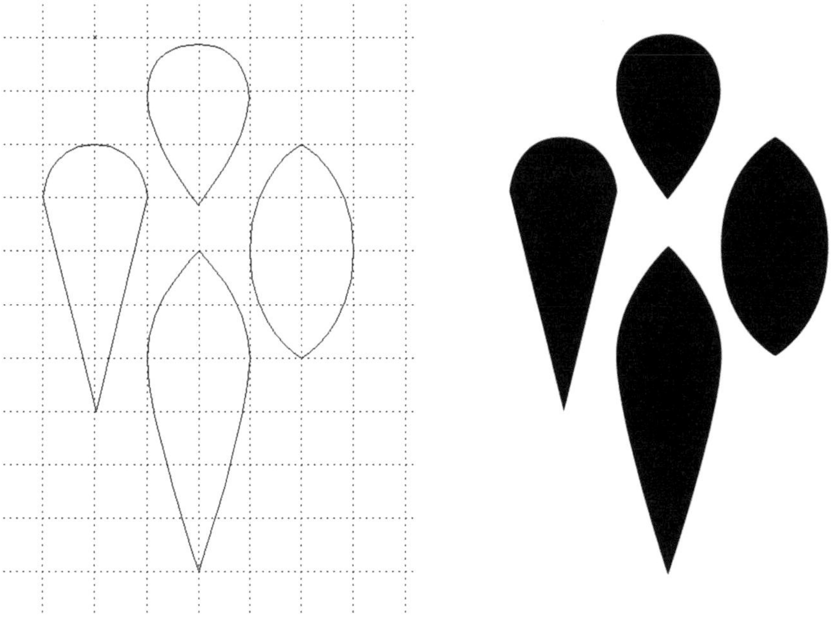

STEP 2

View > Preview.
Fill your shapes with black.
Select one petal.
Edit > Copy.

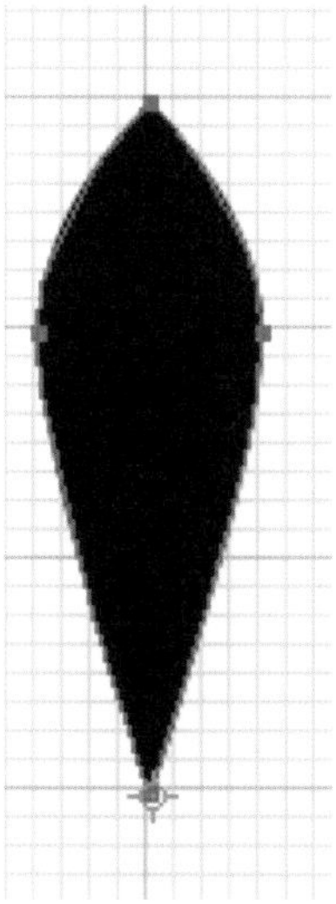

STEP 3

Open up a new document, and again reveal the grid.
Edit > Paste.

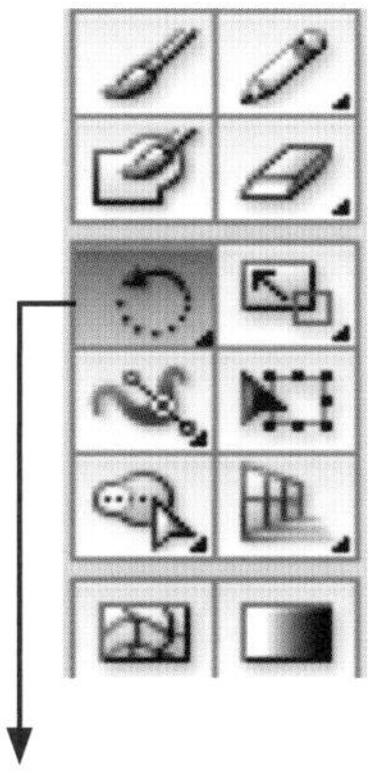

Rotate tool

STEP 4

Now build the flower up.
Window > Info.
With the petal selected, select the Rotate tool from the Tool panel, and place it at the bottom of the petal.
Hold down the Option/Alt key and rotate the petal (this will make a copy of your petal as you rotate it).

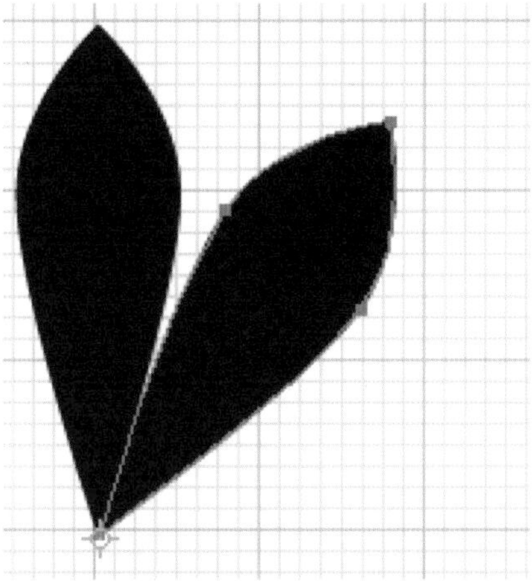

STEP 5

To enter an accurate angle for your petal to rotate, with the Rotate tool still selected, place the reference point at the bottom of the petal. Now press Option/Alt and click, and the Rotate dialog box will appear. Enter an angle that is a division of 360 degrees. Click on the Copy button, and a second petal will appear.

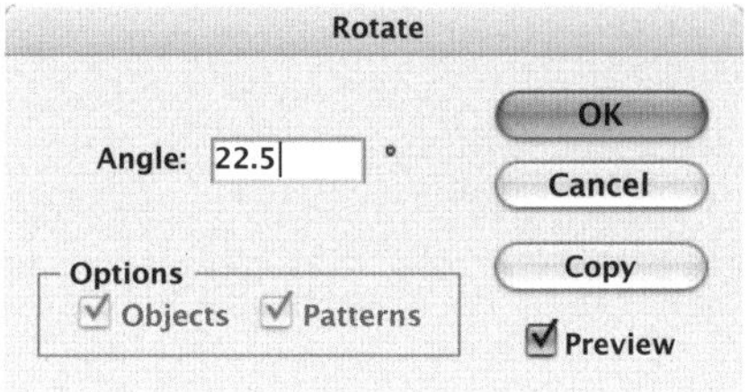

STEP 6

Once you have placed the second petal correctly, you can build up the other petals to complete the flower. Press Command + D; this keyboard shortcut will repeat the last command.
Once you have a complete flower, group the petals together.
Object > Group.

STEP 7

Now apply a color fill. Copy and paste several times to build the flower up, changing the scale and color of each copy.

STEP 8

Window > Align.
Select Vertical Align Center and Horizontal Align Center.

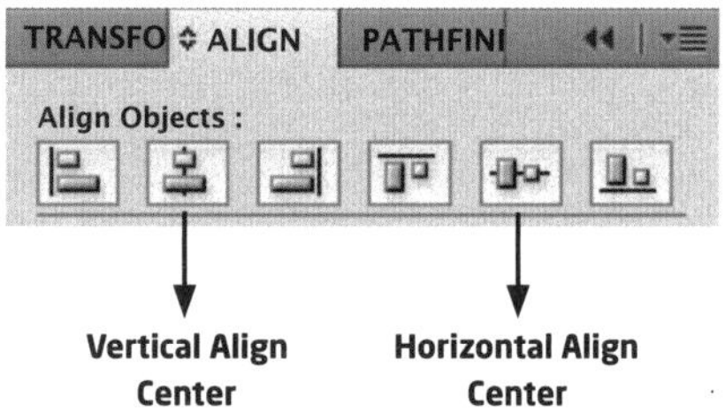

STEP 9

With the Rotate tool, rotate the flowers.
Alter the transparency of the petals to give an impression of depth.
Finally, group the completed flower.
Object > Group.

STEP 10

Draw a line and a circle for the stamen.
Object > Group.
Now copy and rotate the stamen, using the same method as for the petals.

STEP 11

The flower is complete.
Object > Group.

STEP 12

Create more flowers using the same techniques, selecting different colors and sizes of petals.

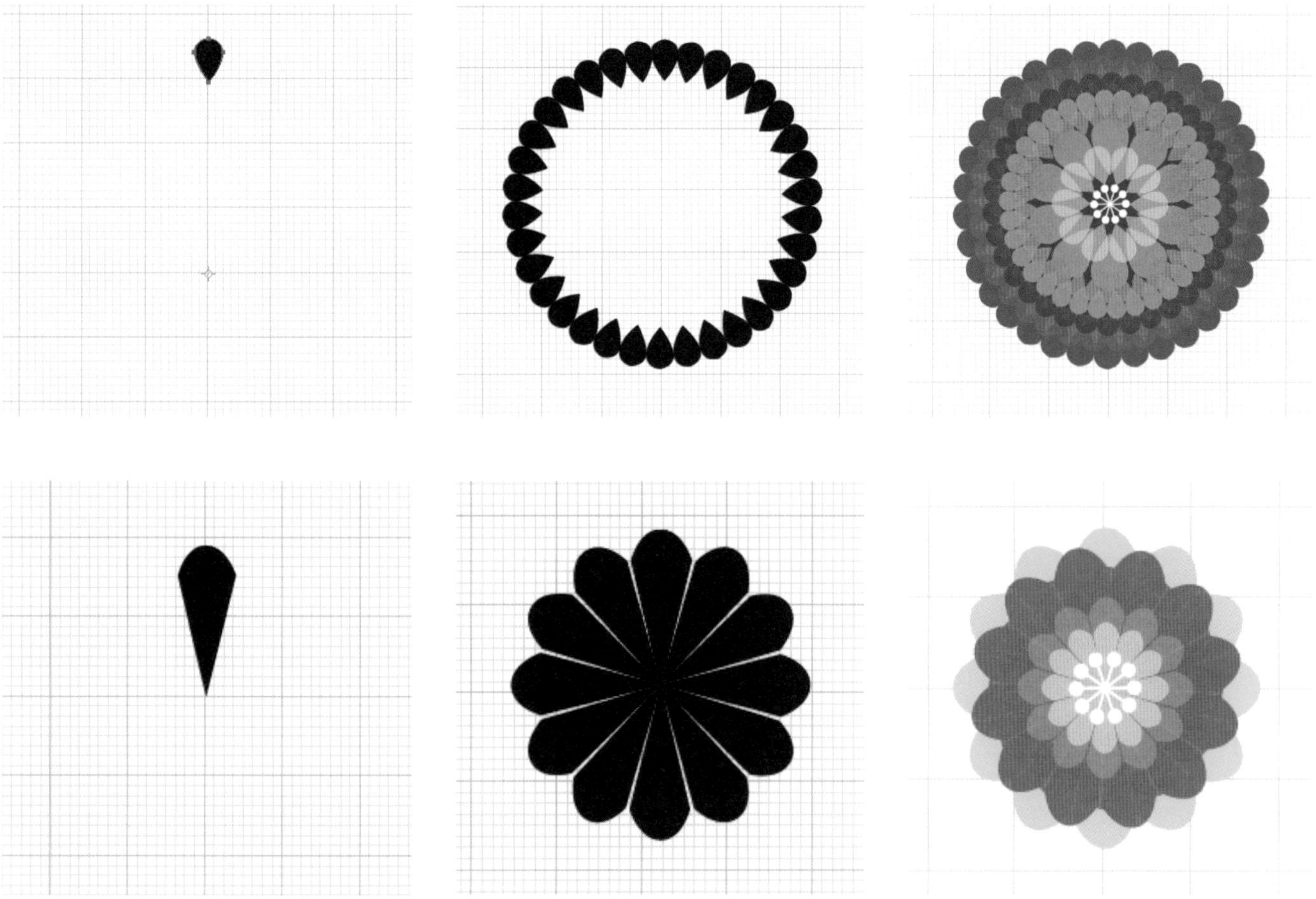

TUTORIAL 4

CROSS-STITCH EFFECTS

Claire Thorpe devised this effective technique in Illustrator to fill motifs with cross-stitch without even touching a needle.

This tutorial demonstrates how to create a cross-stitch from a motif of your choice.

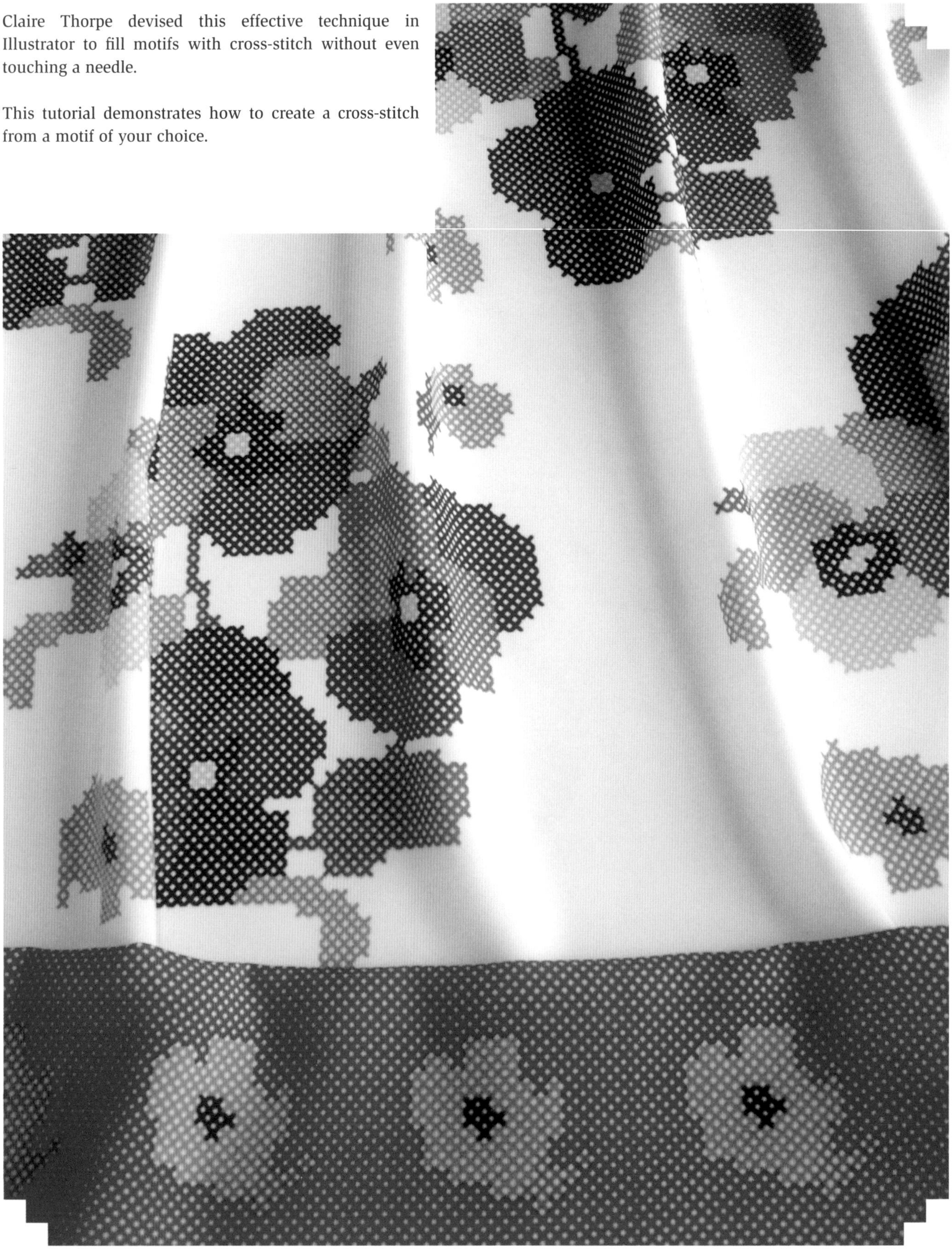

STEP 1

In Illustrator, select the Line tool from the Tool panel.
Draw a 45-degree line by holding down the Shift key while clicking and dragging.

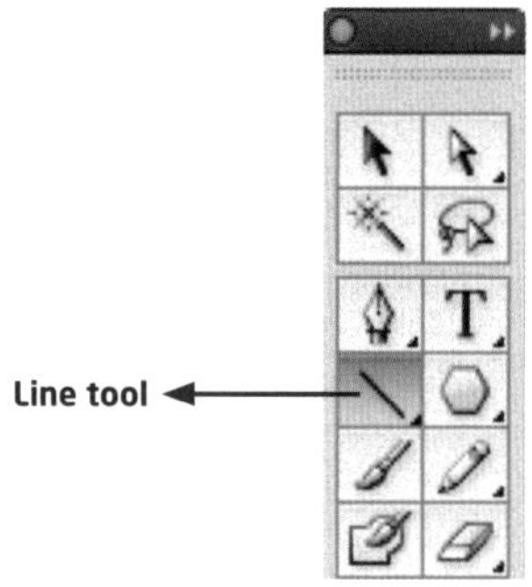

STEP 2

Go to the option bar at the top of the screen. Click on the Link icon between the Width and the Height.
Enter 0.08 in (0.2 cm).

STEP 3

Go to the Stroke panel and enter Weight: 2 pt.
Select Cap: Round Cap and Corner: Round Join.

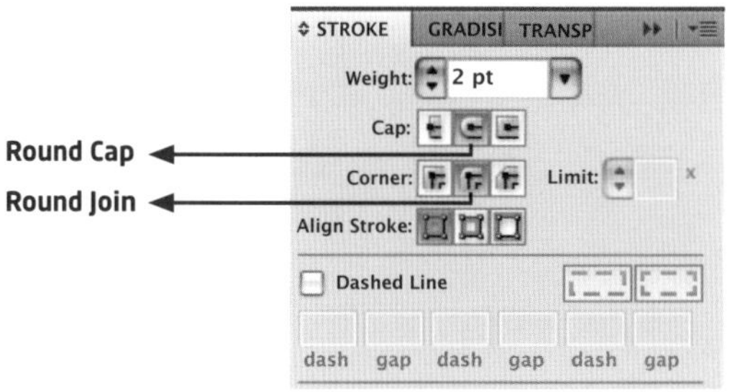

STEP 4

Select the cross. Double-click on the Reflect tool in the Tool panel to open the Reflect dialog box.
Select Vertical and enter an Angle of 90 degrees.
Click Copy.
Select both lines.
Object > Group.

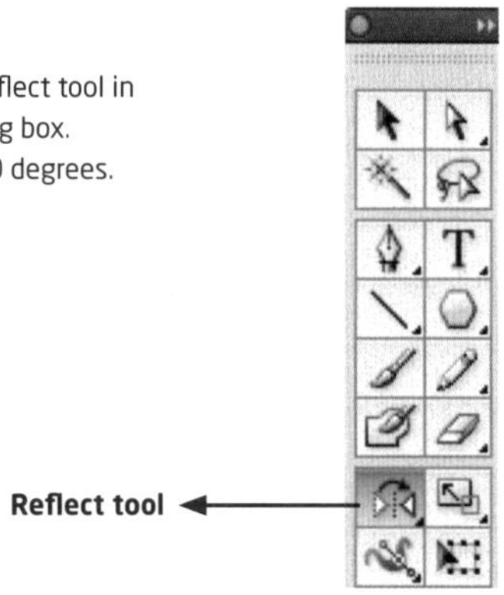

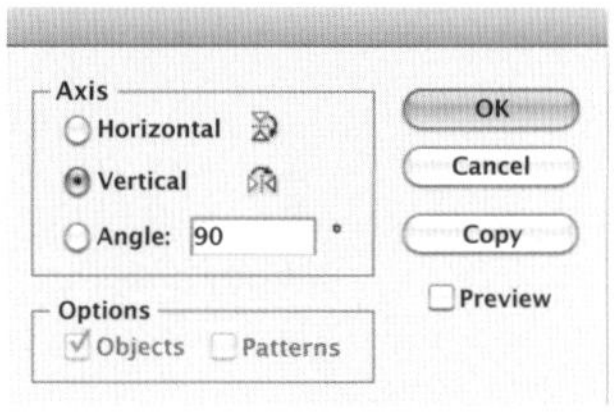

STEP 5

Press the Return key to open the Move dialog box.
Enter -0.11 in (-0.27 cm) in the Vertical field. This is the measurement from the center of the cross to the center of the repeated cross. (In this case it is -0.11 in. If your cross is bigger, the measurement to your repeated cross will be larger, depending on the gap you want between them.)
Click on Copy, and the second cross will appear.
Press Command + D repeatedly to build up a vertical line of crosses.

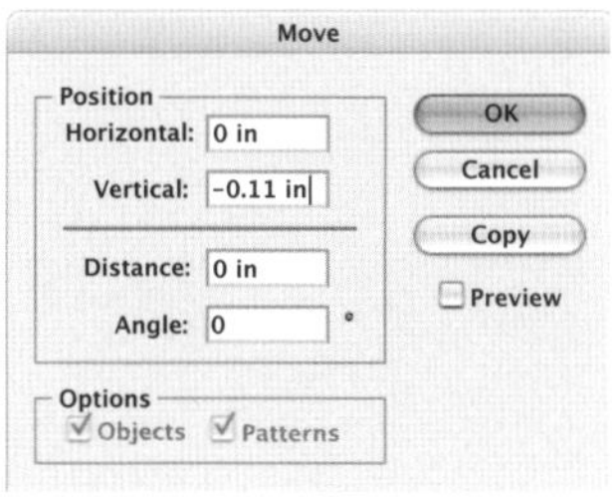

STEP 6

Select the vertical line of crosses. Press the Return key to bring up the Move dialog box. Enter 0.11 in (0.27 cm) in the Horizontal field and click on Copy.
Press Command + D repeatedly to build up horizontal rows of crosses. Your cross-stitch grid is now complete.

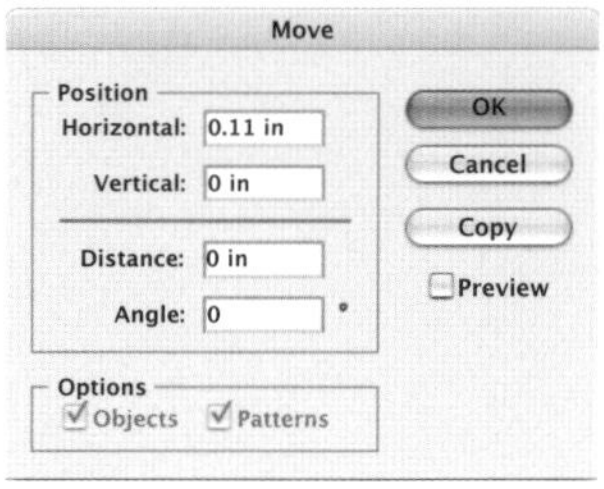

STEP 7

Create a new layer and place it underneath your stitch grid. Choose a motif you wish to work from.
File > Place.
Go back to the stitch grid layer.
Select > All.
Color the stroke gray.
Lower the Opacity to reveal the motif template.

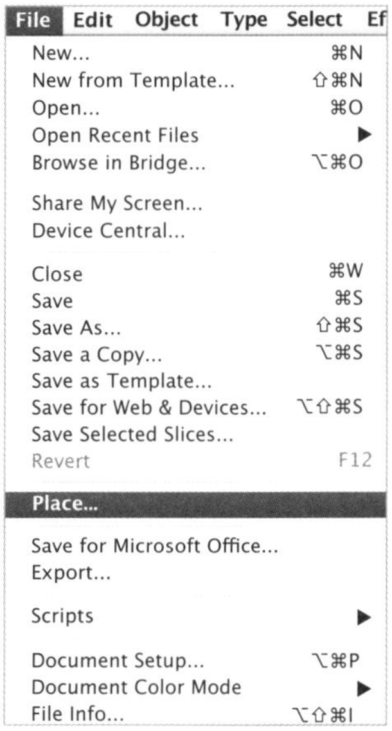

STEP 8

Now carefully color individual stitches and build up the motif (select groups of stitches by holding down the Shift key). Once colored, select all the stitches and raise the Opacity back to normal.

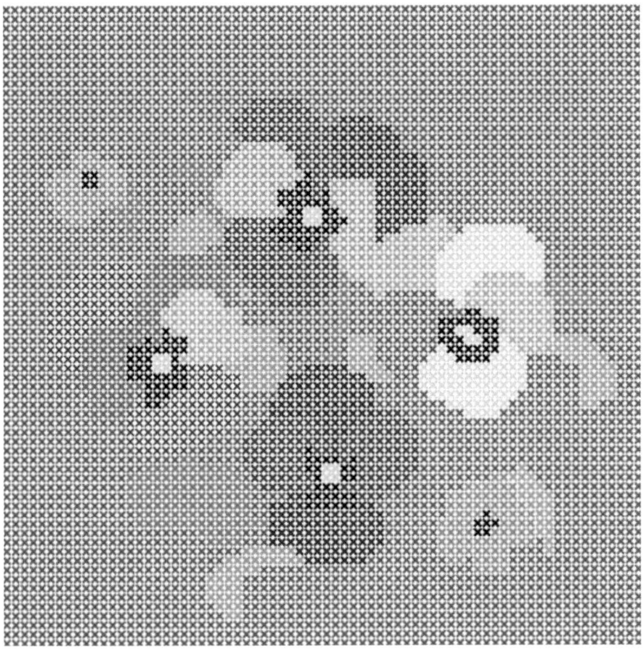

STEP 9

Select one of the grid stitches. **Select > Same > Stroke Color**. All the stitches of that color will be selected. With this method you can recolor your design or delete any stitches you wish to.

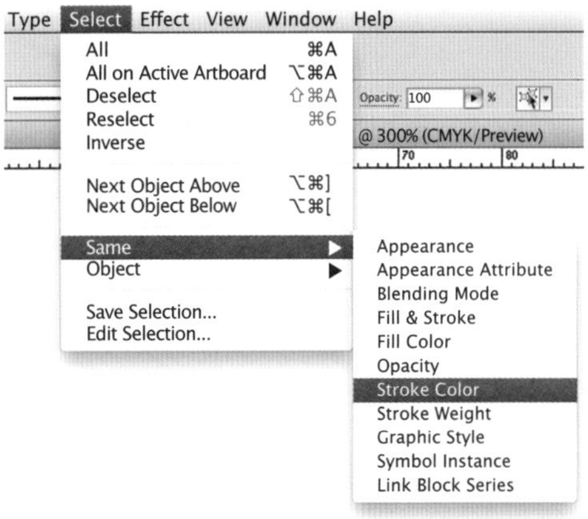

TUTORIAL 5

ENGINEERED PRINTS

"Jemima's World" is an inspirational fashion collection by Jemima Gregson, based on her love of vintage costume jewelry. Jemima places photographs of her jewelry onto the garment shapes in Photoshop to create a stunning trompe l'oeil effect, which also shows the exceptional photographic qualities that can be achieved with digital printing. The garment shapes are digitally printed onto silk satin using a Mimaki TX2, and then made into a garment.

This tutorial demonstrates the process of engineering a print onto a garment shape using Photoshop.

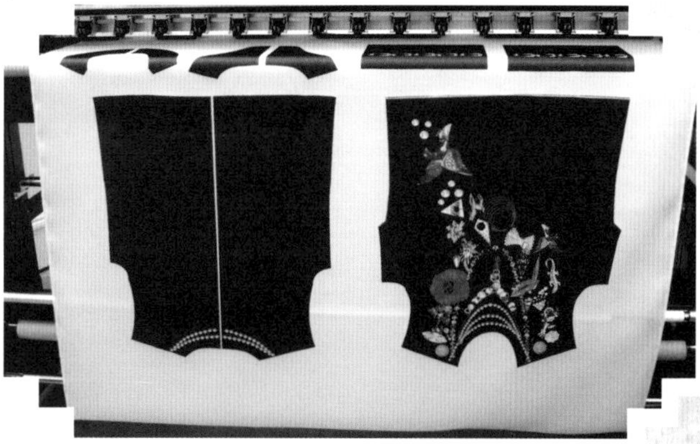

STEP 1

Scan your pattern pieces at 300 dpi, starting with the front. You will have to do this in several sections. Once they are scanned, paste the sections together in Photoshop.

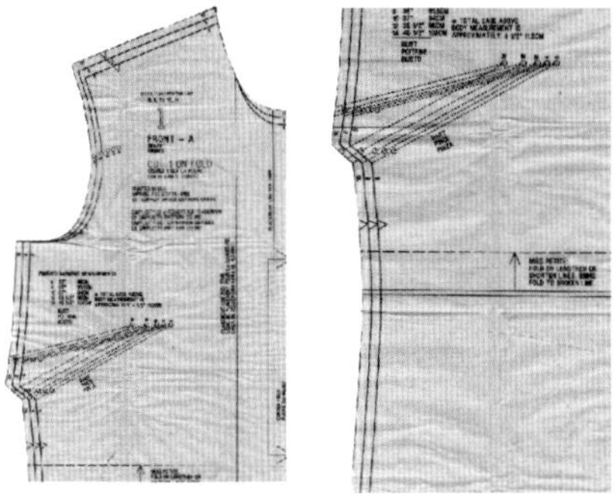

STEP 2

Reposition the top front section of the garment on the canvas by moving it to the top.

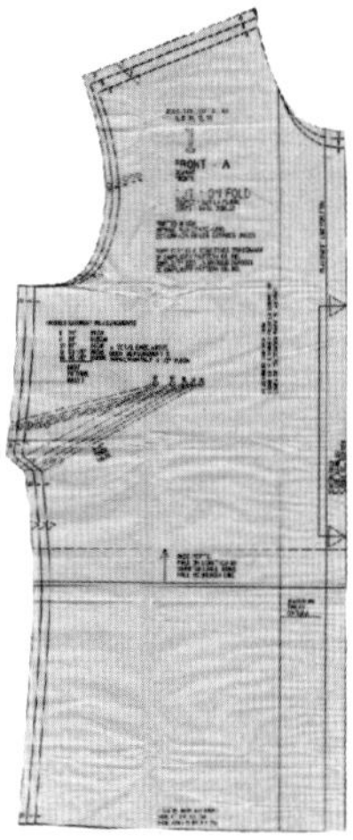

STEP 3

Image > Canvas Size.

In the Canvas Size dialog box, alter the Width and Height measurements sufficiently to allow you to paste in the bottom section of the garment.

Once this is done, flatten the image.

Layer > Flatten Image.

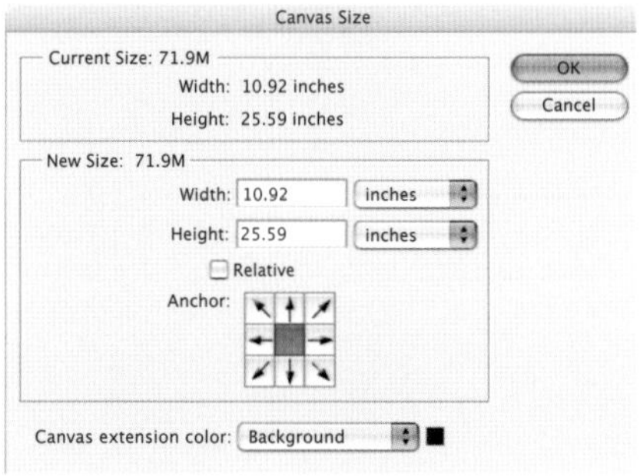

STEP 4

Now increase the canvas size to fit the complete garment shape.

Image > Canvas Size.

Change the Width to 200 percent.

Click OK.

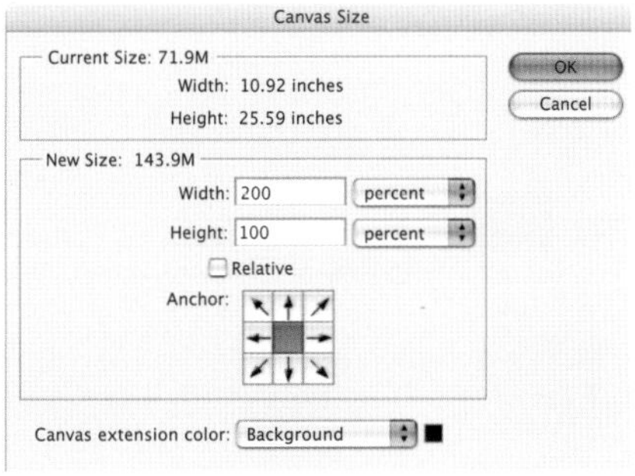

STEP 5

Select the garment piece with the Marquee tool.

Copy and Paste.

Edit > Transform > Flip Horizontally.

Piece the two shapes together so that they match up.

Flatten the image.

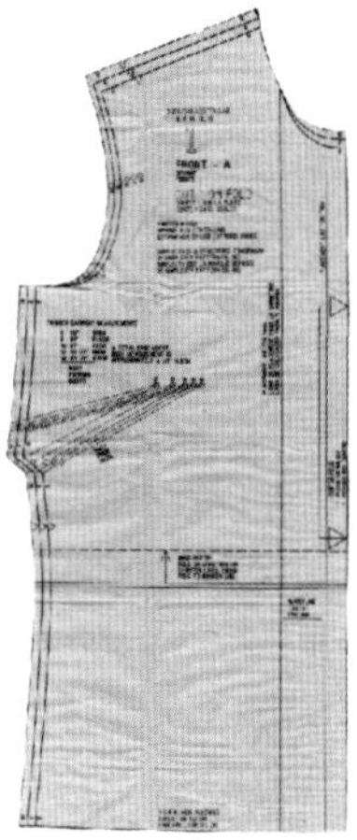

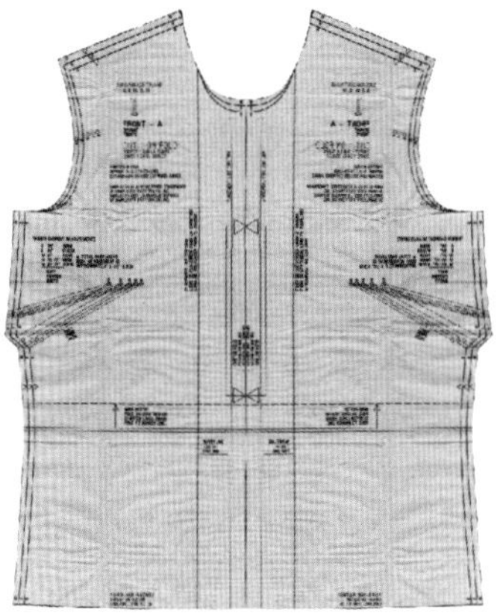

STEP 6

Select the Pen tool, and the Pen tool option bar will appear. Select the Fill option with black as the foreground color in the toolbar.

Pen tool

Fill option

Pen tool option bar

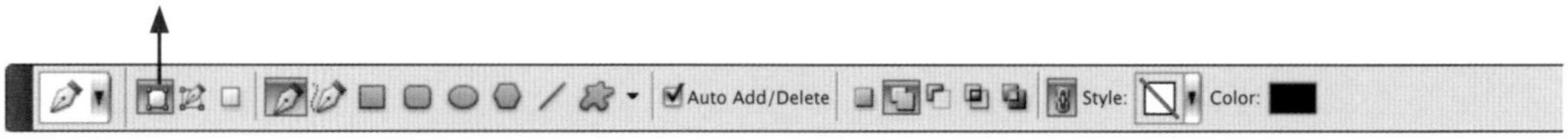

STEP 7

Carefully trace around the garment using the Pen tool, to create a series of anchor points around the garment shape. Use the Convert Point tool (in the Pen tool menu) to create the curves around the neck and armholes. It may take some time and practice until you are happy with the results.

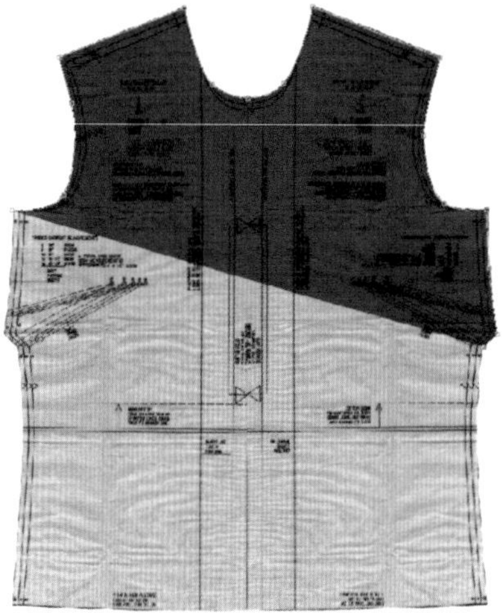

STEP 8

When you use the Pen tool, a shape layer will appear in the Layers panel. Change the Opacity of this layer to reveal the pattern shape so you can trace over it.

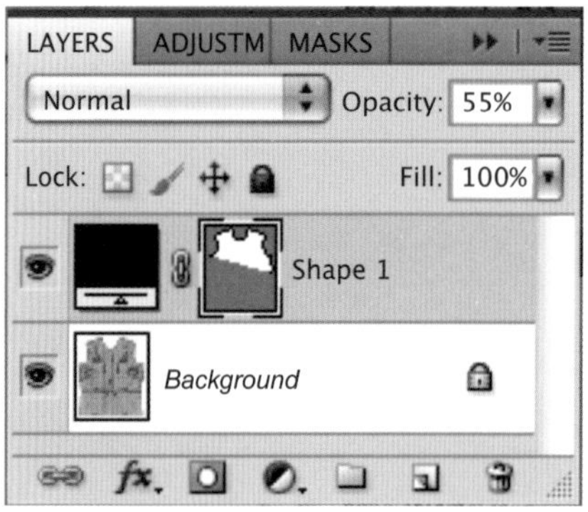

STEP 9

Continue to draw around the garment shape with the Pen tool until it is complete. When you use the Pen tool, you create a new path. Go to the Paths panel to see your new path. Click on the menu button at top right to reveal the drop-down menu. Save your new path so you can edit or select it at any time.

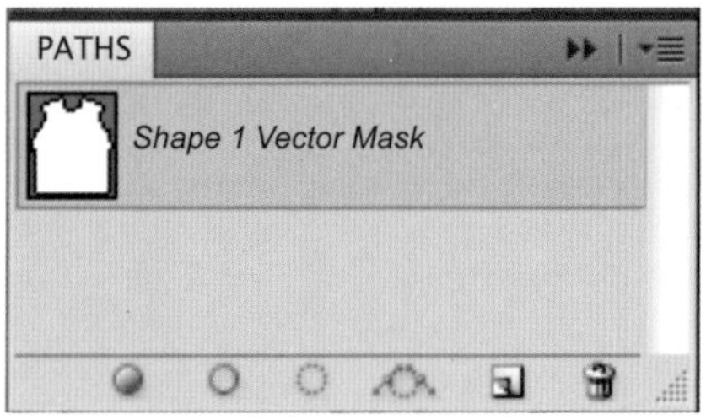

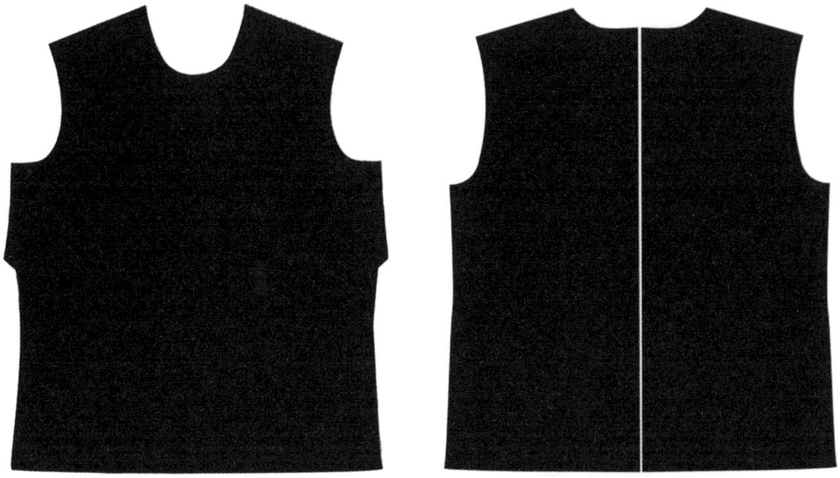

STEP 10

Repeat the entire process with the back sections of the garment.

STEP 11

Arrange a selection of costume jewelry onto a mannequin covered in black material. Using a digital SLR camera and studio lighting, photograph the mannequin at the highest possible resolution. This will allow the image to be reproduced at the maximum size with no compromise in quality.

STEP 12

You could also photograph some extra jewelry against a black background to add to the mannequin jewelry.

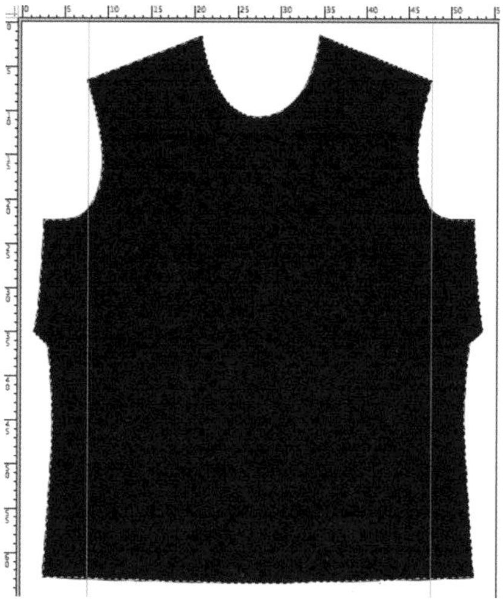

STEP 13

Open up the front garment shape. Your path is drawn but you need to make it into a selection so you can start to paste your jewelry into the pattern piece.

STEP 14

On the Paths panel, highlight your path and click the Path Selection icon at the bottom of the panel. This will create a selection for you to paste your jewelry into.

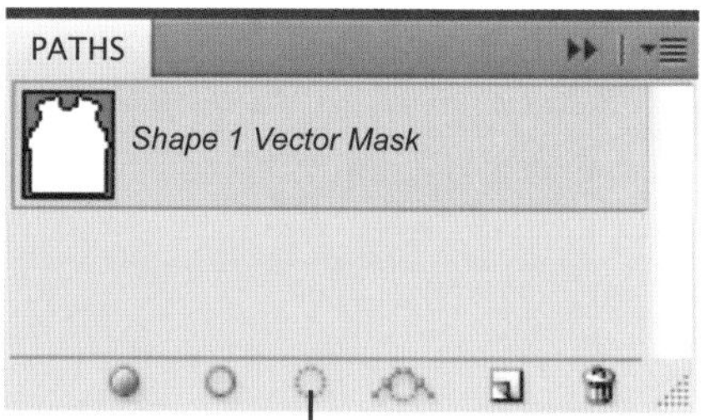

Path Selection icon

STEP 15

Open up the mannequin photograph.
You may wish to brighten the jewelry.
Image > Adjustments > Brightness/Contrast.
Alter the sliders to adjust the tonal range until you are happy with the effect.
Select > All.
Edit > Copy.

STEP 16

Now open up the front garment image.
Select the garment shape.
Edit > Paste Special > Paste Into.
With the new pasted-in layer selected, select the Move tool and position your jewelry to fit into the garment shape.
Scale it to fit.
Edit > Transform > Scale.

STEP 17

Merge the shape layer and the jewelry layer using the Merge Visible command in the Layers panel drop-down menu.

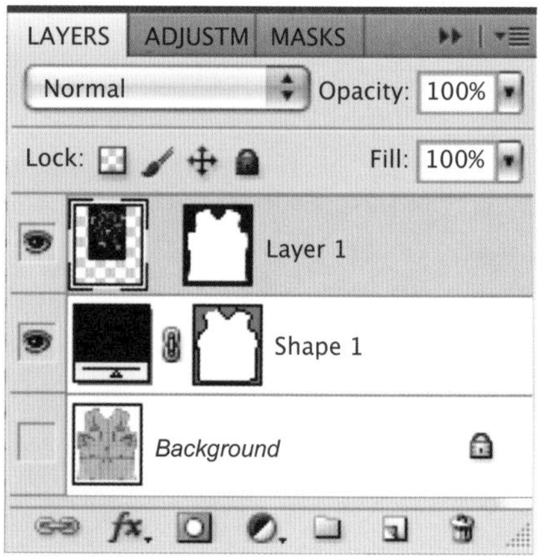

STEP 18

With the Clone tool, carefully clone the necklace to make it continue around the neckline.

STEP 19

Open the extra photographs, and select items with the Lasso tool. **Edit > Copy**.

STEP 20

Now go back to the garment shape and paste on new jewelry.
Edit > Paste.
Merge the new layers as you go.
Lower the Opacity of the jewelry layer so that it reveals the pattern piece beneath.
Continue to add more images to build up the design.

STEP 21

Once you have completed the front, use the same techniques to complete the back and cuffs. When they are all finished, flatten the layers.
Now open a document with a Width of 55 in (140 cm)—the width of fabric on the digital printer—and a Height of 59 in (150 cm). Set the Resolution to 200 dpi.
Open each garment piece.
Select > All.
Edit > Copy.
Go to your new fabric length document and paste the garment piece on.
Edit > Paste.
Paste all the garment shapes and arrange them across the final document.

STEP 22

Once the shapes are placed, flatten the layers. Now you are ready to prepare the document for printing.

TUTORIAL 6

SEQUIN EFFECTS

"You Can't Hurry Love" is a fashion collection created by Tennessee-born Katie Irving Jones. The collection is intended to elicit a sentimental attachment, and draws inspiration from nostalgic heirlooms that Katie incorporates into her designs. She recreates vintage embellishments using digital techniques in Photoshop.

This tutorial demonstrates how to create a sequin motif. Once the technique is mastered, it can be applied to any design.

STEP 1
Scan a sequin at 300 dpi and open the image in Photoshop.
Select > Image > Adjustments > Levels.
Adjust the shadow and highlights by moving the sliders in the dialog box.

STEP 2
Add a lens flare on the corner of the sequin to give it an extra twinkle.
Filter > Render > Lens Flare.

STEP 3
Select the sequin with the Magic Wand tool. Set the Tolerance in the option bar to 30 and select an area around the sequin.
Edit > Cut.
Cut away the background. Select the sequin with the Marquee tool.
Edit > Define Brush.
Name the sequin and press OK.

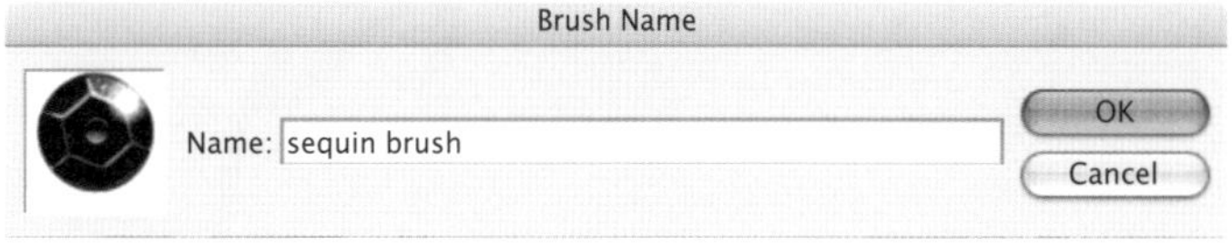

STEP 4
Make a drawing of a heart and banner and scan it into Photoshop. Create a new layer.
Select the new sequin brush.
In the Brush Options panel, change the Opacity to 93 percent and the Size to 70 pixels.

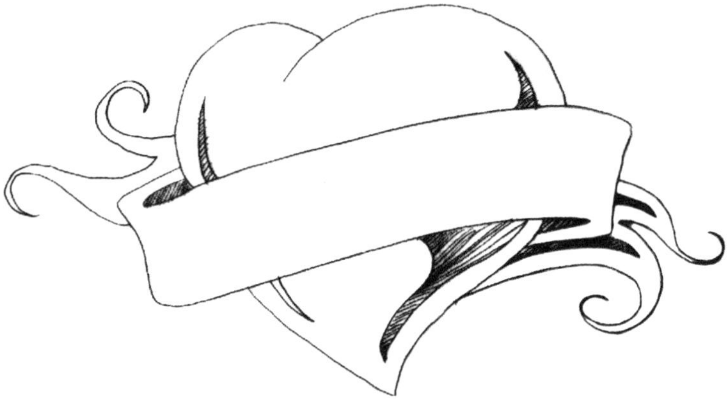

STEP 5
Select black as the brush color and "stamp" around the outline of the heart in black sequins, by clicking once to apply each.

STEP 6
Now add a slight shadow to this layer to give it a three-dimensional effect.
Click the Layer Style icon at the bottom of the Layers panel.

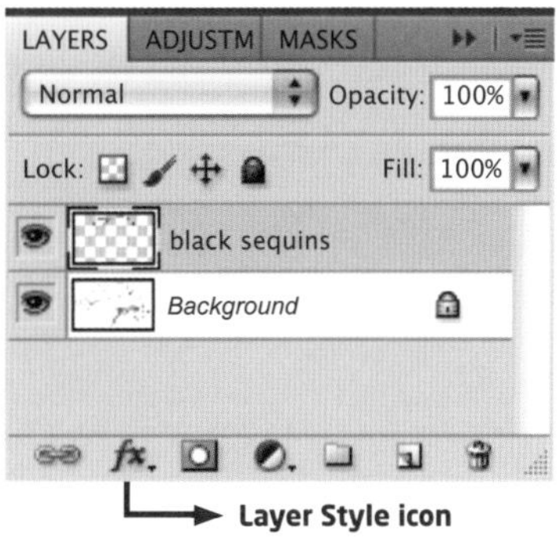

STEP 7

In the Layer Style menu, select Drop Shadow.
A dialog box will appear.
Change the Opacity and the Distance values to create a soft shadow.

STEP 8

Create a new layer.
Select the sequin brush and choose a dark red color.
Stamp inside the heart as shown.

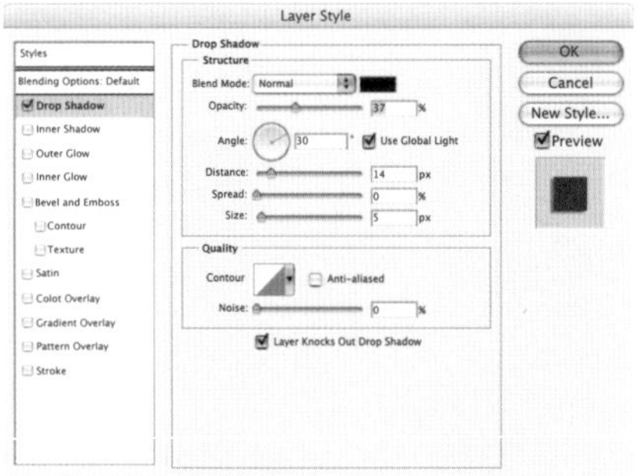

STEP 9

Create a new layer.
Fill the rest of the heart with the sequin brush colored bright red.
You should now have four layers.
Turn the Background layer off and merge the visible layers.

Line tool option bar

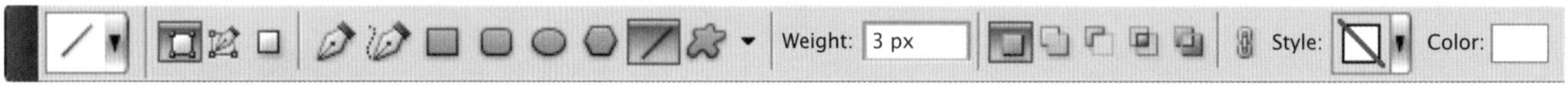

STEP 10

Next, create the stitches that appear to fasten each sequin to give the hand-sewn effect. This is a fairly time-consuming process, but is still a lot quicker than actually sewing them!
Select the Line tool from the Tool panel.
Make sure the Fill option is selected in the Line tool option bar.

Fill option

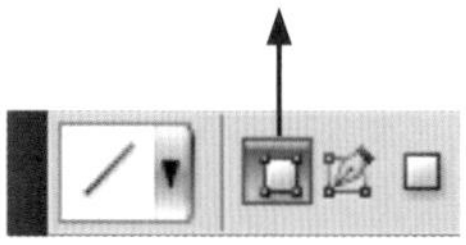

STEP 11

The Line tool option bar will appear at the top of your screen. For Weight, enter 3 px. Select a color for the stitch. Now draw in every stitch, working on each separate layer. Make them slightly irregular to achieve a truly hand-sewn effect.
Your sequins are now complete. Fill in the background layer with white and flatten the image.
Layer> Flatten Image.

STEP 12

Next you need to create the "LOVE" lettering. Scan your chosen lettering into Photoshop.

STEP 13

Use the same technique as before to stamp around the lettering with the sequin brush, varying the scale of the brush.

STEP 14

Once the lettering is complete, flatten the layers and cut it out with the Marquee tool.
Edit > Copy.
Open the heart motif.
Edit > Paste.
Position and adjust the lettering with the Transform tools to fit inside the banner.

STEP 15

Finally, add an extra glow to the finished heart motif.
Filter > Render > Lens Flare.

STEP 16

Print the design onto opaque transfer T-shirt paper through a desktop inkjet printer. Carefully cut the motif out and press it onto your fabric with an iron or heat press.

TUTORIAL 7

PHOTOMONTAGE

Photomontage is the technique of combining photographic elements together to create new compositions. The introduction of Photoshop has made achieving a photomontage effect faster and easier. There is now a trend toward combining illustration, graphics, and photography to create complex designs.

Creating a photomontage in Photoshop depends on developing a theme and having a collection of visually strong photographs to work with. Once you have these, you need to select elements from them and start to build new configurations. You will need to work with the more advanced selection tools to achieve the best edge quality. The most effective tool for selecting areas of photographs is the Quick Mask tool. By using the Airbrush to make selections, you can also achieve soft edges; this tool is easiest to control with a stylus pen.

STEP 1

Open your source image in Photoshop (make sure it is in RGB, as you will apply a filter later). Click on the Quick Mask icon located at the bottom of the Tool panel.

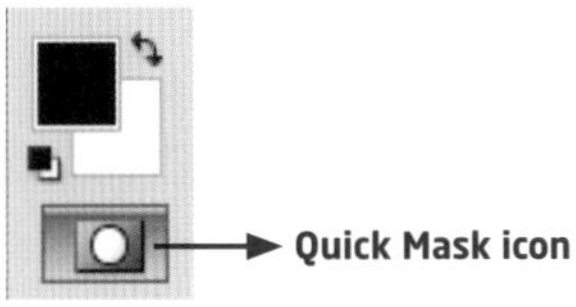

STEP 2

Choose a soft airbrush (using the Brush tool option bar) and paint over the image you want to mask. To change the color of the mask and transparency, double-click the Quick Mask icon to open Quick Mask Options.

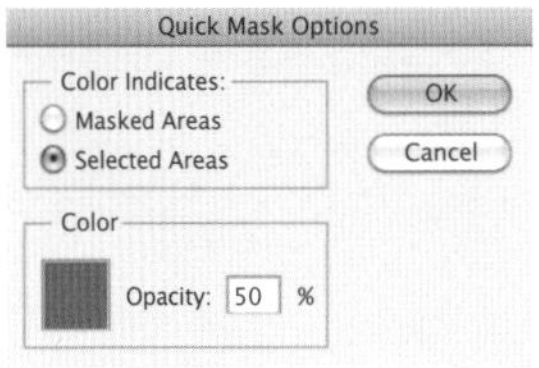

Brush tool option bar

STEP 3

Switch the foreground color to white to use the Mask Eraser tool. Select a small, soft brush and start to clean up the edges of the mask.

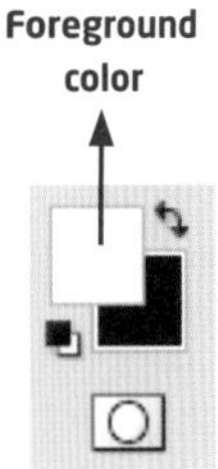

STEP 4

Click on the Quick Mask icon to exit Quick Mask. The area outside of the mask will now be selected.

STEP 5

Now select the pansy.
Select > Inverse.

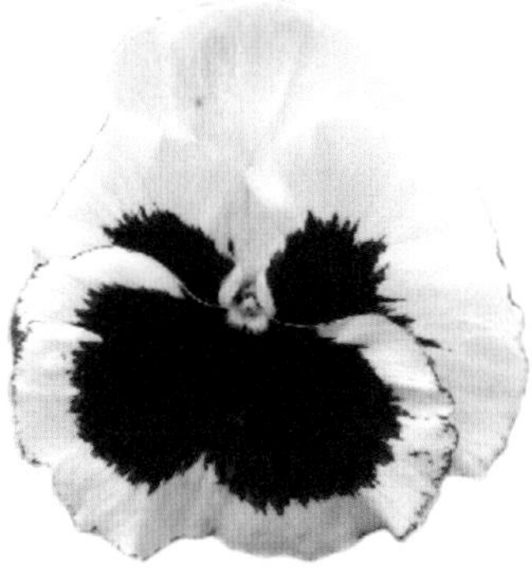

STEP 6

Open a new document.
Edit > Copy.
Edit > Paste.

STEP 7

Continue to build a posy from the photographs you have, using the same Quick Mask process to select a flower from your photograph. Copy and paste the flowers and arrange them into a posy with the Move tool.

STEP 8

Turn the background layer off and merge the visible layers.

STEP 9

To achieve a collage effect, apply the Cutout filter. **Filter > Artist > Cutout**.
Experiment with the levels until you are happy with the result.

STEP 10

Open a new document sized 0.4 x 0.4 in (1 x 1 cm) and create a spot.

STEP 11

Define > Pattern.
Name the spot pattern and press OK.

STEP 12

Select the background layer.
Edit > Fill > Pattern.
Find your spot.

STEP 13

Finally, scan in another image and copy and paste it into the center of the design.

Good photography and careful selection of areas is the basis of creating successful photomontage designs. This group of photographs by Daisy Butler formed the basic elements of her design. The photographs are all 300 dpi to maintain a high-resolution image.

TUTORIAL 8

BUILDING A BRUSH PALETTE

The Brush panel is one of the most versatile tools for textile design in Photoshop. It allows you to create your own custom brush from almost any mark or motif, and then paint freely with it. Designs can be created instantly using your custom brush, or the brush may just be a useful tool to add your own elements to a design.

The inspiration behind this whimsical textile collection, by Korean-born Hong Yeon Yun, came from childhood memories of her garden. Her designs are mainly produced using brushes created in Photoshop from her drawings.

The Brush panel in Photoshop affords the same fluidity and spontaneity that painting does. This, combined with Hong's quirky drawings, adds a magical element to her work. The design shown here is made up from 23 brushes produced in Photoshop; by layering the brushes and changing their scale, rotation, and scattering, she has created a rich and complex collection of designs that maintain the lyrical feeling of her drawings.

This tutorial demonstrates how to use brushes and also shows how to create a basic half-drop with the design.

STEP 1

First, create the series of brushes that you will use to produce your design. You may choose a motif for each brush from a shape you have drawn in Illustrator or from a drawing scanned into Photoshop. Either way, it is best if the initial motif is black to allow maximum definition when you come to customize it. If you are following the tutorial exactly, you may wish to scan in the motifs shown here.

STEP 2

In Photoshop, use the Magic Wand tool to select a motif. (In this case, the butterfly.)

STEP 3

Edit > Define Brush Preset.
Name the brush and press OK.
Your new brush will be saved in the Brush panel.
Create a whole series of brushes in the same way.

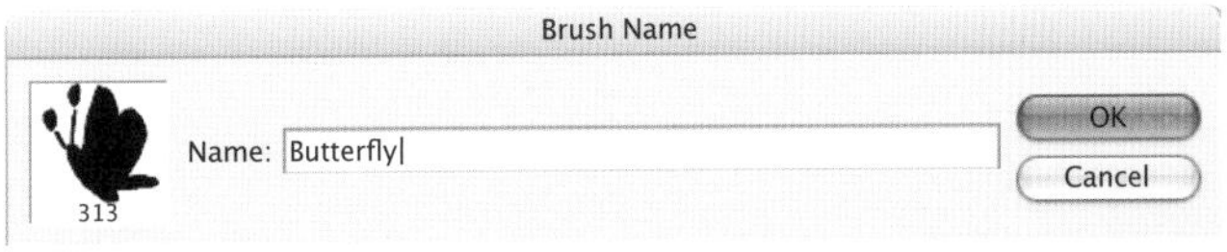

STEP 4

Open the Brush panel.
Windows > Brush.
Within this panel you have endless choices for editing your brushes. Do this by adjusting the various sliders; it is worth experimenting with these options to see the effects that can be achieved.

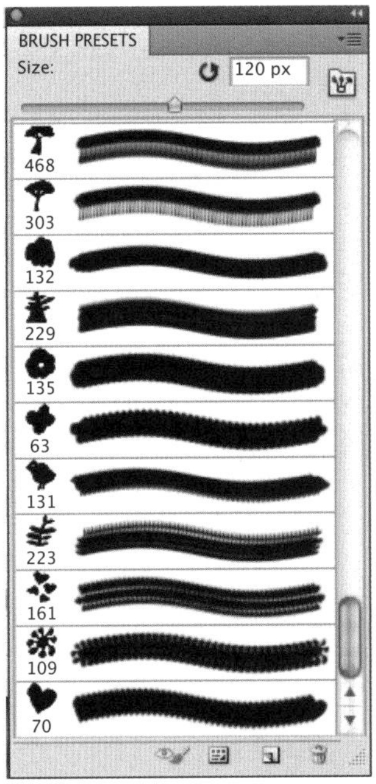

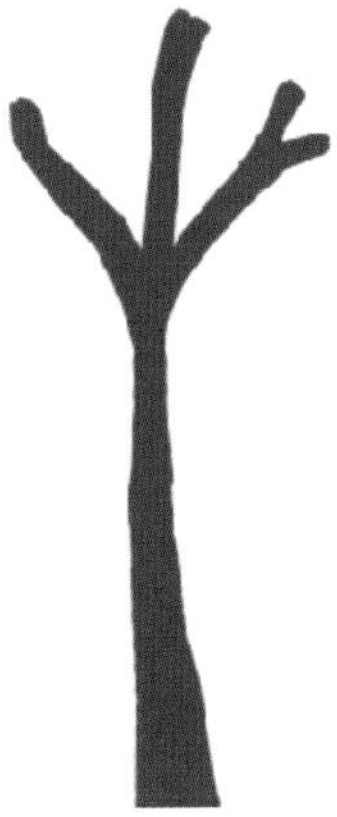

STEP 5

Open a new document and a new layer. With the tree-trunk brush (or one of your own brushes), choose a color and size and paint a tree trunk by clicking once.

Open another new layer. This will give you the chance to try a few effects, deleting and remaking layers until you are satisfied.

STEP 6

Choose the leaf brush from the Brush panel and select Shape Dynamics. Change the Size Jitter and Angle Jitter.

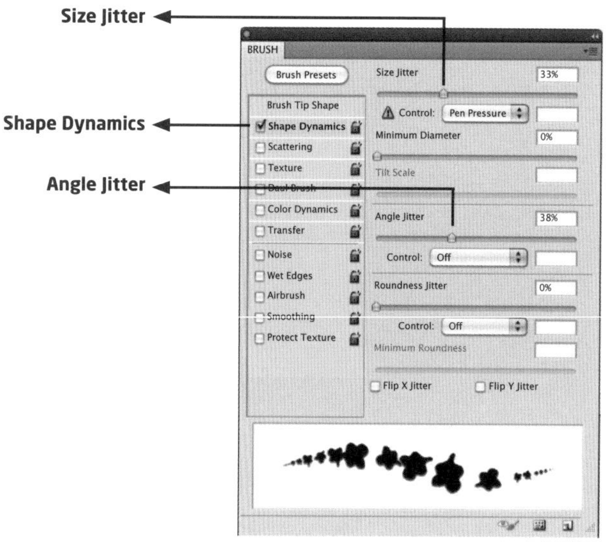

STEP 7

Select the Scattering option. Adjust the Scatter, Count, and Count Jitter.

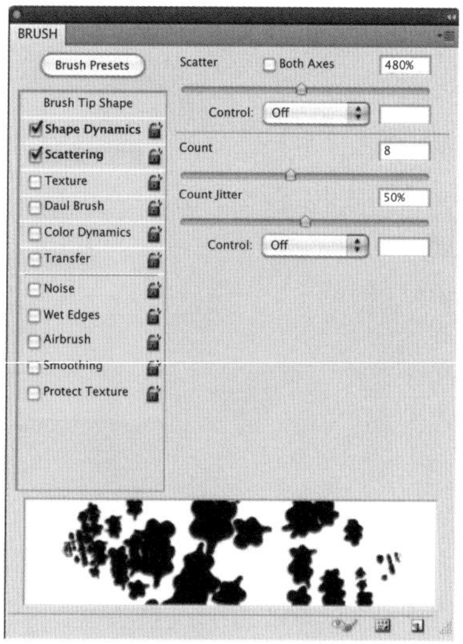

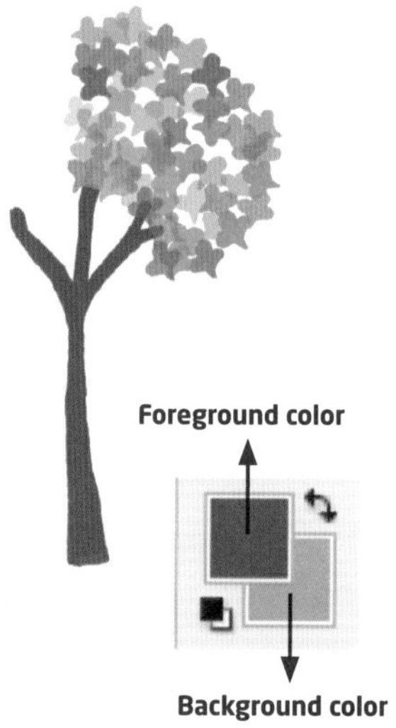

STEP 8

Select Color Dynamics. Select a foreground and background color in the Tool panel. Adjust the sliders in the Color Dynamics dialog box.

Finally, determine the Opacity by clicking on Color Dynamics and moving the Opacity slider. Your leaf brush is ready; start scattering the leaves.

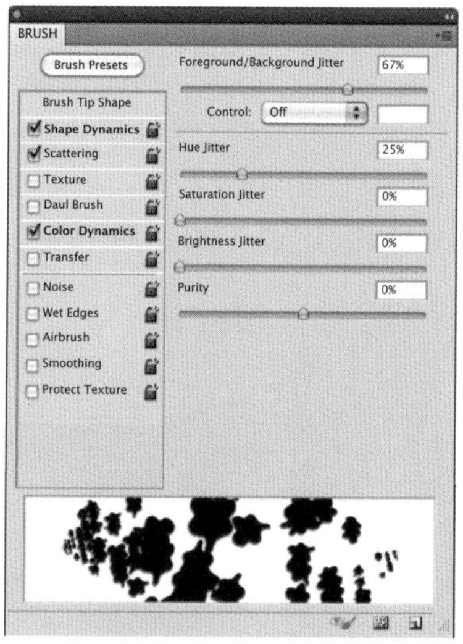

STEP 9

Continue to scatter the leaves until the tree is complete.
Fill the background layer with a color.

STEP 10

Create a new layer and select the flower stem brush. Select the Shape Dynamics option and slightly change the Angle Jitter. Paint the flower stems, changing the scale as you go if you wish.

STEP 11

Create a new layer for the flowers. Again, change the foreground and background colors to change the color effects in the Color Dynamics option.

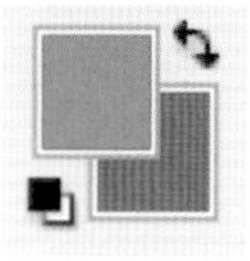

STEP 12

Build up the flowers to surround the tree.

STEP 13

Create a new layer and scatter some hearts around the tree.

STEP 14

Now that your design is nearly complete you will have several layers. Turn the background layer off and flatten the visible layers. You should now have two layers: the background layer and the design layer. Save a copy of the image with a new name.

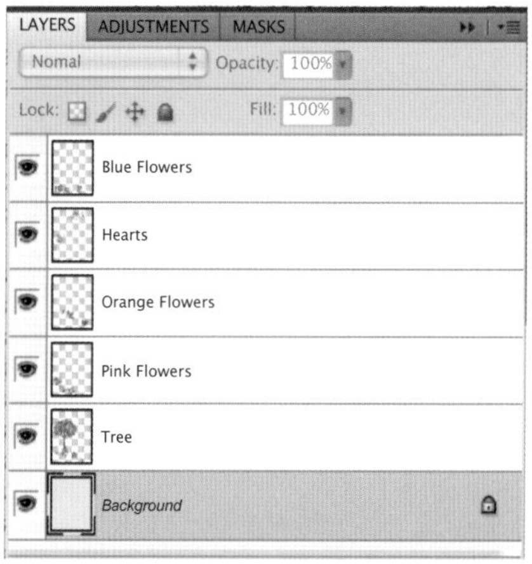

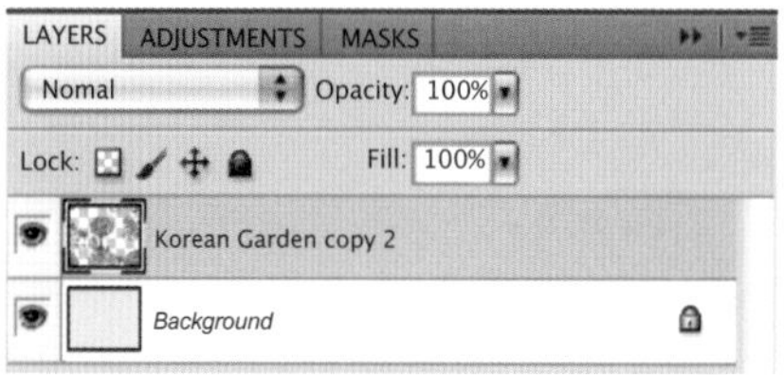

STEP 15

Create another new layer and place it under the design layer. Add other motifs to fill in the spaces. Do not let any of the motifs go over the edges of the design.

STEP 16

Now go to the background layer and change the color if you wish.
Finally, flatten the image.
Layer > Flatten Image.

STEP 17

The next stage is to put the design into a simple half-drop repeat.
Select > All.
Edit > Copy.

STEP 18

Filter > Other > Offset.
Move the Vertical slider to cut the image in half. (Ensure Wrap Around is selected.)

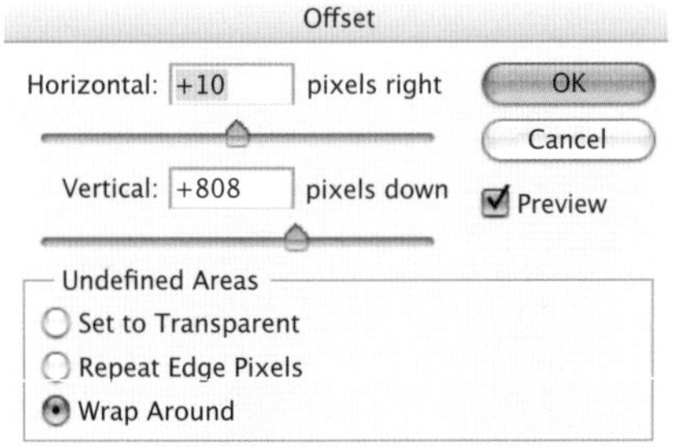

STEP 19

Go to the Tool panel and make sure the background color is the same as your design background color.

STEP 20

Image > Canvas size.
Highlight the middle box on the left-hand side of the Anchor grid.
Change the Width to 200 percent.

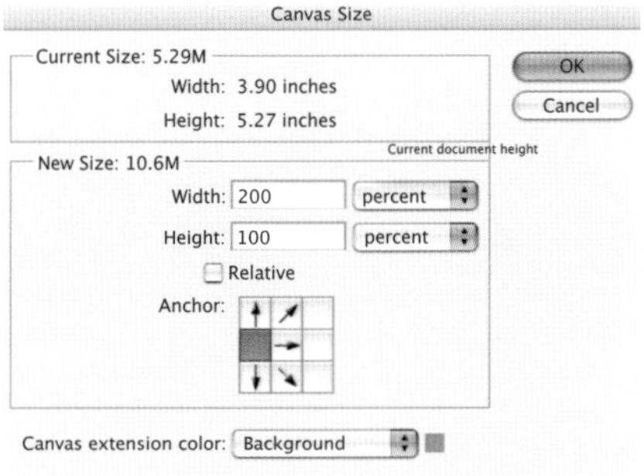

STEP 21

View > Snap To > All.

STEP 22

Edit > Paste.
Snap your design into position. Flatten the layers.

STEP 23

Your half-drop repeat is now complete. If you wish to change the unit size, go to **Image > Image Size**.

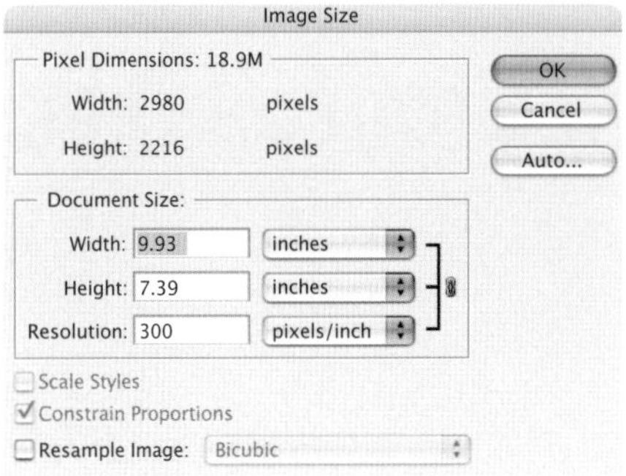

STEP 24

Select > All.
Edit > Define Pattern.
Name the pattern and press OK.

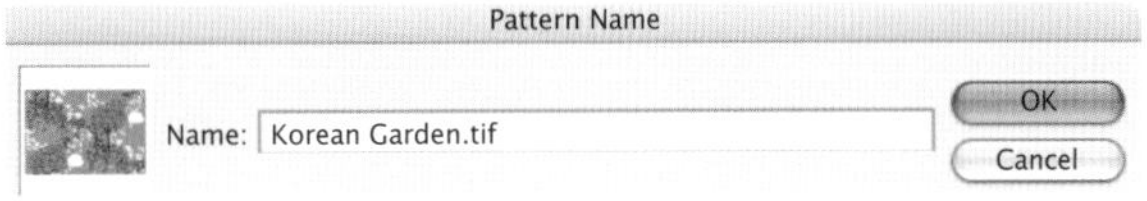

TUTORIAL 9

TEXTURED EFFECTS

Claire Turner's collection is a quirky mixture of screen-printed fabrics and digital prints. She combines digital photography with her lovely freehand drawings. Her grass-printed dress (above right) is an example of an allover texture print, and shows how effective a photographic print can be. This technique can also be useful for creating a background onto which you can apply images or motifs.

STEP 1

To create a textured grass repeat, take a good-quality photo of a patch of grass and open it in Photoshop.

STEP 2

With the Marquee tool, select a section of the image.
Image > Crop.
Image > Image Size.
Jot down the pixel size of your image.

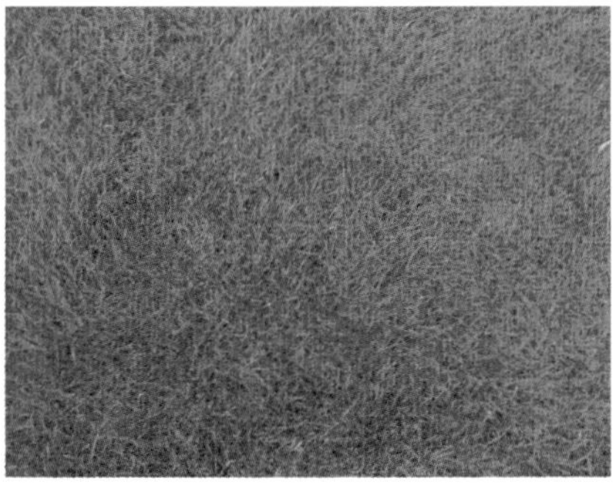

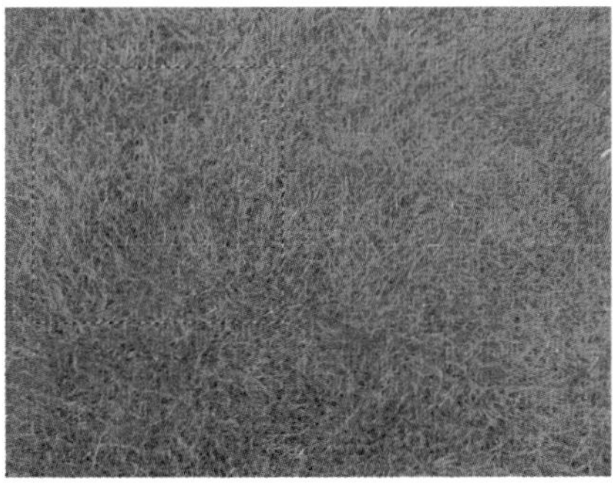

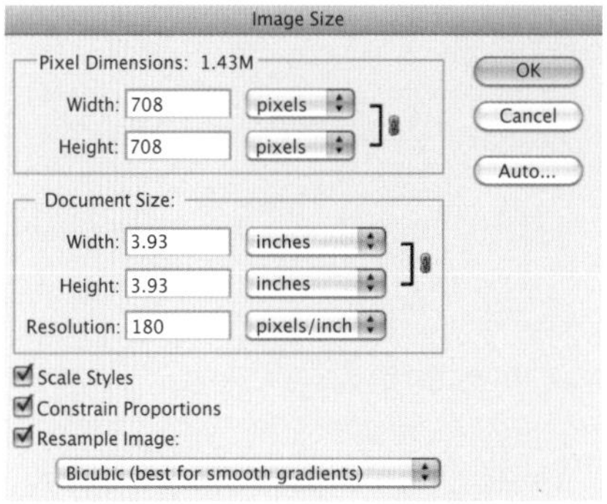

STEP 3

Filter > Other > Offset.
In the Offset dialog box, divide the Horizontal and the Vertical pixel image sizes by two and enter the new values.

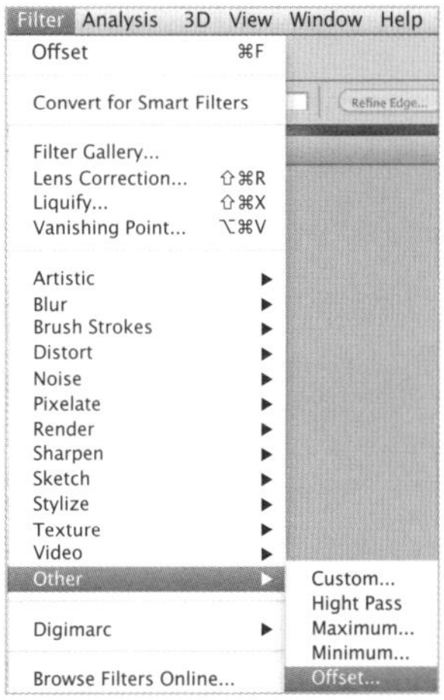

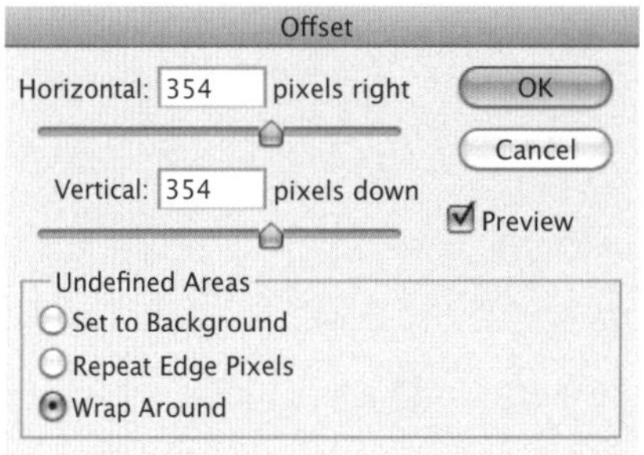

STEP 4

Your image will be cut into four and flipped round so the outside of the image is in repeat. You will see a seam appear.

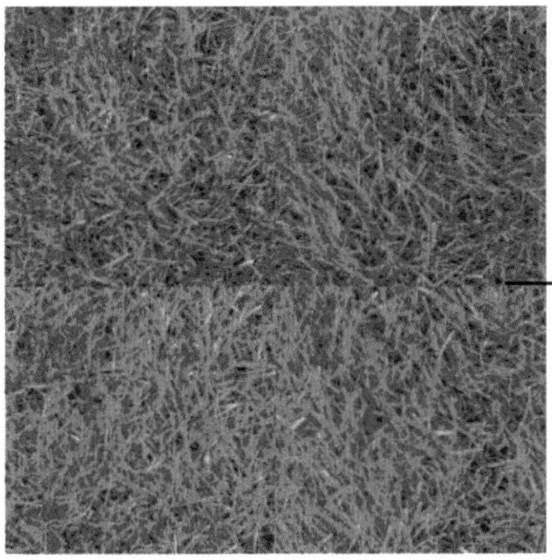

Seam

STEP 5

To mend the seam between the repeat sections, you can use Content-Aware Fill. This will copy and color-match data from another part of the image to fill in a selected area.
Select the Lasso tool from the toolbar and select an area of the seam.
Edit > Fill > Content Aware. Click OK.
Repeat this process until the seam has been completely mended.

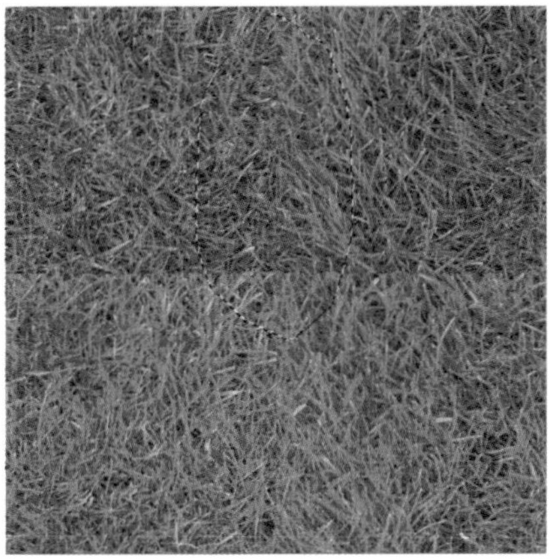

Lasso tool

STEP 6

Content-Aware Fill is a quick and easy method to mend seams between sections of a repeat. You can also use the Clone tool to mend any individual areas. The Clone tool will copy one area to another using the Brush tool.

Select the Clone tool and choose a brush, size, and opacity—the airbrush will give a softer and more forgiving effect. Choose an area you want to clone and press the Alt/Option key to set the copy target point. Move the Clone tool onto the seam and start mending the seam.

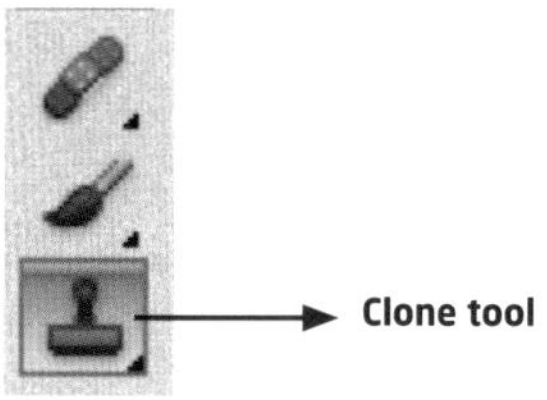

STEP 7

One you are happy with your mended seam you can put the unit into repeat. At this point you can change the unit size.

Image > Image Size.

Change the unit of measurement to percent and adjust as required.

STEP 8

Edit > Define Pattern.

Name your design unit and press OK.

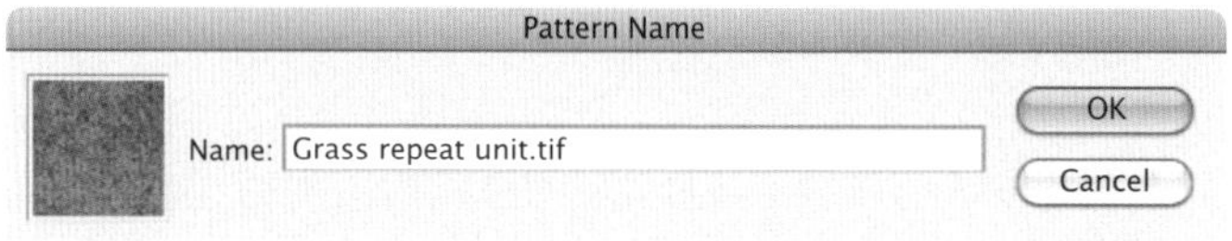

STEP 9

Open a new document.

Edit > Fill.

Select Pattern and find your design unit under Custom Pattern.

Check your repeat for any obvious seams or lines of patches. If you see any you can go back to the original unit and amend, then remake your pattern until you are satisfied.

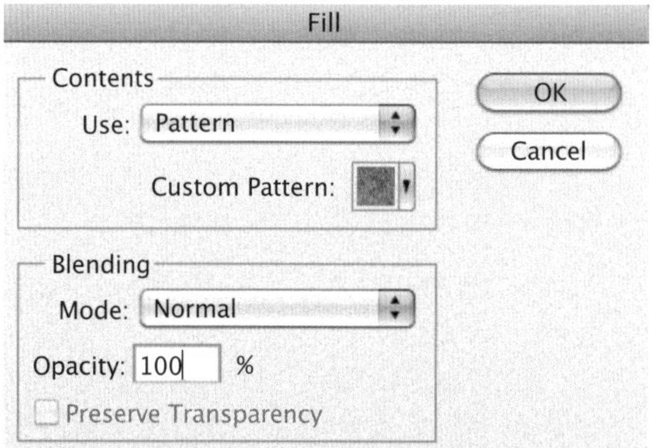

CREATING A GOOD REPEAT

When putting a textural design into repeat, the aim is to create a continuous pattern. There should be no clumsy interruptions that stand out and make a design look awkward. After a few attempts it should be perfectly possible to create repeats where the repetition of the unit is not apparent unless the viewer really searches for it. Rhythm and balance are the key to a good repeat.

The photograph on the right was the starting point for this example. The largest possible area, containing only the shells, was cropped and put into a half-drop repeat (see page 96). A half-drop is the best method for disguising the joins of textural repeat. In this process the seams are blended using the Clone tool.

The best method for checking your repeat is successful is to reduce the file size and tile-out as large an area as possible (at least two units across and down), then stand back and see if any unintentional patterns emerge.

BAD REPEAT

This example is not as successfully crafted as it could be. This is because certain elements, such as the emptier patches of sand and the diagonal line of larger white shells, stand out too obviously. One way of avoiding this is to scatter any eye-catching elements so they do not line up and so that the eye moves around the design rather than focusing on an isolated element.

GOOD REPEAT

In this example of a successful repeat, some of these same shells were carefully selected, copied, and repositioned around the unit and finally blended into the background so that they were more evenly distributed. Some were also rotated so they look like slightly different motifs.

TUTORIAL 10

CREATING A COLOR PALETTE

Color is one of the most important elements in creating a successful textile design, and it is essential that the designer is a confident colorist. Textile designers often have to design with a season in mind and follow color forecasts, but there are plenty of sources of inspiration for building color palettes.

A movie of the Broadway musical *West Side Story* was designer Andrea Patterson's starting point for her winter womenswear collection. Set in New York, the musical centers around rival teenage gangs of different ethnic and cultural backgrounds. The urban tones of gritty city life mixed with flashes of jewel brights gave the designer a rich palette to work with, but it was also the mood, atmosphere, tension, and passion of the movie that she wanted her designs to evoke.

This tutorial shows how to extract a color palette from a photograph, create a geometric pattern, and apply coloring effects and filters to create a sense of mood and atmosphere.

STEP 1

Open your photograph in Illustrator.
Select > All.
Object > Create Object Mosaic.

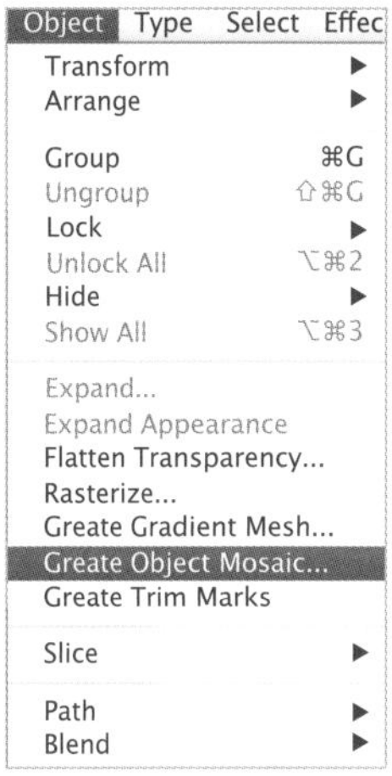

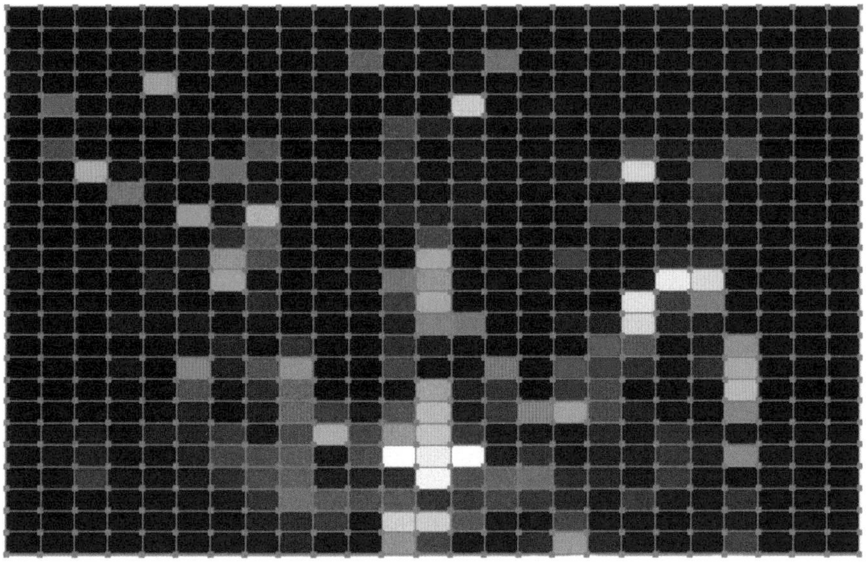

STEP 2

A dialog box will appear. Choose how many tiles you want vertically and horizontally. In this example 25 have been selected.
The tiles will be grouped; you will need to ungroup them.
Object > Ungroup.

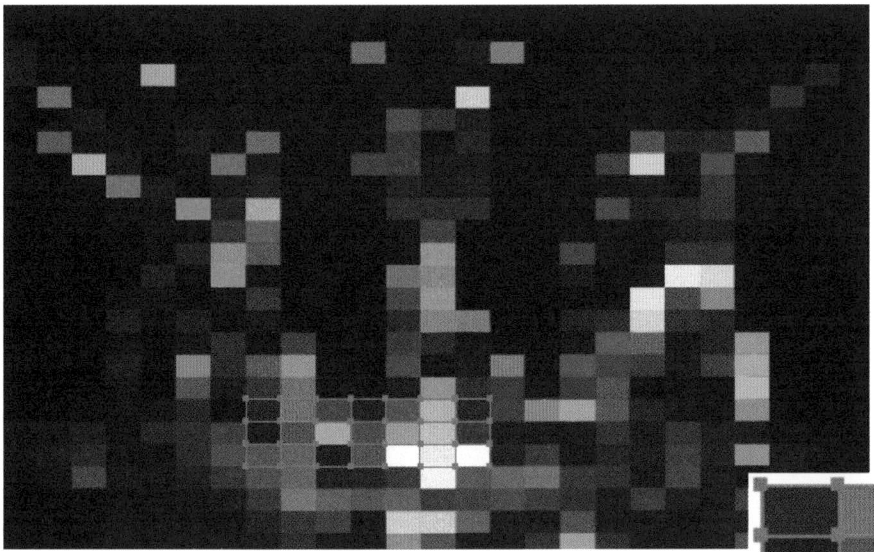

STEP 3

Select a series of tiles from the mosaic that represent a color grouping you like.
Edit > Copy.
Edit > Paste.
Select individual tiles and, with the Eyedropper tool, move across the mosaic and select and drop colors to create a palette. Alternatively, you could use a combination already together in the mosaic.

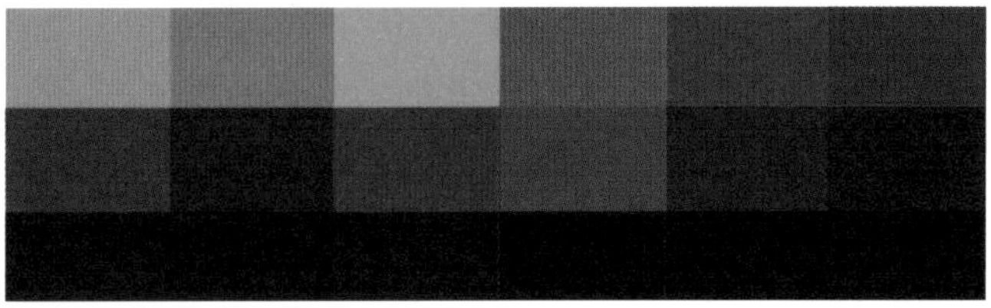

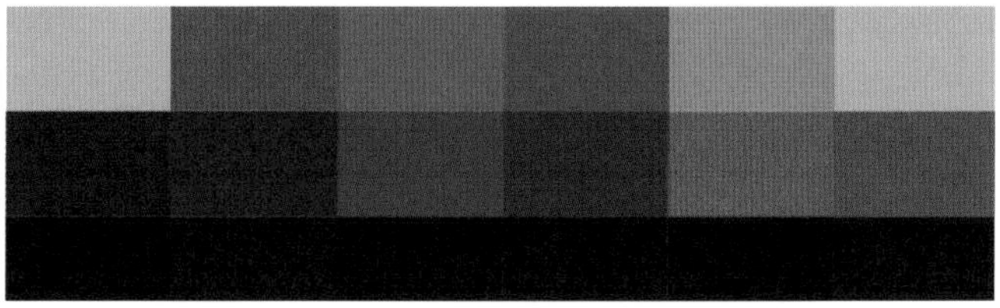

STEP 4

Here the designer has created two separate palettes from the mosaic that capture the mood she wants to evoke. To create a new palette, open up the Swatches panel if it is not already visible.
Window > Swatches.
Delete colors from the Swatches panel. Now highlight the individual tiles from your selected colors and click on the New Swatch icon at the bottom of the panel to create new swatches.

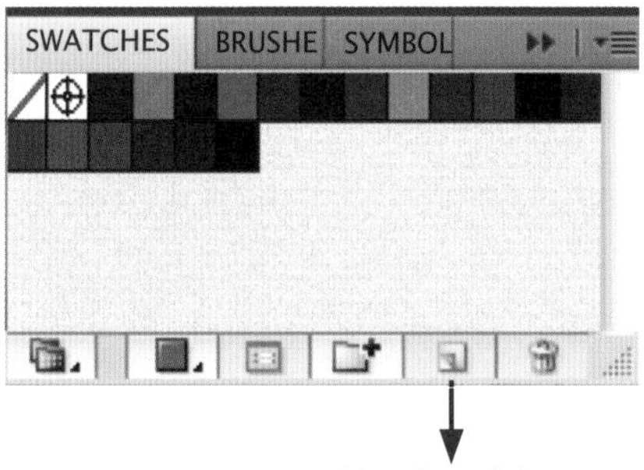

New Swatch icon

STEP 5

Click on the menu button in the top right-hand corner of the Swatches panel to reveal the drop-down menu. Scroll down to Save Swatch Library as AI. Name your new swatch palette. This will now be saved and you can access it at any time from the Swatch Library.

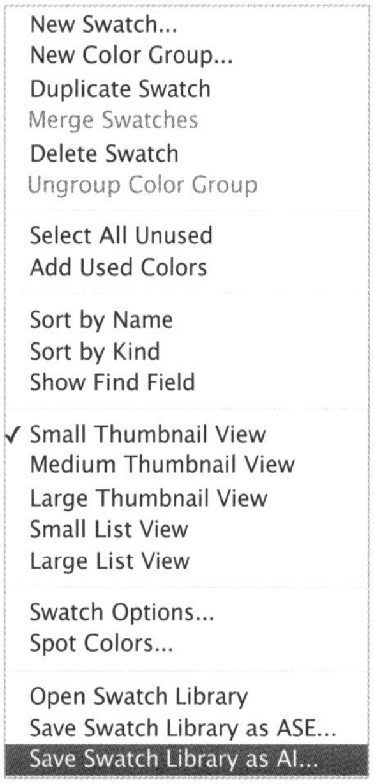

STEP 6

Open the Swatches panel and find your saved color palette in the Swatch Library.

STEP 7

Open up a new document.
View > Show Grid.
View > Snap to Grid.
View > Smart Guides.
With the grid as a guide, begin to draw a cube. Your points will snap to the grid.

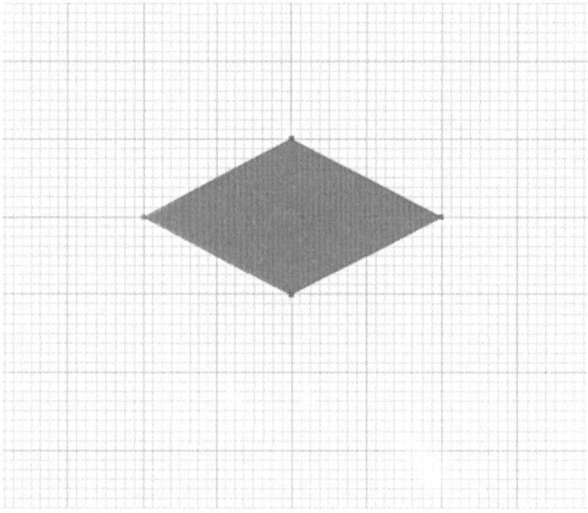

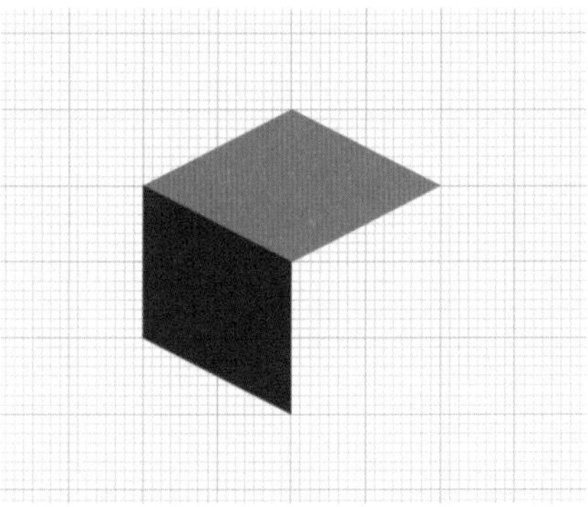

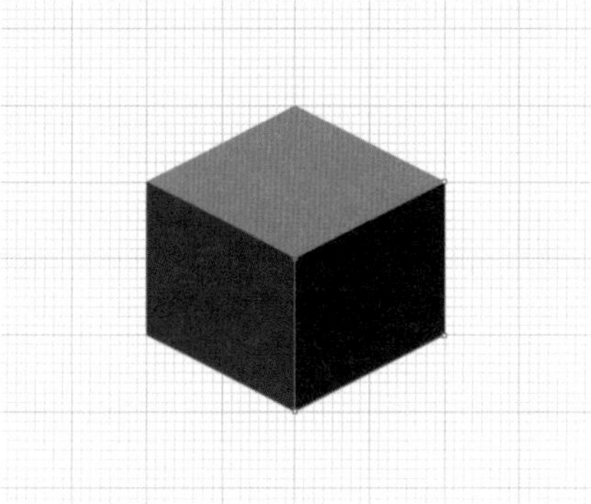

STEP 8

Once your cube is complete, select the whole cube.
Object > Group.
In the View menu, deselect Snap to Grid and select Snap to Point.

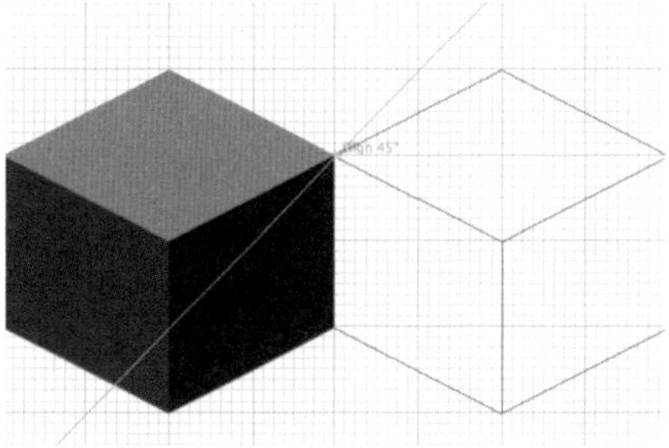

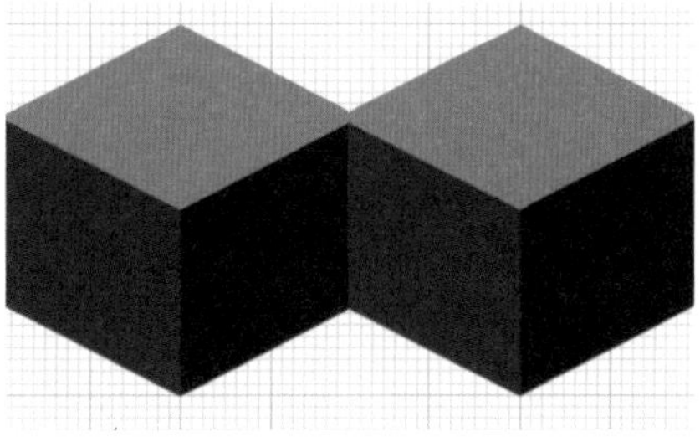

STEP 9

Select the cube, with the Selection tool placed directly on the far left anchor point. Hold down the Shift key and the Option/Alt key and drag and copy the first cube until it snaps into place on the right-hand anchor point of the cube and leaves a copy. When the double arrow goes white it has snapped to point.

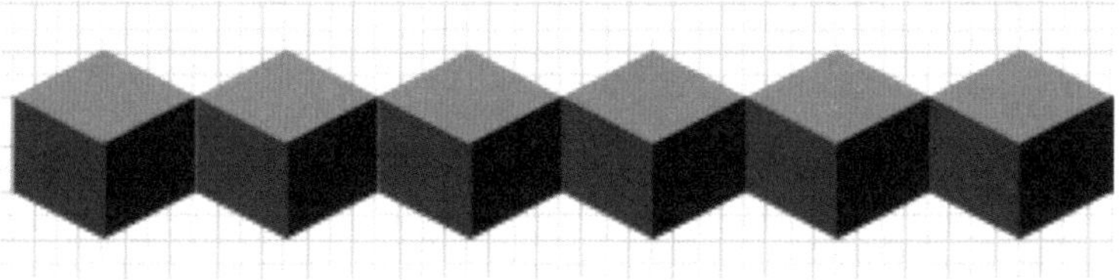

STEP 10

Press Command + D to repeat the last command and duplicate your cube.
Build up a row.

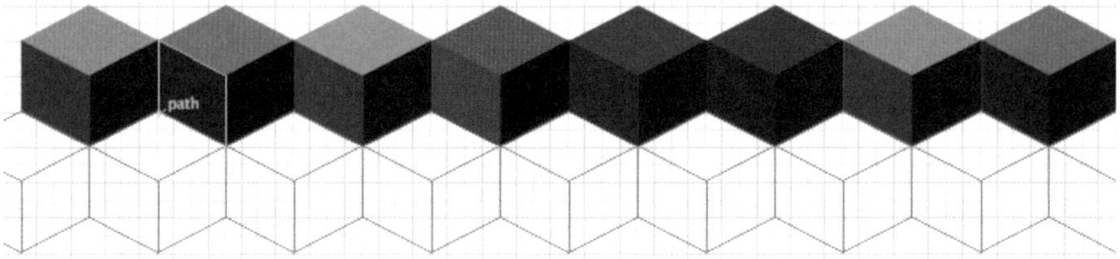

STEP 11

Once you have a row, ungroup the cubes so you can color individual sides with your color palette.
Object > Ungroup.
When your row is colored, regroup the cubes.
Select > All.
Object > Group.

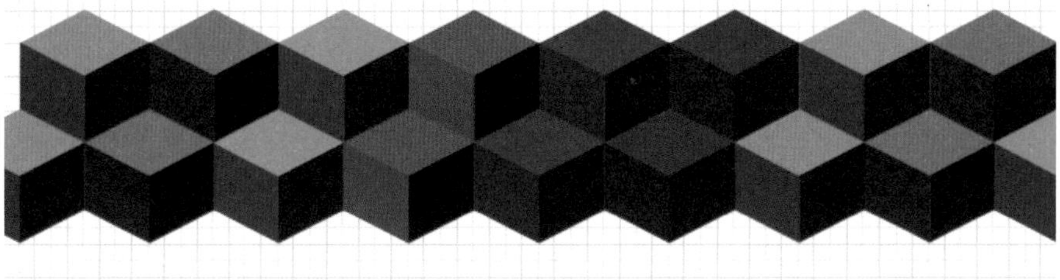

STEP 12

Select the row and, holding down the Shift and Option/Alt keys as before, duplicate the entire row this time. Continue until you have built up a unit of cubes.

STEP 13

Use a Clipping Mask to tidy up the edges of your design. Using the Rectangle tool, draw a rectangle (with no Stroke or Fill) over the design.

Select > All.

Object > Clipping Mask > Make.

Save your design. Export it as a TIFF file.

File > Export.

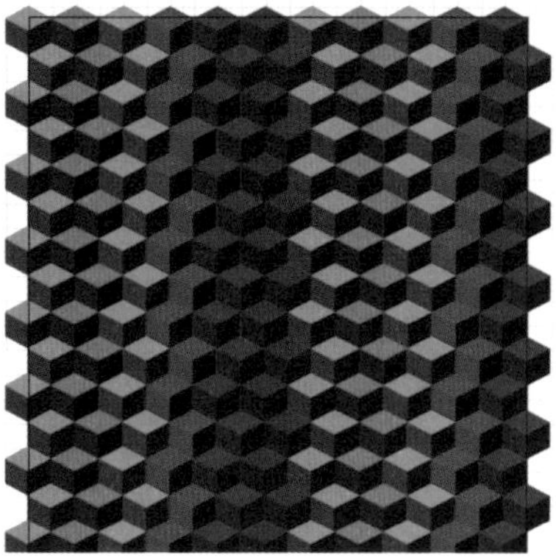

ADDING FILTERS AND EFFECTS

There are many effects and filters that can be used in Photoshop, but Andrea wanted to maintain the color and energy of the musical that initially inspired her. Her aim was to give the design a sense of movement and rhythm that the dance scene evokes.

TRANSPARENT OVERLAYS

STEP 1

Open the design in Photoshop and duplicate the layer twice.

Layer > Duplicate Layer.

Select the second layer.

Edit > Transform > Scale.

Enlarge the layer. Alter the Opacity in the Layers panel to reveal the underneath layer. With the Move tool, slightly shift the layer across to reveal the layer beneath.

STEP 2

With this layer still selected, click on the drop-down menu at the top left of the Layers panel to reveal the Blend Modes.

On Layer 3, apply the Hue blend to heighten the color. Experiment with the Opacity in the Layers panel to enhance the effects of transparency and movement.

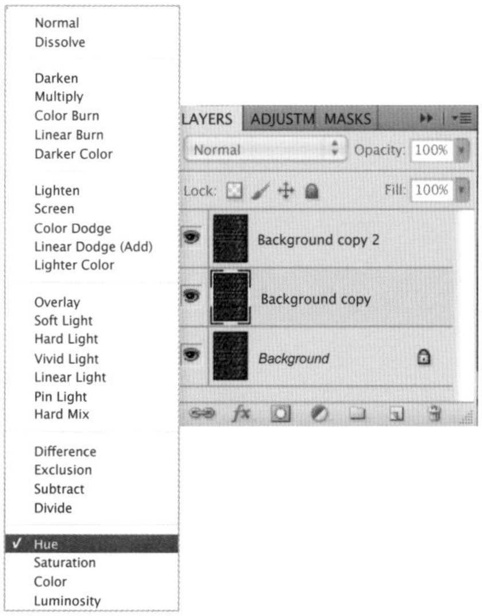

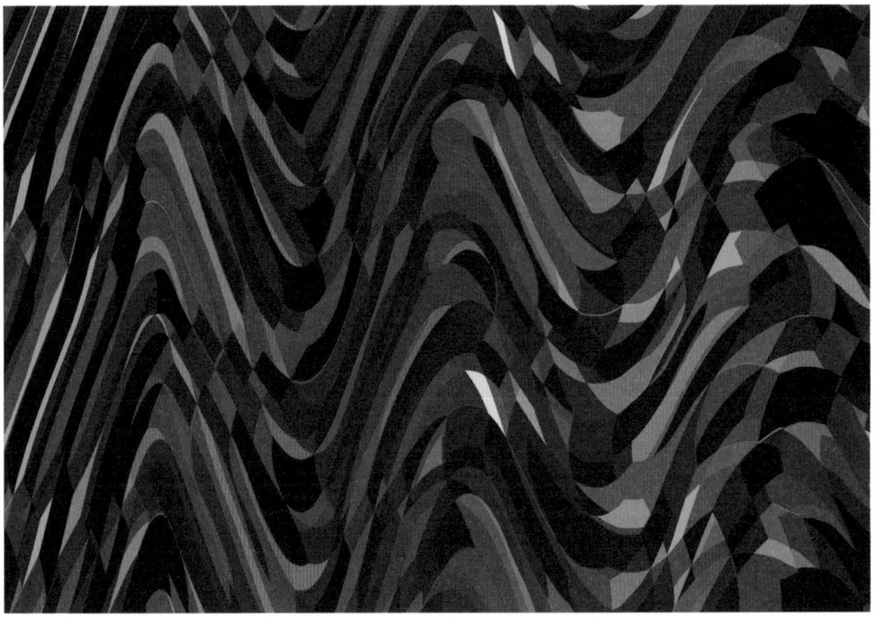

MAKING WAVES

Flatten all the layers.

Filter > Distort > Wave.

Alter the sliders in the Wave dialog box until you are happy with the effect.

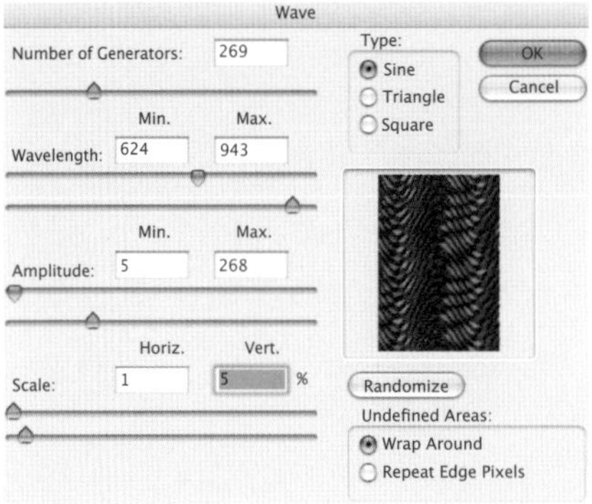

COLOR BLENDS

Here, a different color palette has been used to create the cube design.

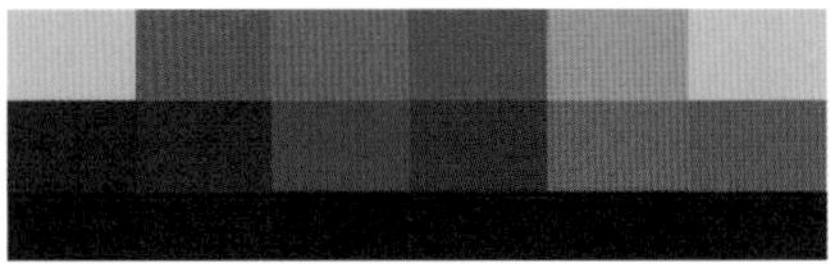

After exporting your design to Photoshop, again duplicate the layers, changing the Scale and Opacity in the Layers panel, and add the Blend Modes settings Difference and Lighten to create the effect shown on the left.

Finally, flatten the image and apply the Liquify filter to create fluidity and color blending. **Filter > Liquify**.

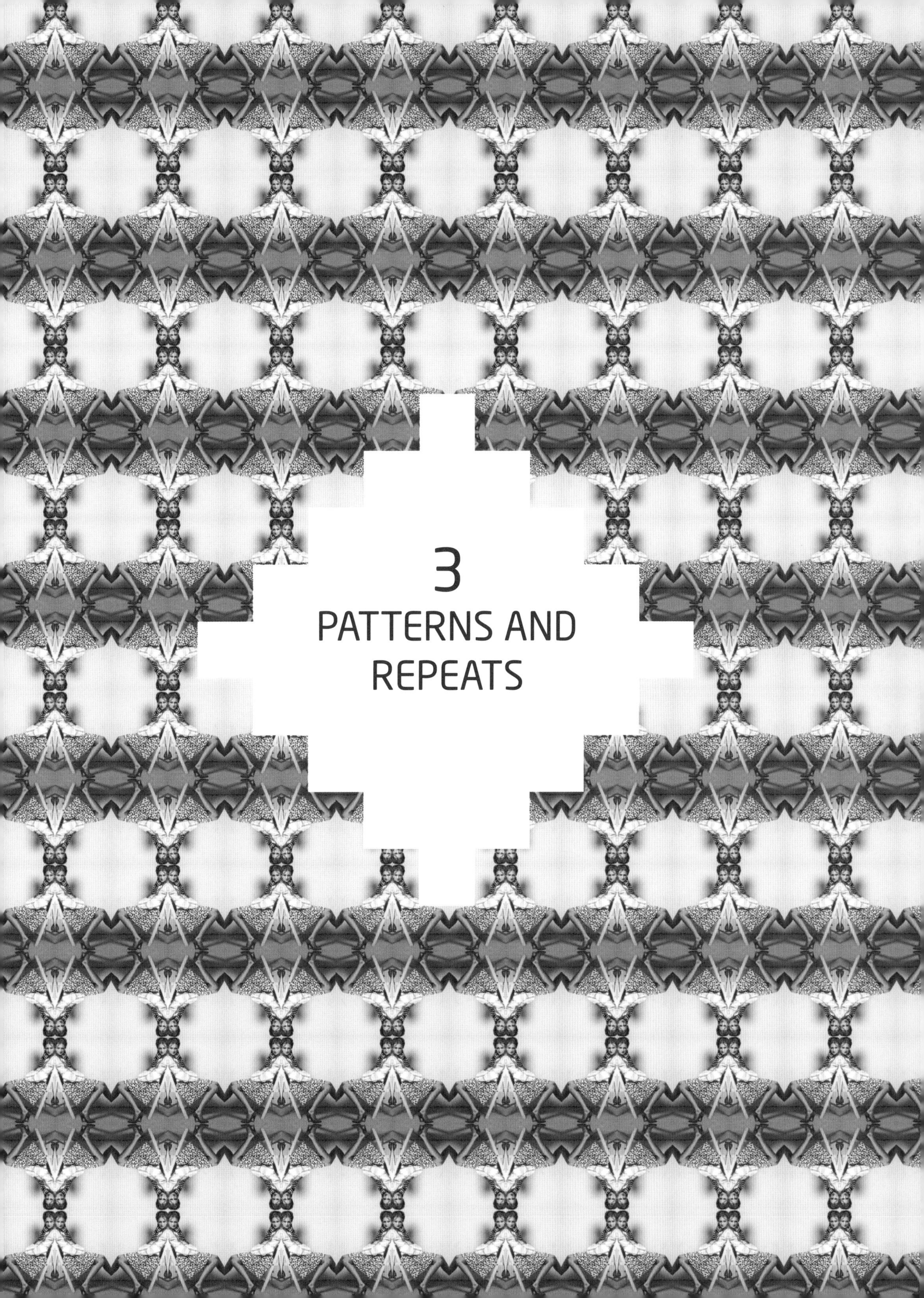

3
PATTERNS AND REPEATS

PATTERNS AND REPEATS IN DIGITAL TEXTILE DESIGN

Artists and designers have always been inspired by both the natural and man-made textures and patterns that surround them, and repeating patterns have formed the basis of most surface design in the decorative arts. It seems that we are instinctively drawn to designs that mimic the rhythms found in nature.

If a design is hand painted or drawn then the pattern may be made to change continuously, in the same way that ripples in water vary, and yet also seem to follow a predictable structure. In traditional mechanized printing, however, this kind of randomization is not possible and the exact repetition of motifs is an intrinsic part of the process. The introduction of digital printing means that such rigid repetition is no longer necessary. But there are still sound aesthetic and practical reasons for putting a design into repeat.

There are two types of repeat structure used to lay out a design so that, once printed, it will form a continuous length: the block or tile, and the half-drop repeat. It may not seem obvious at first, but all surface designs that have been printed by traditional mechanical methods fit into one of these two structures. Examples of tiled repeats include checkerboards, plaids, and stripes, while half-drops include polka dots, diamonds, and ogees, as well as the familiar pattern in which bricks are often laid.

An obvious and intentional geometric structure is part of the very nature of a plaid or diamond design. In the case of more organic patterns, such as floral or textural designs, where the designer does not intend to lay out the motifs geometrically, a successful repeat is one that is not obvious, but instead creates an illusion of randomly scattered motifs or unbroken texture (see page 79). Such textural designs tend to be more meditative and restful to the eye, in contrast to patterns in which the repeat structure is intended to dominate the design, making a bold statement. Both styles can be equally pleasing.

A skilled repeat artist is able to put an organic design based on pebbles or woodgrain together in such a way that a viewer who is not searching for the repeat unit will not be aware of it. In an example of a repeat that has not been well constructed, a particularly bright pebble might perhaps stand out from the rest as it was repeated, drawing the viewer's eye to this one element and destroying the illusion of a natural surface.

This problem, known as "tracking" within the surface design industry, where an unintentional stripe or diagonal has been created, can be resolved by scattering copies or variations of noticeable elements in a design in such a way that they appear to be randomly placed and equally balanced with other similar motifs or colored areas. An important factor in carrying out this randomization is to make sure that the initial size of the repeat unit is large enough to contain enough elements with which to work. This may be accomplished by joining several images together to form the unit that will then be repeated. All of us have seen this type of repeat in the textures often used in kitchen Formica or linoleum, based on photographs of marble, for example. In the case of a floral, a balanced rhythm can be created by rotating and mirroring motifs until the overall effect is fluid and the eye is not distracted by a rigid structure. A balanced distribution of negative space is also crucial.

By using digital techniques and "stepping out"—or tiling—your design in repeat on-screen, prior to printing, you have the option of rectifying any visual mistakes such as tracking. If tracking does occur, then you should rework and retile the repeat until you achieve a balanced effect.

CREATING REPEATS IN PHOTOSHOP AND ILLUSTRATOR

Putting your design into repeat is the final stage of preparing your work for production. It is vital that you understand repeat structures and how they can change the look of a design, and the different approaches that can be explored. Prior to the introduction of software such as Photoshop, repeats were created by tracing or photocopying the original artwork, cutting up the page, and collaging or retracing motifs to work across the seam. Once the repeat unit was deemed successful, the design would be recreated by painting or photocopying. The methods explained in this chapter for creating a repeat digitally follow the same principles, although they are obviously far less time-consuming.

Even though Photoshop and Illustrator were not created for textile designers, there are many methods for creating repeats using these programs. Photoshop offers a painterly approach to design work; for example, the Clone Stamp tool may be used to maintain the hand-drawn or photographic qualities of an original design. The tools can help when mending any of the seams that are inevitably created during the repeat process, which must be done with skill.

Illustrator, on the other hand, is a vector-based program and the software maintains a mathematical "memory" of elements so that they never become distorted during manipulation. It is easier to set up groups of motifs in Illustrator than in Photoshop so that they may all be moved or manipulated together. Accurate and complex graphic patterns and constructions can be built in this program, providing an infinite range of possibilities.

This chapter presents tutorials designed to explain the basic principles of setting up block and half-drop repeats in both Photoshop and Illustrator; examples include stripes and plaids. Once you have mastered the mechanical processes in both

Vicki Murdoch created an eccentric textile collection for furnishing her 1969 caravan, the owner of which is her cat! She is inspired by retro prints of the era. Repeat patterns are intrinsic to her design process and allow her designs to work together in harmony with their somewhat bizarre surroundings.

programs they should become second nature, allowing you to concentrate on designing and constructing successful repeats. Photoshop is better suited to organic, painterly, or photographic designs, while Illustrator works well with geometric and hard-edged styles.

Specialist textile design software geared for production and the preparation of designs for traditional print production, such as AVA, Pointcarré, and Lectra, does exist and will be covered more fully in Chapter Six. Many of these systems have the advantage of providing functions for creating repeats that are considerably faster and more sophisticated than off-the-shelf packages such as Photoshop and Illustrator.

TUTORIAL 11

PHOTOSHOP REPEAT: BASIC BLOCK REPEAT

The quickest way to make a basic block pattern in Photoshop is with the Define Pattern function. This simply puts a motif into repeat and stores it in the Pattern Library for you to use at any time.

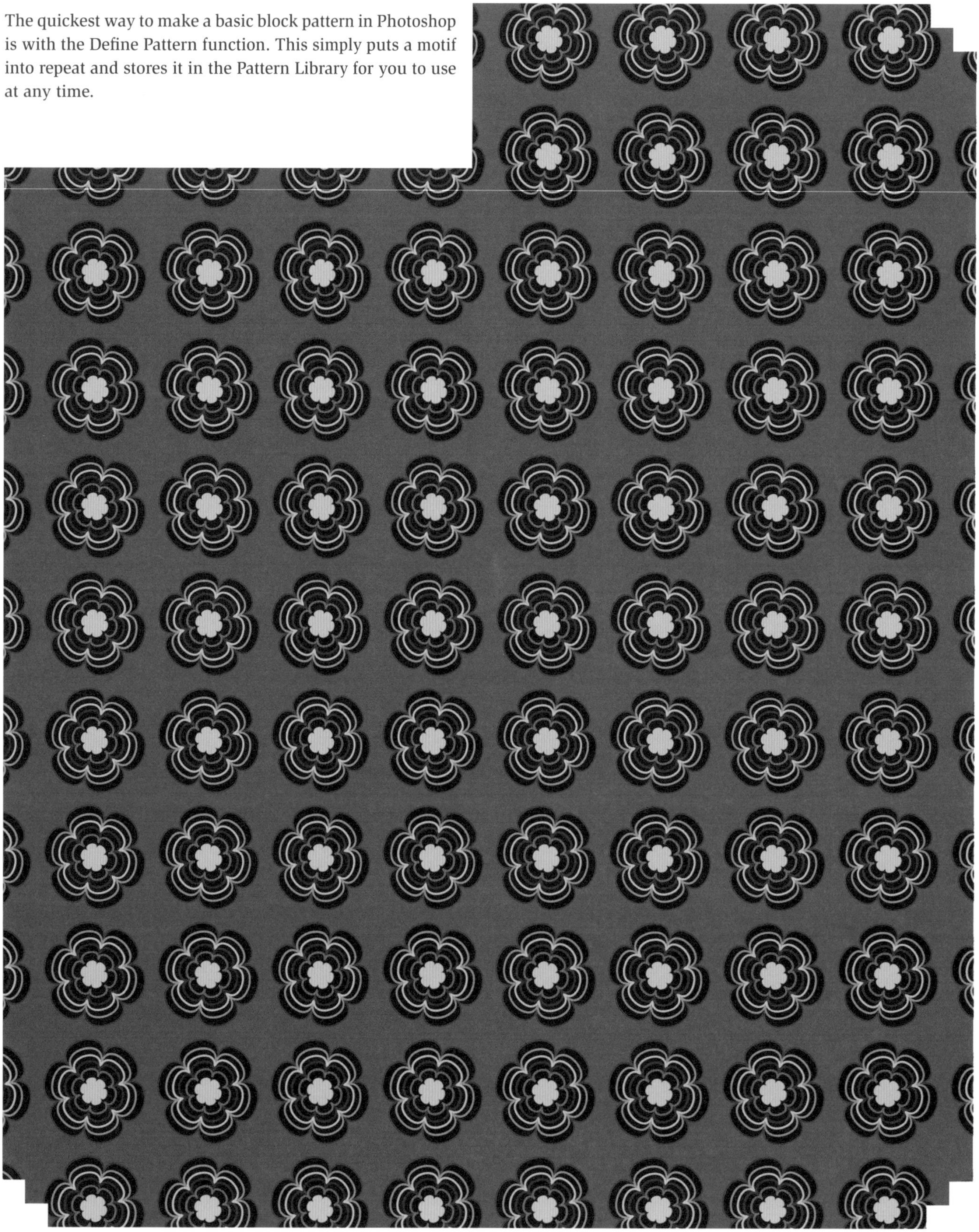

STEP 1

Choose a motif and resize the unit to the required size. Here the image was scaled down to 0.8 x 0.8 in (2 x 2 cm).
Image > Image Size.
Select > All.

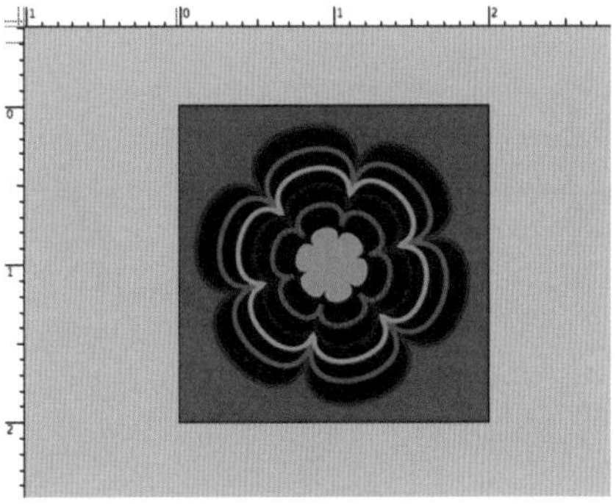

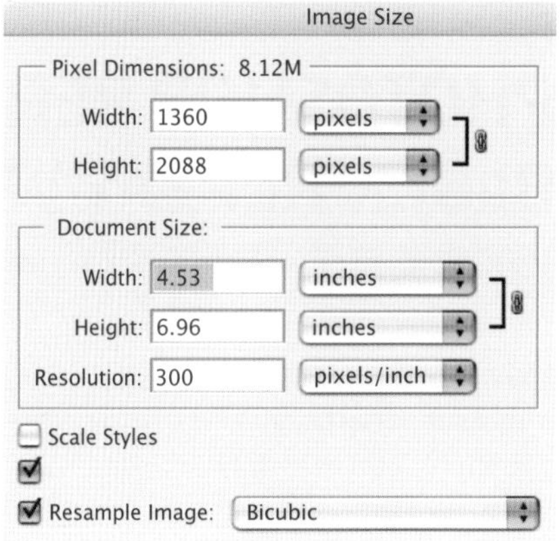

STEP 2

Edit > Define Pattern.
Name your new pattern and press OK.

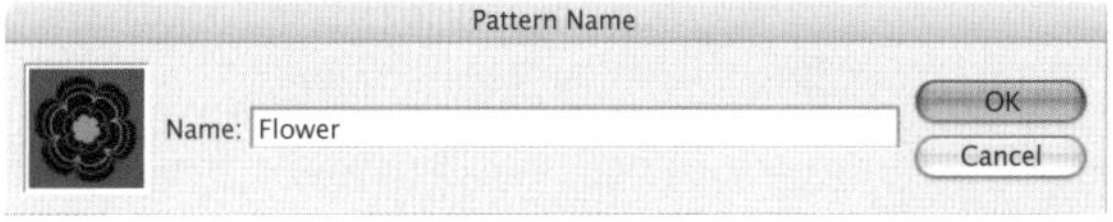

STEP 3

Open a new document or select the shape you want to fill with your new pattern.
Edit > Fill.

STEP 4

In the Fill dialog box, select Pattern.

STEP 5

Click on Custom Pattern to reveal the patterns stored in the Pattern Library. The last pattern shown will be the one you have just made.

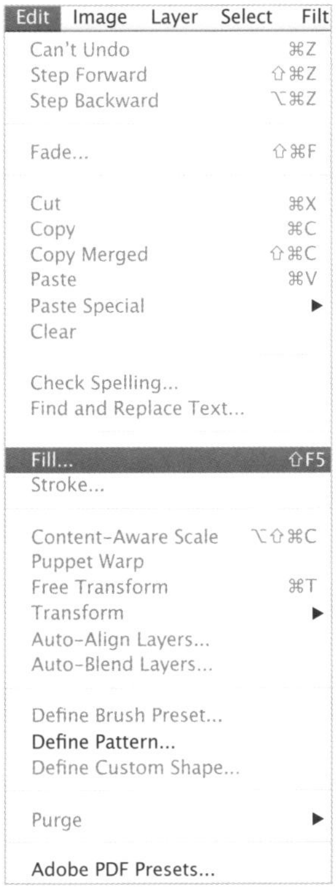

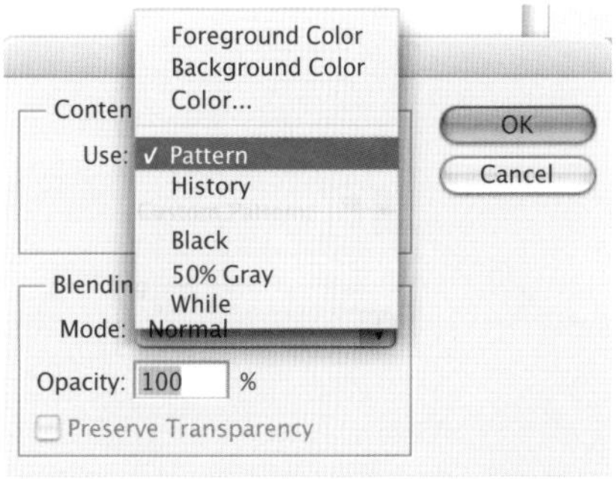

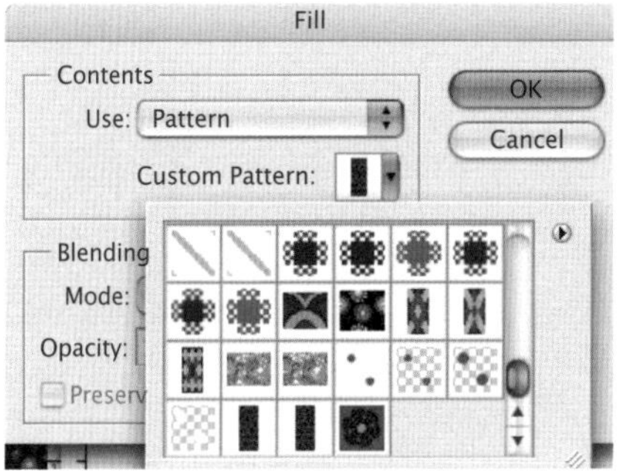

TUTORIAL 12

PHOTOSHOP REPEAT: BLOCK REPEAT WITH OFFSET FILTER

You can create an easy block repeat by defining your design unit as a pattern. However, if your design is not a simple, flat motif and has texture, you will see a seam appear. By offsetting the design you can carefully mend the seam and avoid any ugly lines passing through the repeat. The mending of a seam can take time and patience, but it is an important part of the process of achieving a beautiful and natural pattern.

This tutorial demonstrates a floral painting being put into a repeat. The painting is built up with layers of acrylic paint, and it is crucial to maintain the feel and quality of the painting in the mending process.

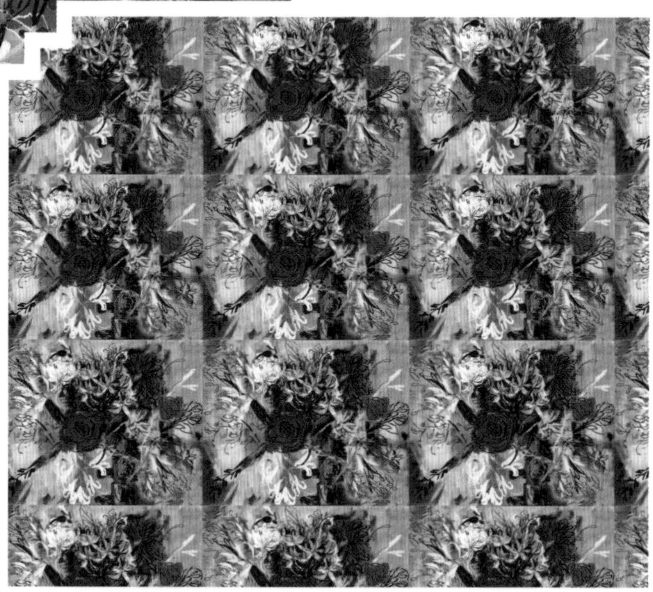

STEP 1

Open the artwork in Photoshop and apply the Offset filter.
Filter > Other > Offset.
In the Offset dialog box, ensure that Wrap Around is selected. Divide the Horizontal and the Vertical pixel image sizes by two and enter the new values. Click OK.

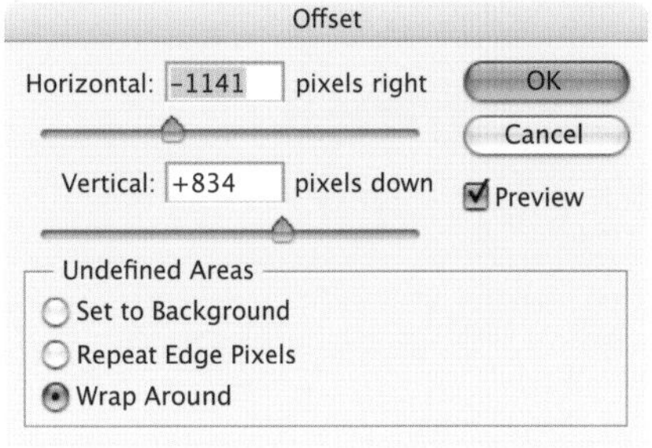

STEP 2

Your artwork should now be cut into four and flipped so the outsides of the design will match edge to edge. However, seams now run through the design.

STEP 3

You need to carefully mend the seams, using any tools you think are appropriate for the job. Here, the Clone tool is used to retain the painted textures. Select a soft brush option to avoid creating hard edges. Paint and draw back into the seams using the Eyedropper tool for color-matching. You can also copy and paste parts of the design to rebuild an area around the seams.
The Spot Healing Brush tool will copy the texture from a selected area and match it to the color and tone of the area you are mending.
With Content-Aware Fill, you can copy and color-match data from one area of the image to fill in another selected area. The selected area changes to match the area around it and fills in the selection with actual image detail.

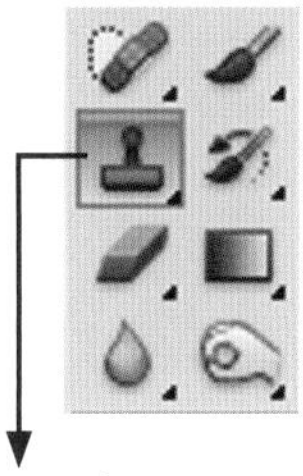

Clone tool

STEP 4

Once you are happy with your mending you can offset again (steps 1 to 3) to check the repeat unit.
Finally, flatten the artwork.
Layer > Flatten Image.

STEP 5

Before you define the pattern you can change the unit size.
Image > Image Size.

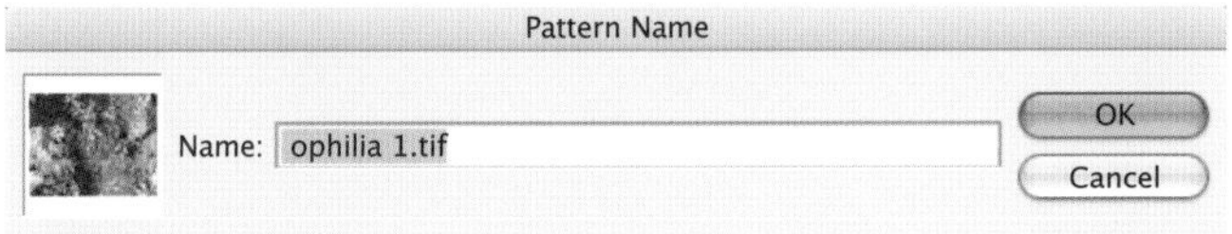

STEP 6

Edit > Define Pattern.
Name your pattern and click OK.

TUTORIAL 13

PHOTOSHOP REPEAT: SIMPLE HALF-DROP MOTIF

This tutorial shows a simple method for creating a half-drop if you have a motif you wish to put into repeat. As the motif is self-contained, there are no seams to mend and no need to use the more complex method for making a half-drop repeat shown on page 96. You can use this method to create simple patterns that you can store in your Pattern Library.

STEP 1

Open your motif in Photoshop.

Select > All.

Edit > Copy.

STEP 2

Image > Image Size.

Write down the pixel measurements.

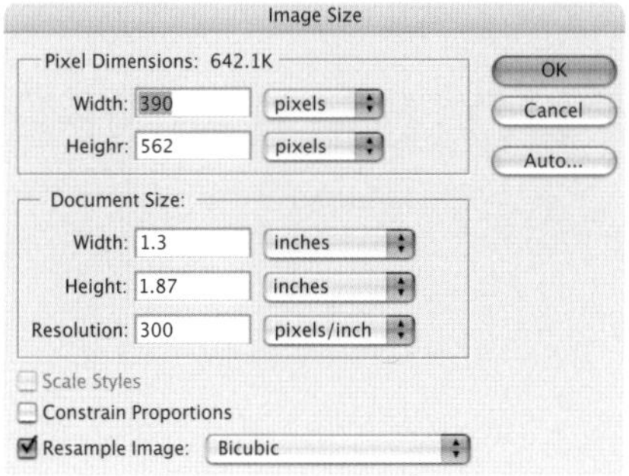

STEP 3

Filter > Other > Offset.

In the Offset dialog box, ensure that Wrap Around is selected. Divide the Vertical pixel image size by two and enter the new value. Click OK.

STEP 4

Image > Canvas Size.

Select the middle box on the left-hand side of the Anchor grid.

For Width, enter 200 percent.

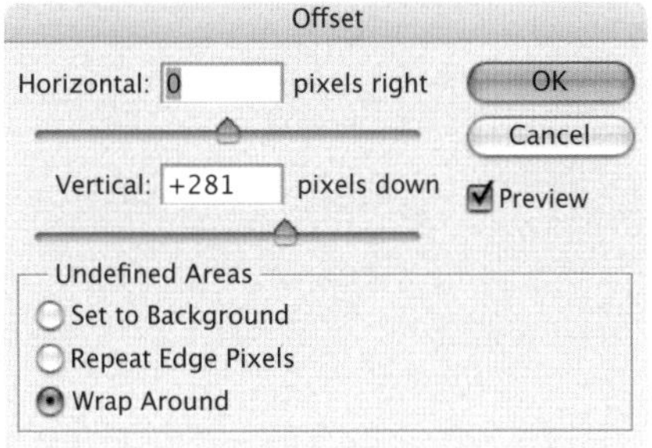

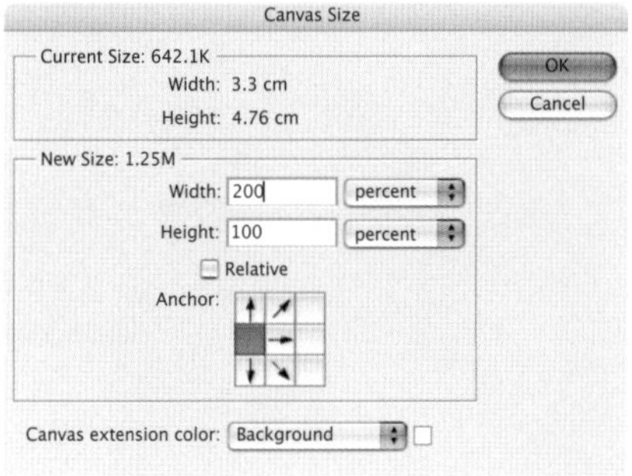

STEP 5

You have already copied the original motif.

Edit > Paste.

Position the new motif next to the first.

Flatten the image.

Layer > Flatten Image.

STEP 6

Change the size of the motif if you wish.

Image > Image Size.

STEP 7

Edit > Define Pattern.

Name your pattern and click OK.

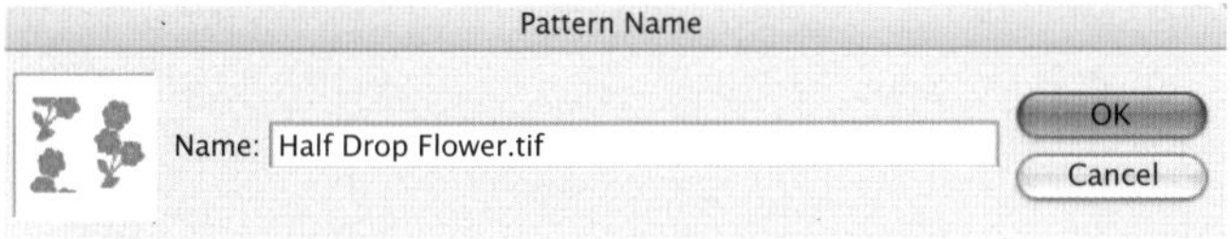

STEP 8

Open a new document.

Edit > Fill.

Cick on Custom Pattern and find your new pattern.

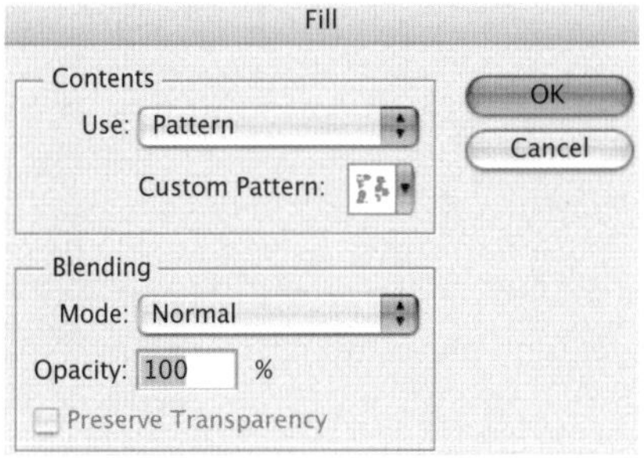

TUTORIAL 14

PHOTOSHOP REPEAT: HALF-DROP REPEAT

The half-drop is the most complex repeat you can do in Photoshop. The process is straightforward, but you will need patience to mend the seams so that they flow with the design to achieve a fluid repeat. In this tutorial, Victoria Purver's floral painting *Ophilia* is used to demonstrate a half-drop repeat.

STEP 1

Open your image in Photoshop.
Layer > Flatten Image.
View > Snap To > All.

STEP 2

Select > All.
Edit > Free Transform.
Notice the crosshairs that appear to mark the central point of your design.

STEP 3

View > Rulers.
Drag a guide down so it clicks into place over the crosshairs.
Press Escape.

STEP 4

Select your design.
Edit > Copy.
Deselect the design.

STEP 5

Image > Canvas Size.
Select the middle square at the bottom of the Anchor grid.
Change the Height to 200 percent.

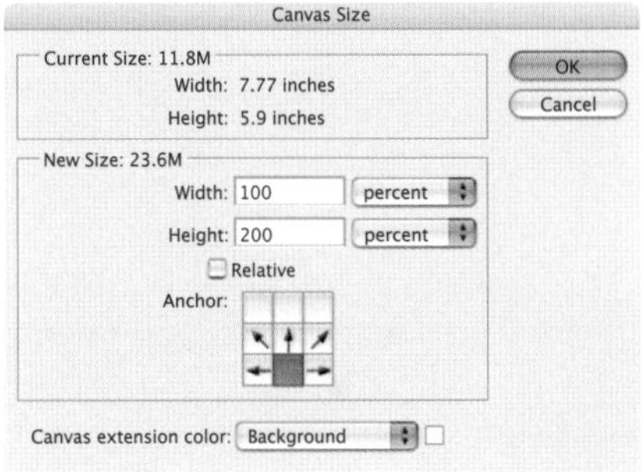

STEP 6

Click OK. You will see the canvas size is doubled in height.

STEP 7

Edit > Paste.
Flatten the image.

STEP 8

Now you need to carefully mend the seams, using any tools you think are appropriate for the job. Here, the Clone tool is used to retain the painted textures. Select a soft brush option to avoid creating hard edges. Paint and draw back into the seams using the Eyedropper tool for color-matching. You can also copy and paste parts of the design to rebuild an area around the seams.
The Healing Brush tool will copy the texture from a selected area and match it to the color and tone of the area you are mending.
With Content-Aware Fill, you can copy and color-match data from one area of the image to fill in another selected area. The selected area changes to match the area around it and fills in the selection with actual image detail.

STEP 9

Select > All.
Edit > Copy.
It can help to copy and paste other design elements during the process. For example, the red flower on the right-hand side was only half an element in the design work and would otherwise have been quite hard to complete using standard Photoshop tools.

STEP 10

Image > Canvas size.
Set the Width to 200 percent so that the canvas doubles in width.

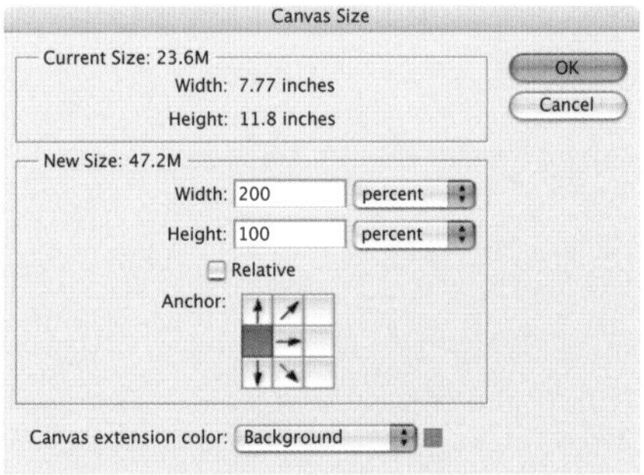

STEP 11
Edit > Paste.
Move the pasted image so the top snaps into place along the guide line.

STEP 12
Duplicate the new pasted layer. Drag this so the bottom snaps onto the guide line. Flatten the layers.

STEP 13
Now mend the seams as before.

STEP 14
Image > Image Size.
Note the pixel size.

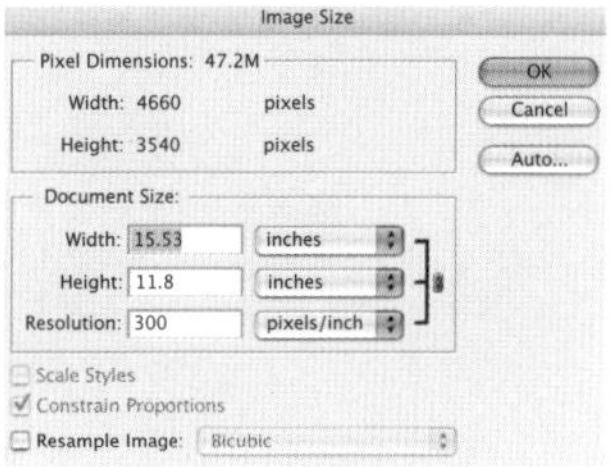

STEP 15
Filter > Other > Offset.
In the Offset dialog box, select Wrap Around. Divide the Horizontal and the Vertical pixel image sizes by two and enter the new values. Click OK. New seams will appear that, once again, you will need to mend.

STEP 16
Image > Canvas Size.
Select the middle square at the bottom of the Anchor grid.
Change Height to 50 percent.

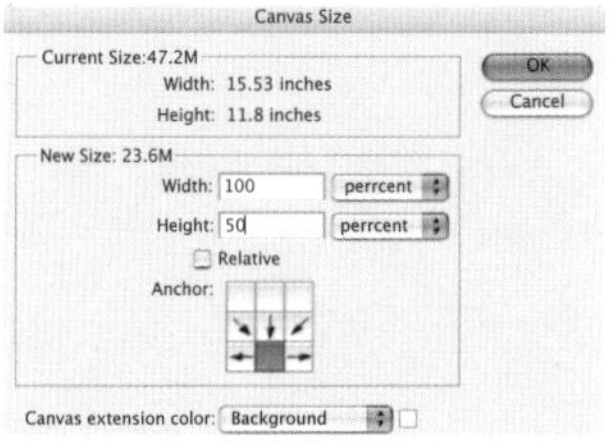

STEP 17
Your design is now in a half-drop unit.
At this point you may alter the image size.
This is the unit that you can give to a digital print bureau to print out in repeat.

STEP 18
Select > All.
Edit > Define Pattern.
Name the pattern and press OK.
Open up a new document to see the repeat effect.
Edit > Fill.
Select Pattern and find your new pattern.

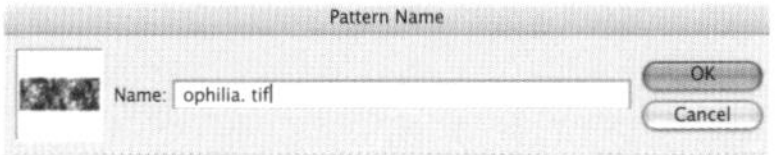

TUTORIAL 15

PHOTOSHOP PATTERN: GINGHAM

This tutorial shows how to create the eternally popular gingham pattern. Once created, it can be filled with any color and changed in scale. It may be used alone or incorporated into a design. However it's applied, it adds a charming, fresh element to a design.

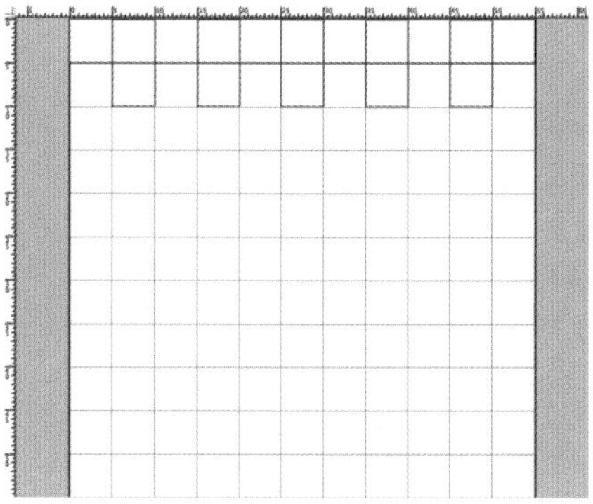

STEP 1

Open a new document in Photoshop at size 2 x 2 inches (5.5 x 5.5 cm).

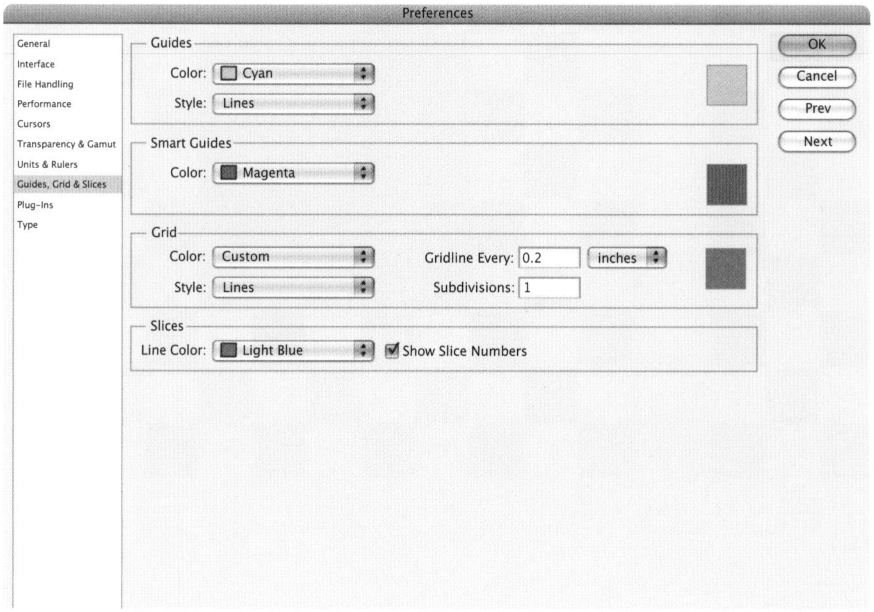

STEP 2

Adjust your grid settings.
Photoshop > Preferences > Guides, Grid & Slices.
A dialog box will appear. Set a Gridline every 0.2 in (0.5 cm), and set Subdivisions to 1.

STEP 3

View > Show > Grid.
View > Snap To > Grid.

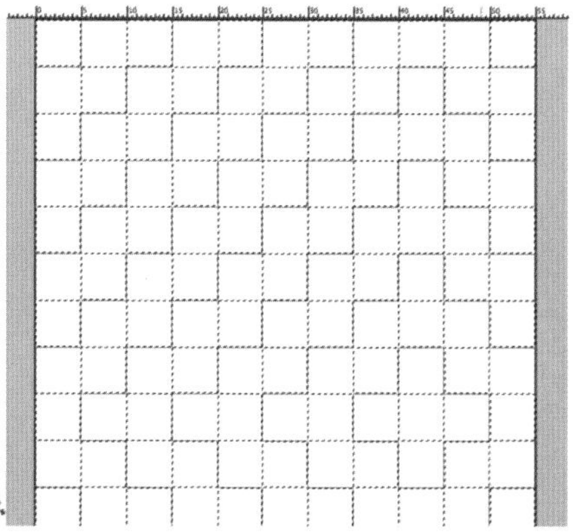

STEP 4

Select the Pen tool from the toolbar.
Use the Pen tool to draw alternating squares, using the grid as a guide to create a checkerboard effect. The anchor point should click automatically to the corner point of each grid square.

Pen tool

STEP 5

Click on the Paths palette to see the paths you have created.
Click on the Selection icon at the bottom of the palette to make your path a live selection.

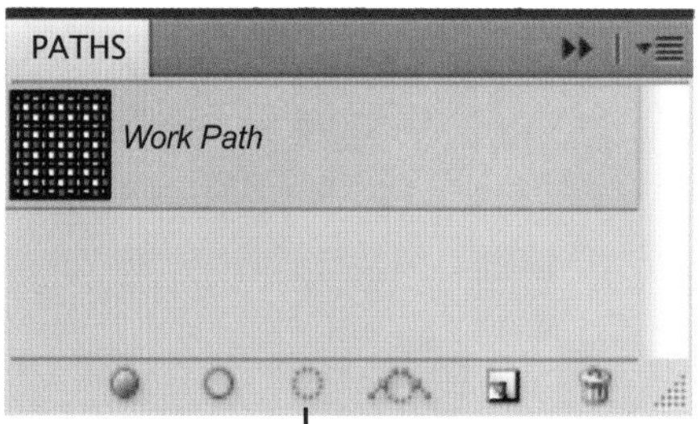

Selection icon

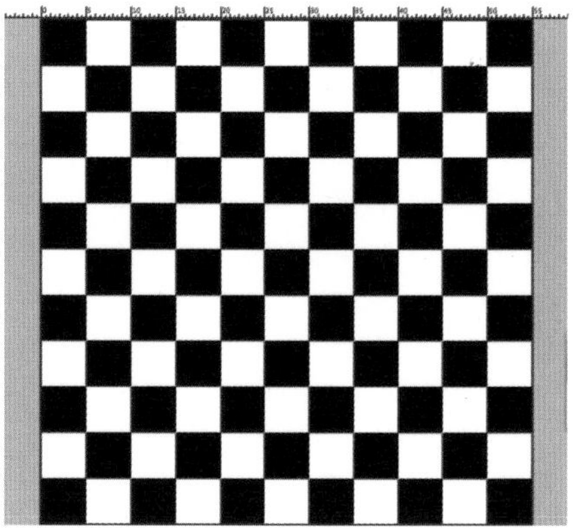

STEP 6

Edit > Fill.
Choose black as the foreground color.

STEP 7

Drag horizontal and vertical guide lines 0.2 in (0.5 cm) from the edge of the design.

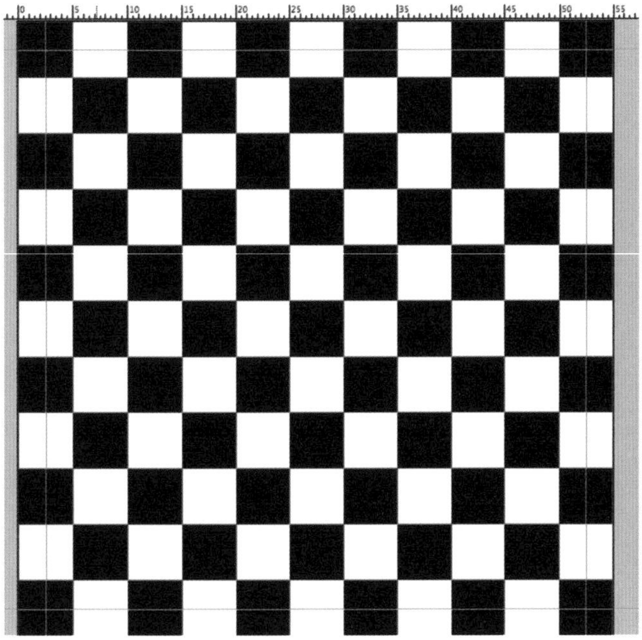

STEP 8

Use the Pen tool draw a central five-by-five square. Make it into a selection in the Paths palette. **Edit > Fill > Foreground Color**.

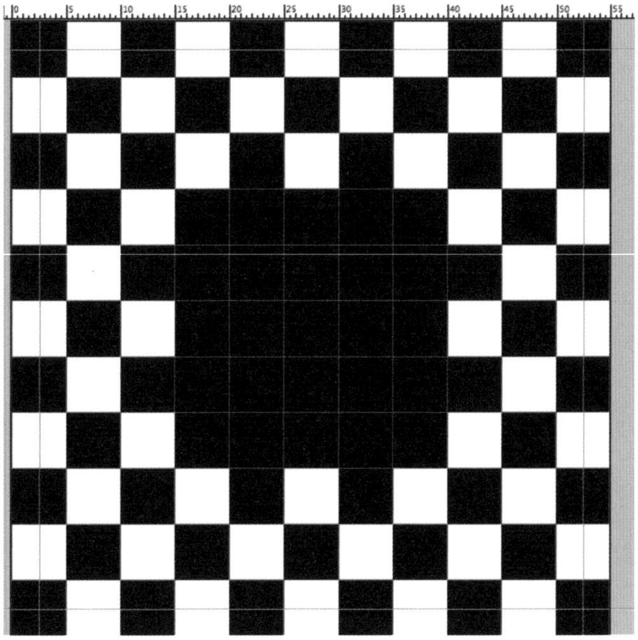

STEP 9

Use the Pen tool again to draw and fill in the corner three-by-three squares and, as before, select them. Fill the squares with white.

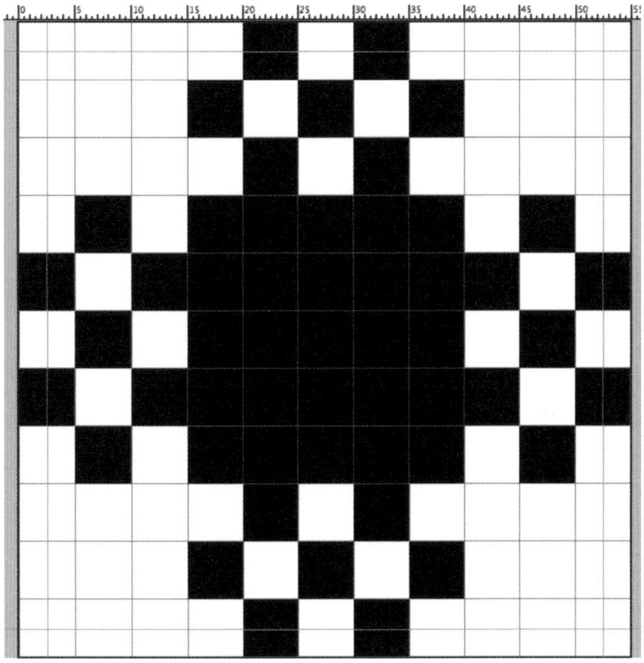

STEP 10

Now, with your guide lines as your guides and, using the Crop tool in the Tool palette, crop your design. You have now created the unit for your gingham pattern.

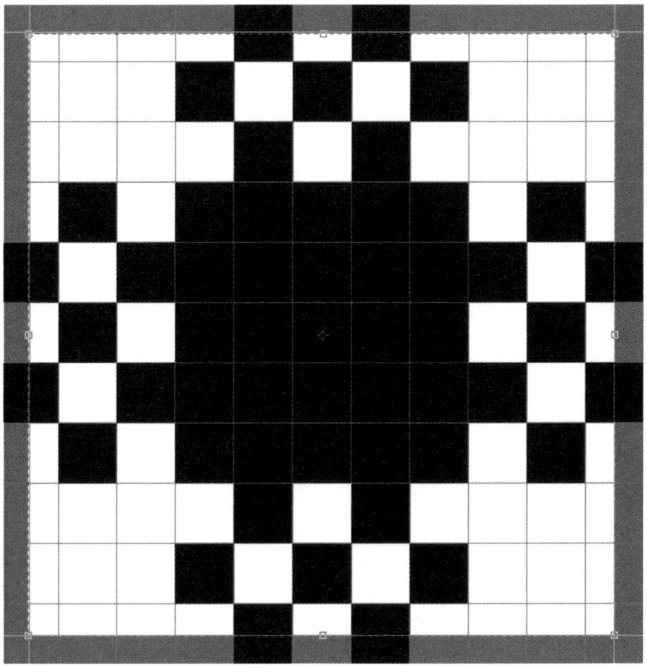

STEP 11

You could now simply select the black and color it as desired. The following method shows a two-tone effect for a woven look.

Select the gingham and fill with white.
Now select it again, and fill with your desired color. However, in the Fill dialog box change the Opacity to 80%.

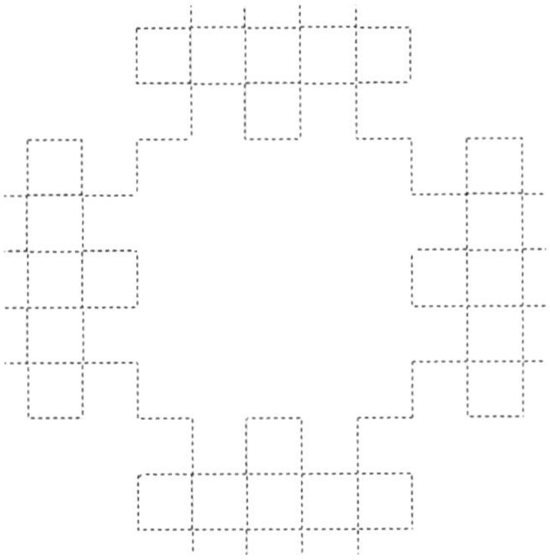

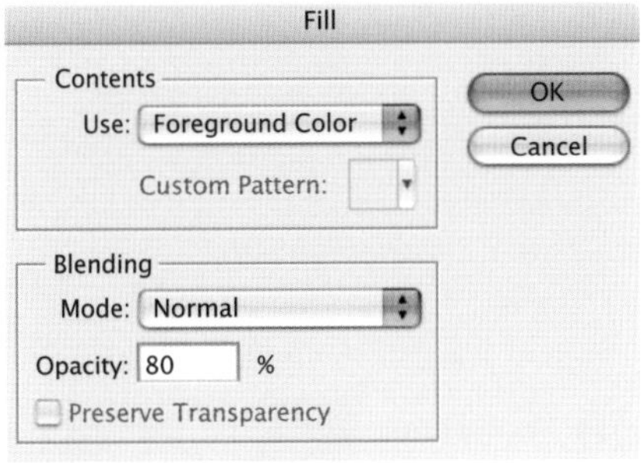

STEP 12

Use the Pen tool to draw the central square. Select it and fill it with the same color but with Opacity set to 100%.

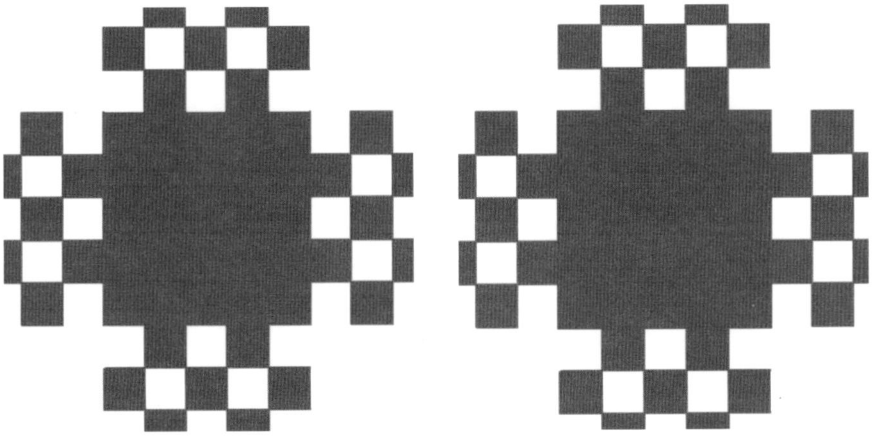

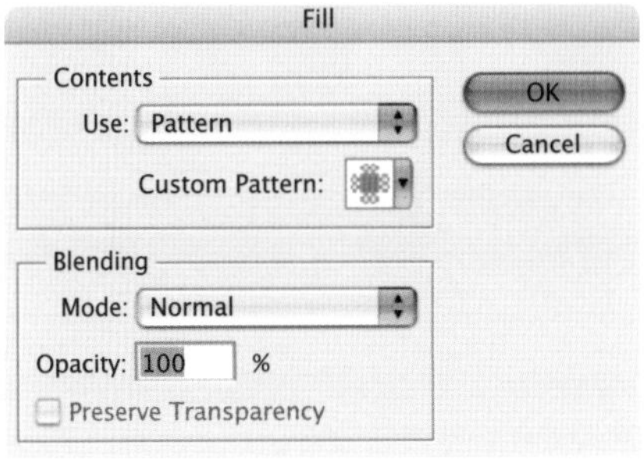

STEP 13

Now your gingham is ready. You can change its size using the Image Size dialog box to vary the scale. **Image > Image Size**.

STEP 14

Select > All.
Edit > Define Pattern.
Name your pattern and click OK.
Create a new document.
Edit > Fill.
Select Pattern and find your gingham.

TUTORIAL 16

PHOTOSHOP PATTERN: CREATING STRIPES

You can create simple or sophisticated stripes in Photoshop and store them in your Pattern Library for later use.

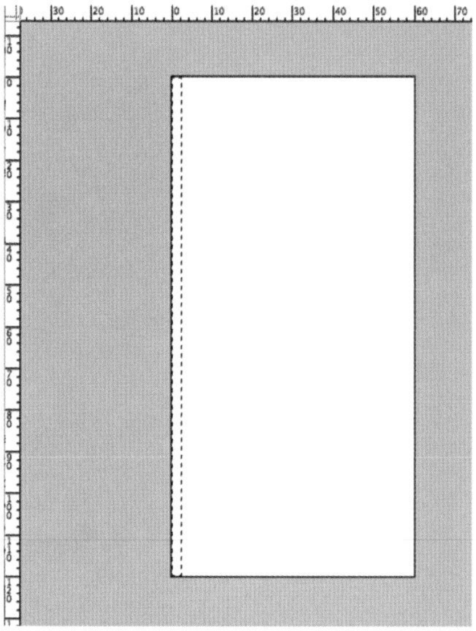

STEP 1

Open a new document. The one shown here is 2.4 x 4.7 in (6 x 12 cm).

View > Rulers.

Select a long, thin area with the Marquee tool.

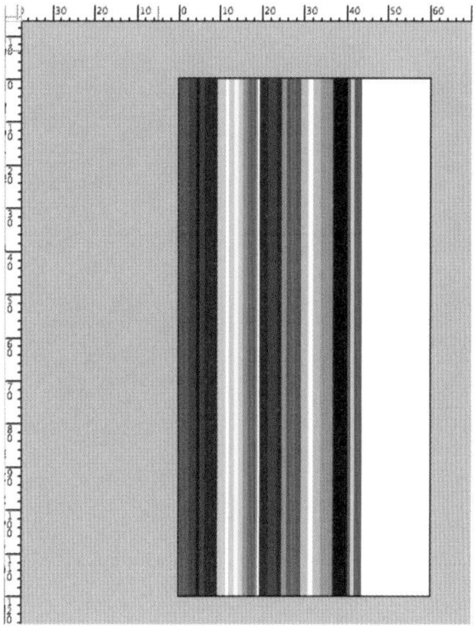

STEP 2

Fill the selected area with color using the Paint Bucket tool. Continue to build up stripes across the area using this method.

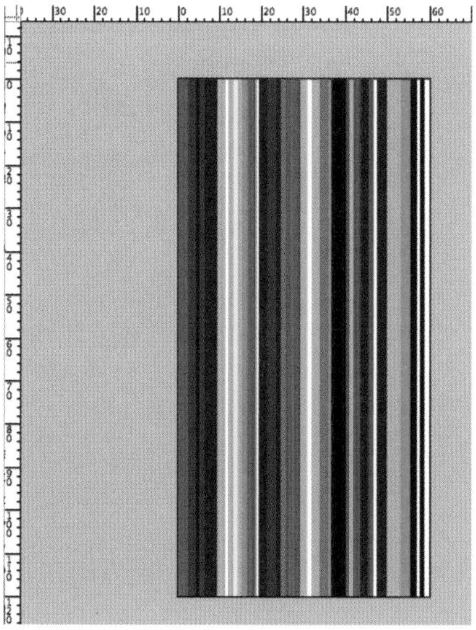

STEP 3

Complete your stripes.

Select > All.

STEP 4

Edit > Define Pattern.

Name your stripe and click OK.

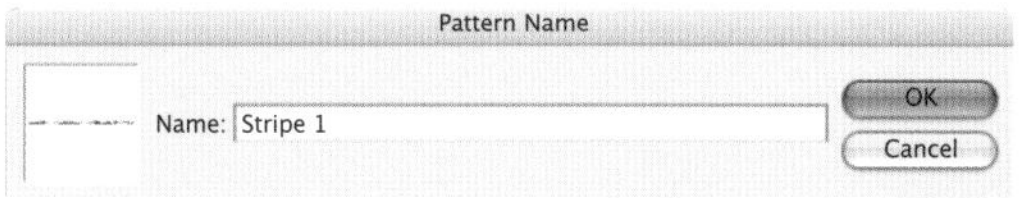

STEP 5

Open a new document.

Edit > Fill.

Select Pattern and find your stripe.

Fill the new document with your new stripe.

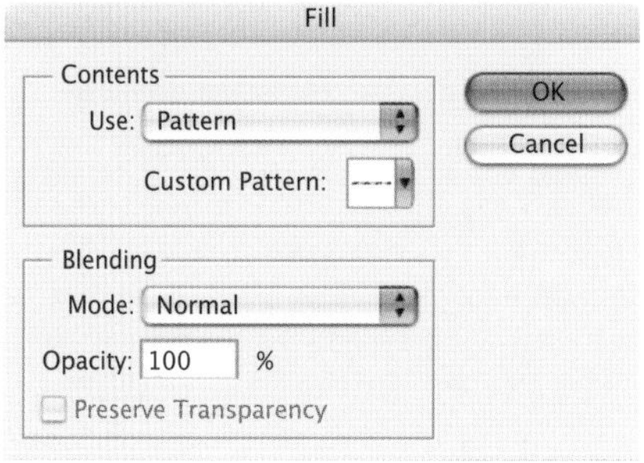

TUTORIAL 17

ILLUSTRATOR REPEAT: BASIC PATTERN SWATCH

Illustrator offers a simple method of constructing a patterned tile. This tutorial explains how to make a block and half-drop tile that can be used to create striking patterns. Working with vector graphic motifs, you can create a library of pattern swatches to use in designs such as patchwork. You can also create different color variations.

STEP 1

Create your motif. If it has several elements, group them together.

Object > Group.

STEP 2

To create a simple block tile, place the motif in the center of a square, and select both the square and the motif.

Edit > Define Pattern.

Name your motif.

STEP 3

To create a half-drop tile, draw a square to place your motif in. Check the View menu and make sure Snap to Point and Smart Guides are selected.

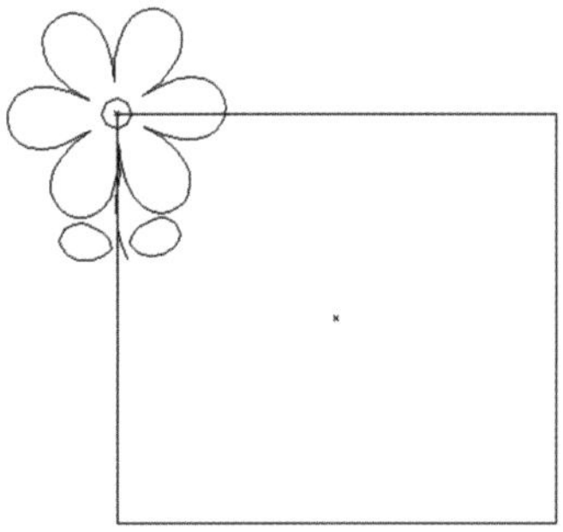

STEP 4

Copy and paste your flower into the square.

View > Outline.

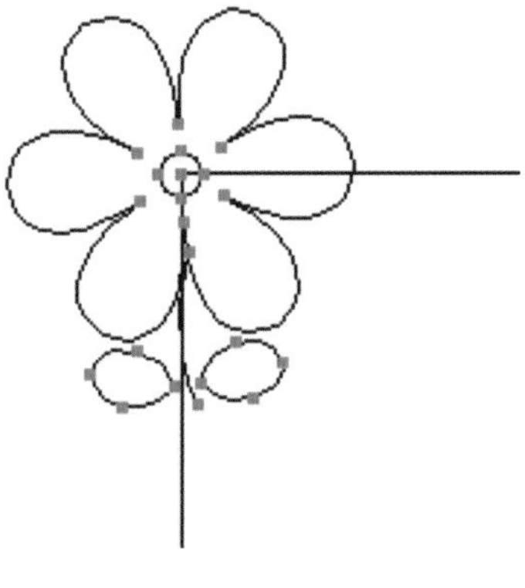

STEP 5

Using the Selection tool, select the center of the flower and drag it over the left-hand corner of the square. It will snap into place and crosshairs will appear.

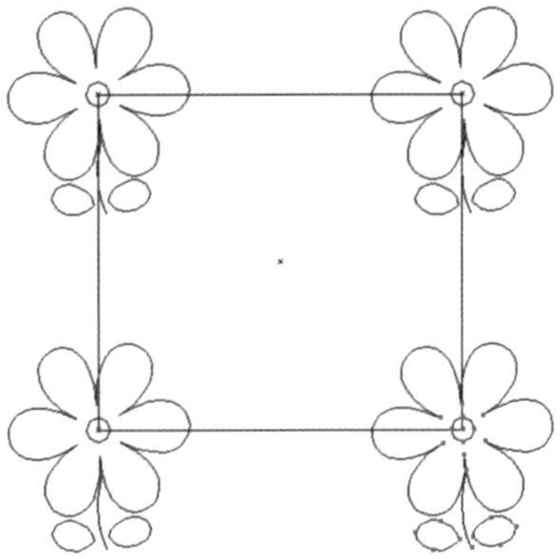

STEP 6

Duplicate the flower. Place one in each corner of the square, and add another one in the center.

STEP 7

View > Preview.
Select your filled square.
Edit > Paste in Back.
With the square still selected, set Stroke and Fill to "None" to create a bounding box.
(If you are already using a transparent square, this step is unnecessary.)

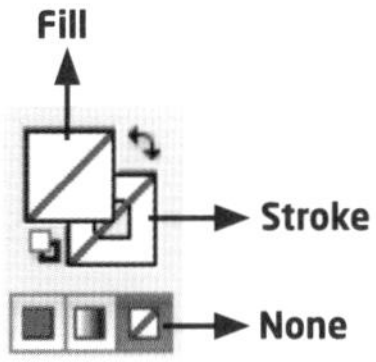

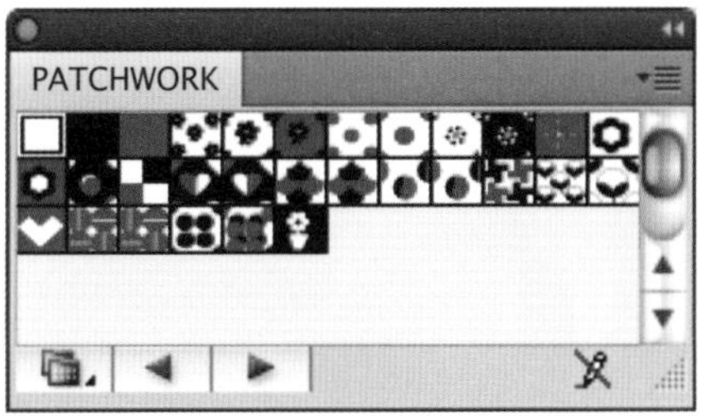

STEP 8

Select the square and patterns.
Edit > Define Pattern.
Name your pattern and click OK.
Your pattern will appear in the Swatches panel.
Once your swatches are made, save them in the Swatch Library for future use.

STEP 9

Create a shape and fill it with your new swatch tile. Experiment with the Transform tools to change the pattern rotation and scale.
Object > Transform > Rotate.
Object > Transform Scale.
Make sure you have the Patterns option selected and Objects and Scale Strokes & Effects deselected.

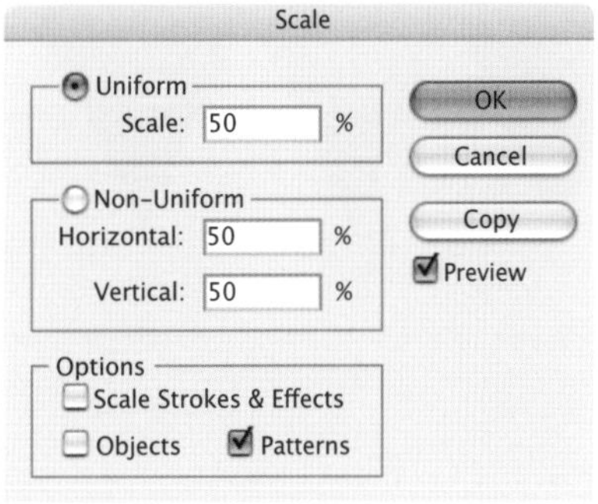

TUTORIAL 18

ILLUSTRATOR PATTERN: DIAMOND PATTERN

There are an infinite number of ways to create a geometric tile in Illustrator. This tutorial shows how to create a classic diamond pattern. By coloring individual diamond shapes you can build a variety of designs that can be saved in the Swatch Library. Once created in Illustrator, you can save the swatches and use them as pattern tiles in Photoshop.

STEP 1

Open a document in Illustrator.
View > Show Grid.
View > Snap to Grid.
Use the Pen tool to draw a diamond with equal sides. The anchor points will snap to the grid.

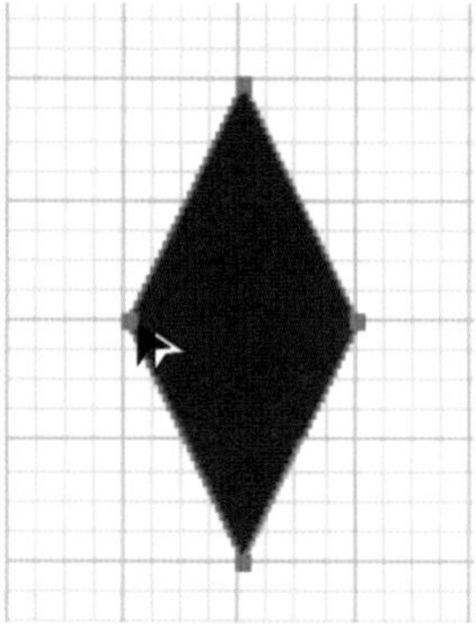

STEP 2

Now go to the View menu and deselect Snap to Grid. Select Snap to Point and Smart Guides instead.

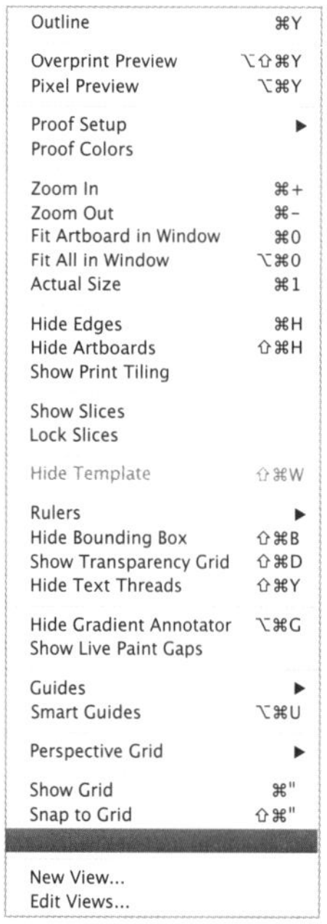

STEP 3

Position the pointer on the left-hand anchor point and begin to drag it to the right. Hold down the Shift and Option/Alt keys to constrain and leave a copy. The cursor will turn white when it has snapped to point.

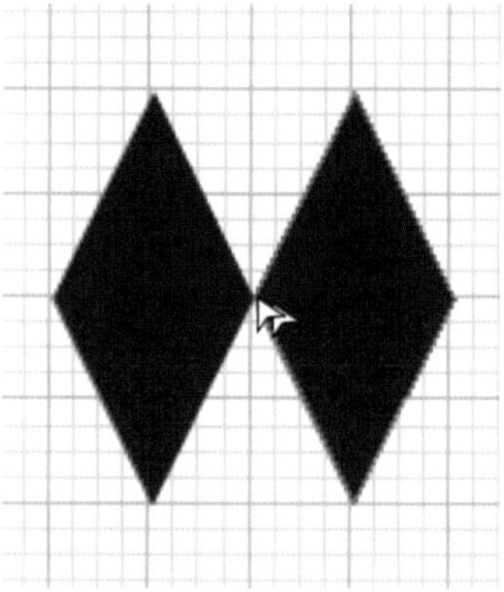

STEP 4

Repeat this action with the keyboard shortcut Command + D to build up a row of four diamonds.

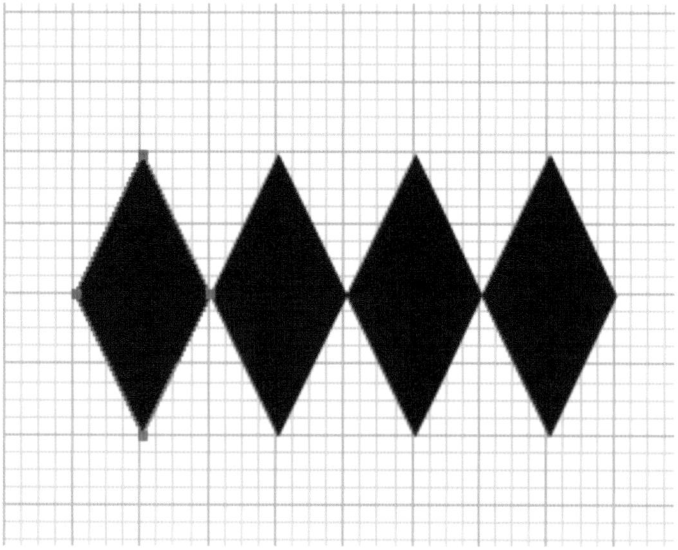

Here, the pattern has been dropped into a fashion illustration by Daisy Butler.

STEP 5

Once your row of four diamonds is complete, select the top anchor point on the left-hand diamond and, holding down the Option/Alt key, drag it until it snaps into place with the right anchor point of the same diamond. Repeat until you have a row of three diamonds.

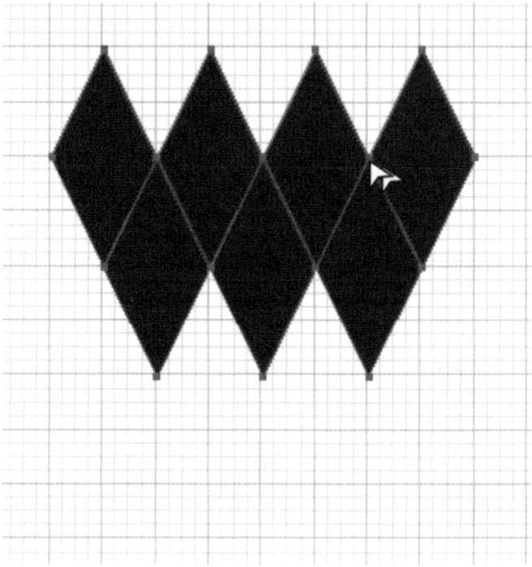

STEP 6

Select all the diamonds. Start at the top left-hand diamond's anchor point and, holding down the Option/Alt key, drag it until it snaps into place with the bottom row's left anchor point. Continue to build a fifth row of diamonds.

STEP 7

Select individual diamonds and color them to create a pattern.

STEP 8

View > Outline.
Window > Attributes.
With all the diamonds selected, click the Show Center icon to display the center point of the diamonds.

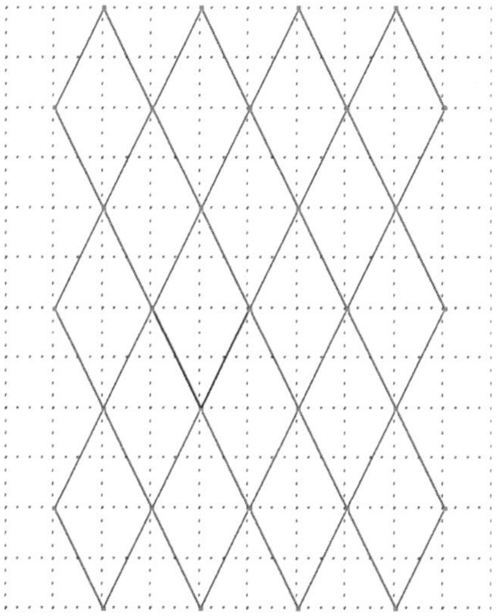

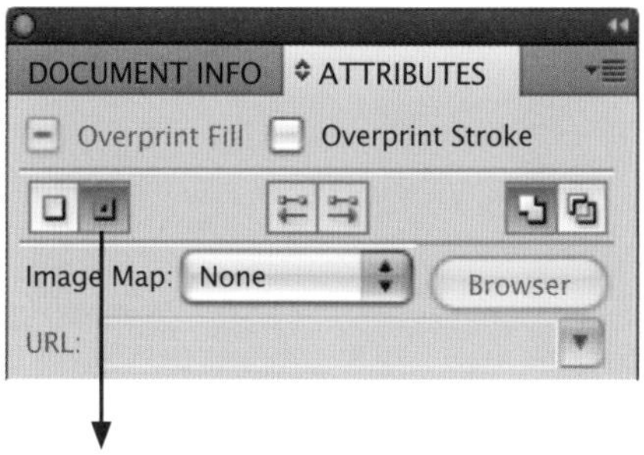

Show Center icon

STEP 9

Select the Rectangle tool from the Tool palette. Set Stroke and Fill to "None." Draw a rectangle, starting from the center point of the top left-hand diamond and ending at the center point of the bottom right-hand diamond.

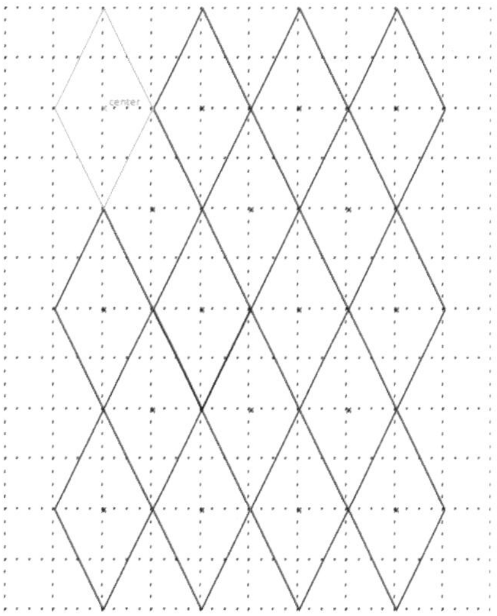

STEP 10

Select the rectangle and all the pattern elements.
Edit > Define Pattern.
Name your pattern and click OK. Your pattern will appear in the Swatches palette.

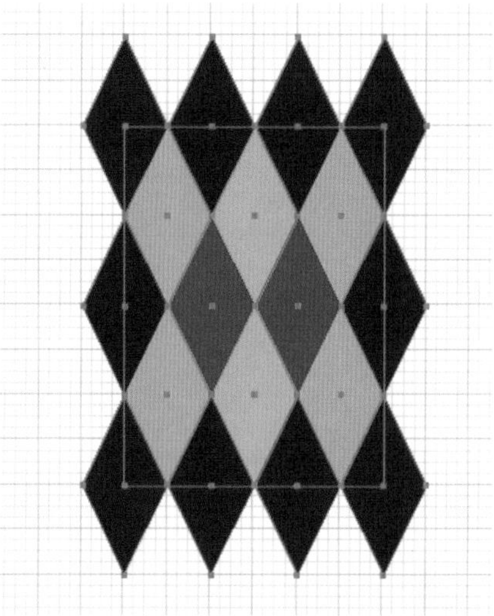

PATTERN VARIATIONS

Once you have your diamond unit, you can make an infinite number of different diamond formations by selecting and changing the fill colors.

Save each pattern as a swatch, draw a rectangle, and fill it with the new swatch patterns to create different effects.

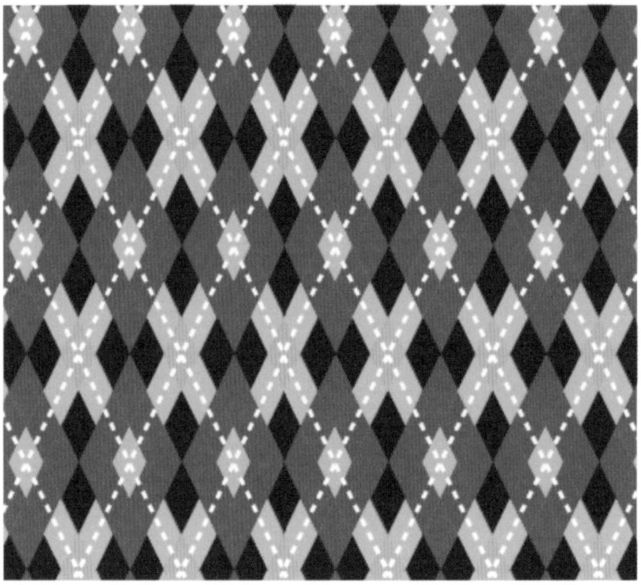

Using the Pen tool, create a diagonal line from the center points in the outside diamond, and apply a dash to the stroke. This will give a stitched effect reminiscent of the classic Argyle pattern.

PUTTING ILLUSTRATOR PATTERN FILES INTO PHOTOSHOP

Once you have made your pattern tile, save it in the Swatch Library so you can use it again. You can also save it in the Photoshop Pattern Library for use in a Photoshop image.

STEP 1

In Illustrator, open your saved swatches from the Swatch Library.

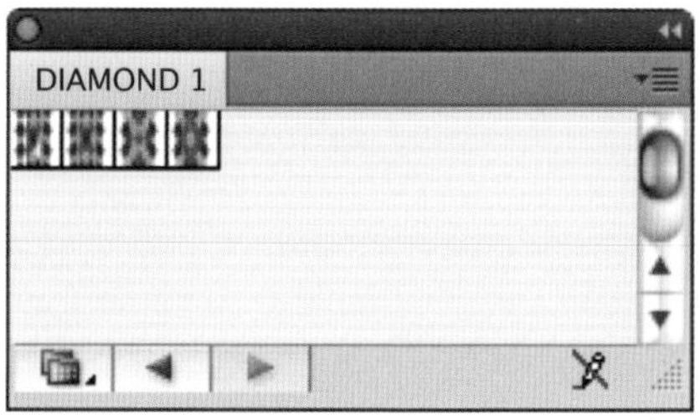

STEP 2

Drag your pattern out.
View > Outline.
Select the bounding box.
If the pattern is grouped, **Object > Ungroup**.
Select the bounding box.
Edit > Copy. Deselect everything.
Edit > Paste in Front.

STEP 3

Select the rectangle.
Object > Create Trim Marks.
Save the file.

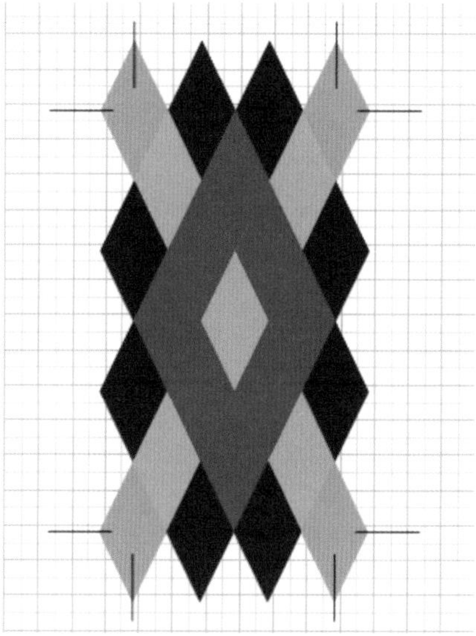

STEP 4

Open Photoshop and then open your Illustrator pattern file. An Import PDF dialog box will appear. Alter the resolution to 300 pixels/inch.

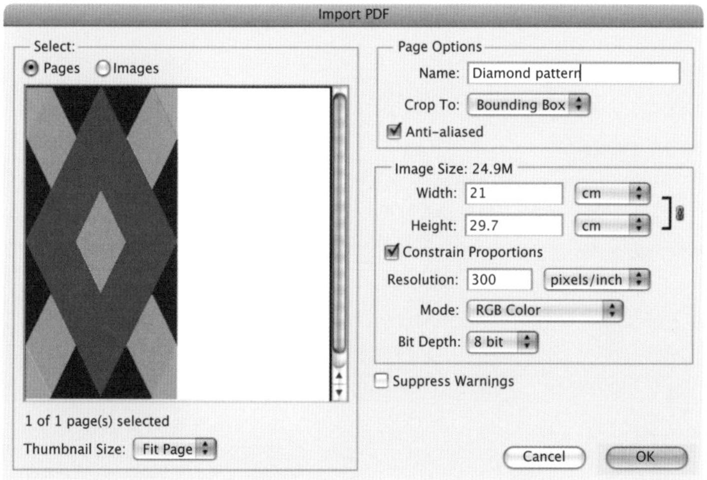

STEP 5

Click OK and your pattern tile will open.
At this point you can change the image size.
Image > Image size.

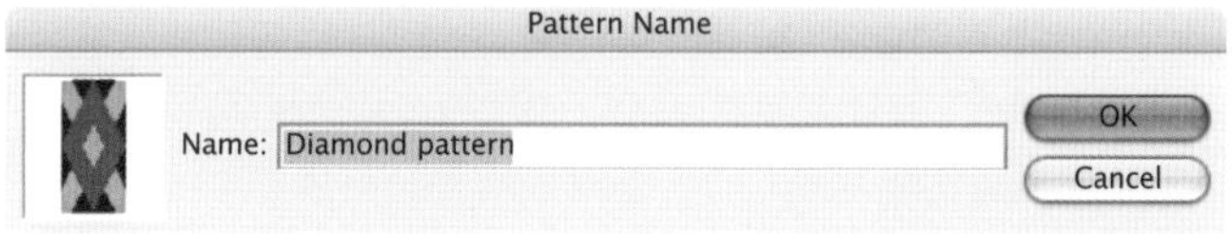

STEP 6

Select > All.
Edit > Define Pattern.
Name your pattern and click OK.
You can now apply your tiles to a Photoshop file.

TUTORIAL 19

ILLUSTRATOR PATTERN: PLAID PATTERNS

This tutorial shows you how to create a traditional plaid design that can be used by a print or weave designer. A plaid is constructed through the threads of the loom; the warp is set up vertically and the weft horizontally. We will work with the same method, but using Adobe Illustrator.

To give your plaid more pattern and texture we will first create some diagonal stripe pattern tiles. Once you have created a pattern tile you can then alter it with any of the Transform tools, and by also creating different color variations you can then build up plaid and check designs.

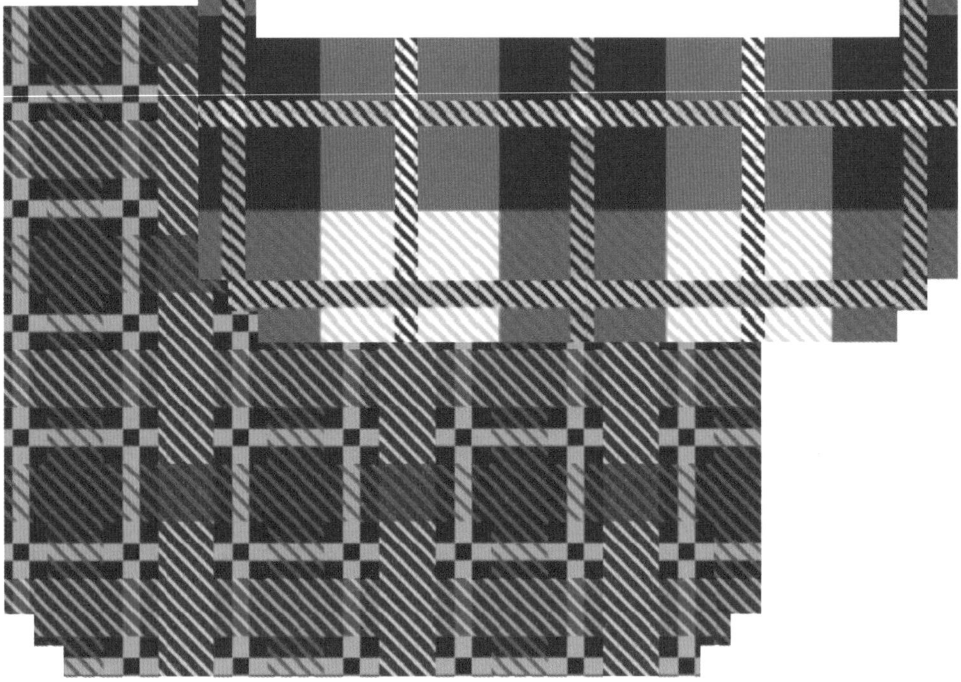

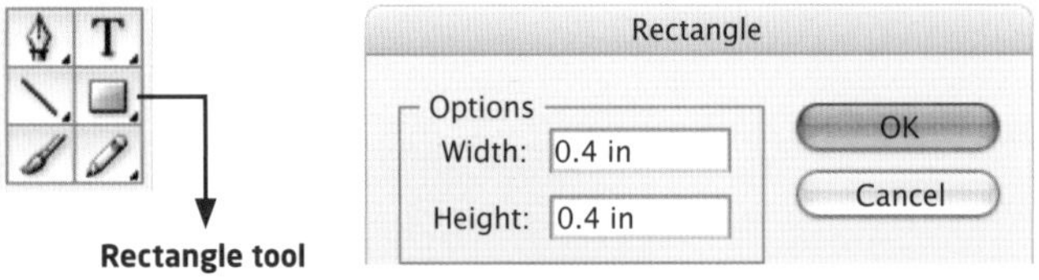

STEP 1

Use the Rectangle tool to create a 0.4 x 0.4 in (1 x 1 cm) square.

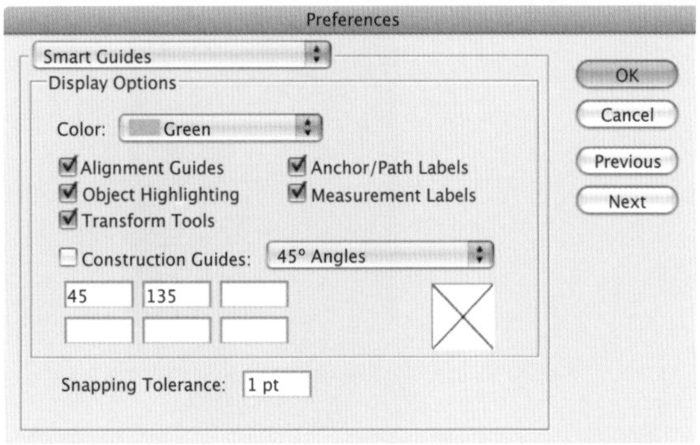

STEP 2

Illustrator > Preferences > Smart Guides.
Set the Construction Guides to 45° Angles.
Check the View menu to make sure Smart Guides and Snap to Point are on.

STEP 3

Set Stroke and Fill to "None."

STEP 4

View > Outline.
Select the Pen tool and drag it across the square until it hits the 45-degree line. Now draw a line diagonally across the square.
View > Preview.
Give the line a 3 pt black stroke.

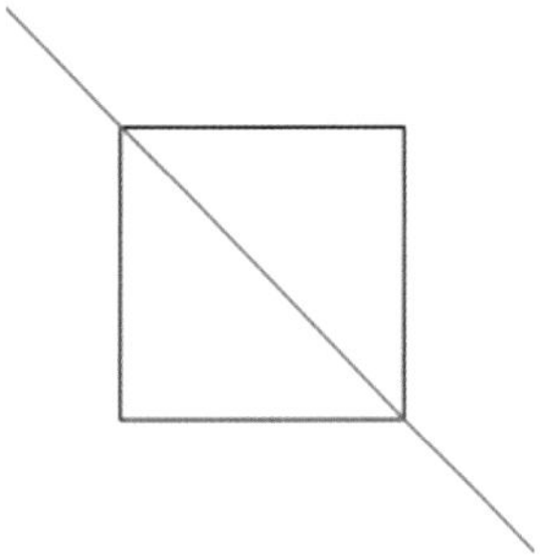

STEP 5

Use the Selection tool to grab the diagonal line. Drag it toward the right-hand corner of the square, holding down the Shift and Option/Alt keys to constrain and copy it.
Do not release the mouse button or the keys until the cursor goes white; this means the line has snapped into place.
Repeat for the left-hand corner line.

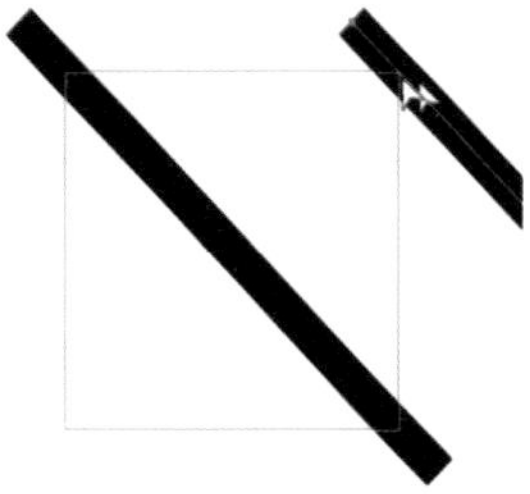

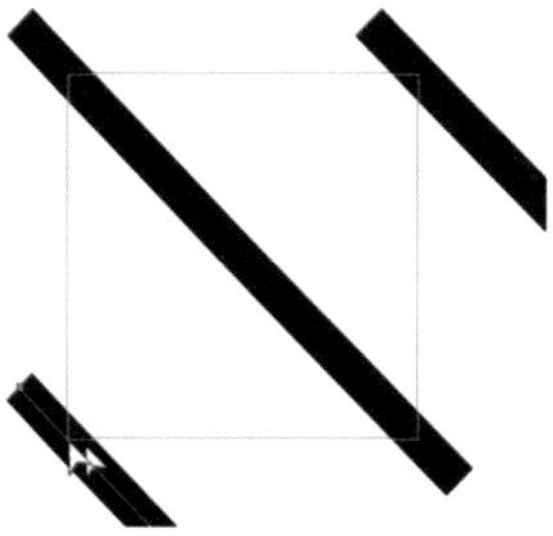

STEP 6

Select all three lines to change the stroke color.

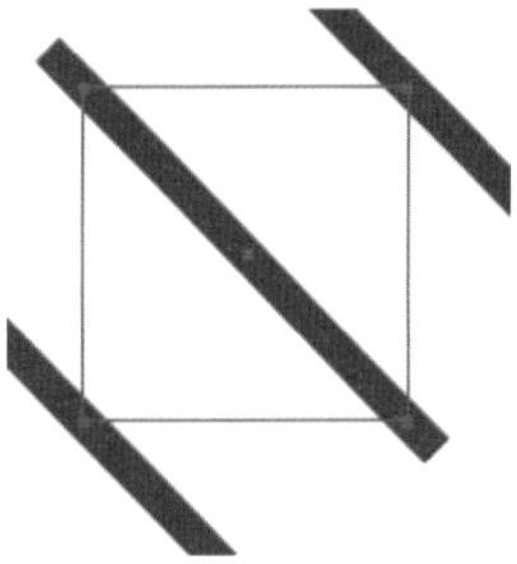

STEP 7

You can alter the background color and the stroke color. Select the three lines and choose a new stroke color. Select the square and fill it with a new color.
Select the square.
Edit > Copy.
Edit > Paste in Back.
This will still be selected; set Stroke and Fill to "None."

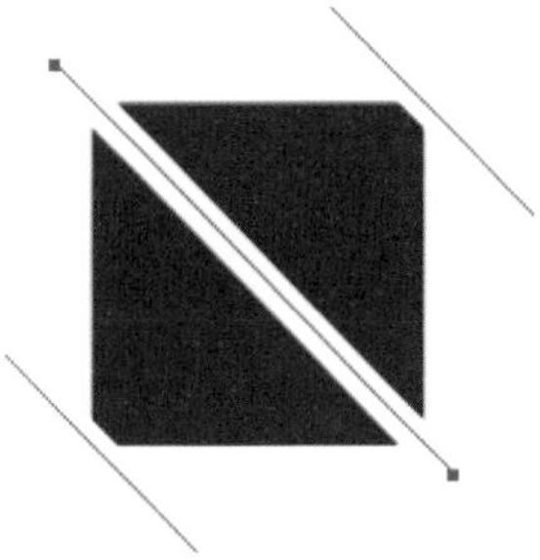

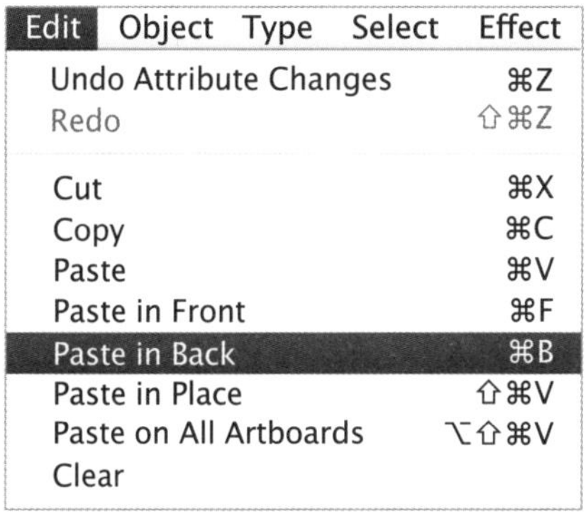

STEP 8

Select > All.
Edit > Define Pattern.
Name your pattern and click OK.
The new pattern tile will appear in the Swatches palette.

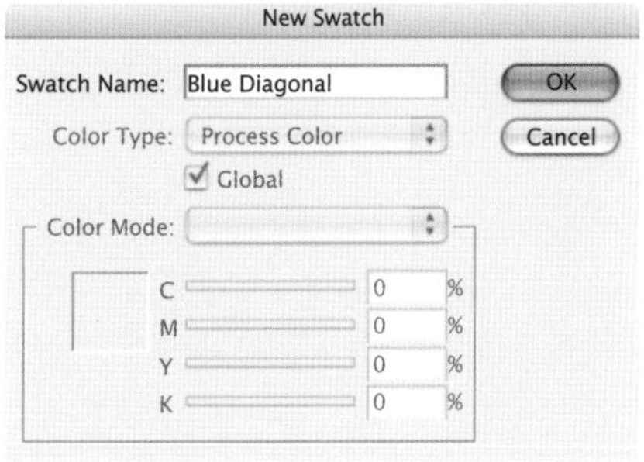

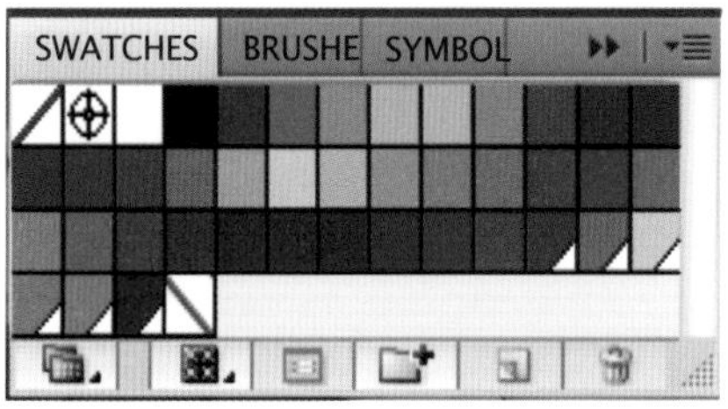

STEP 9

Draw a rectangle and fill it with your swatch.
You can change the scale:
Object > Transform > Scale.
A dialog box will appear.
Under Options, select Patterns. All the other options should be deselected.
Now change the Uniform Scale percentage.

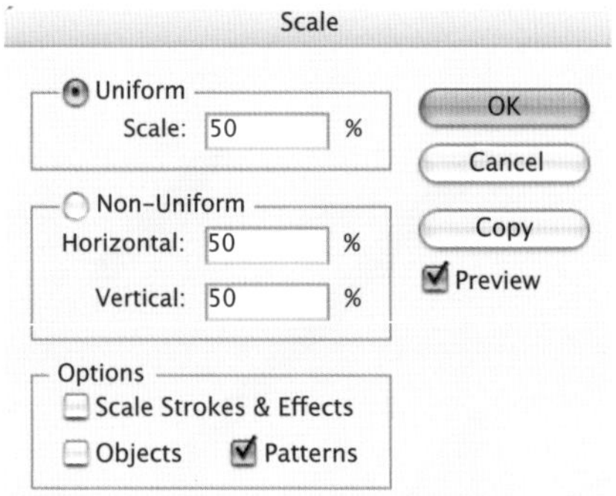

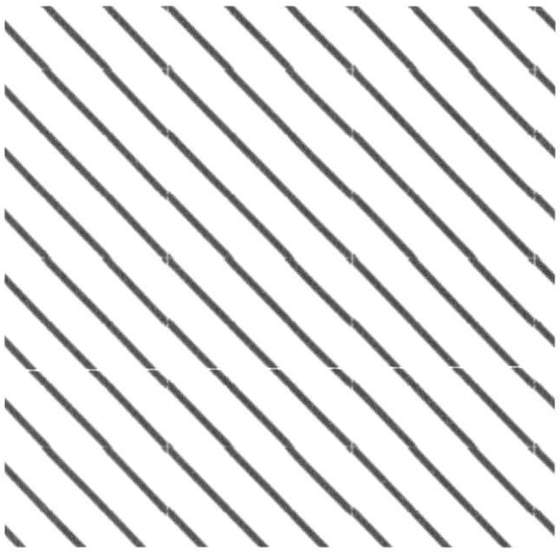

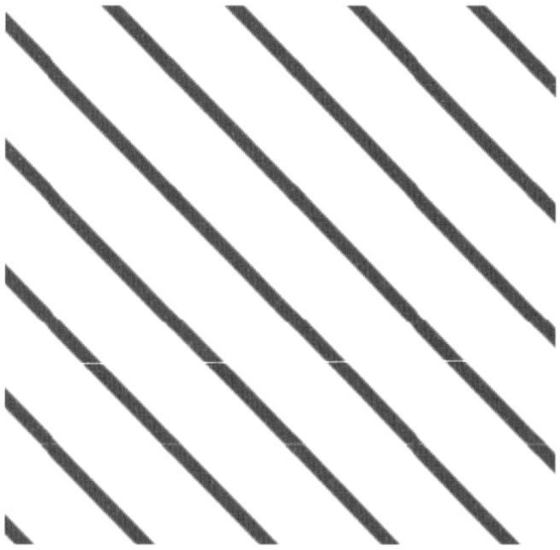

STEP 10

To build up a basic diagonal plaid:
Object > Transform > Reflect.
Select Vertical Axis and the Patterns option, and then click Copy.
With this new box selected, open the Transparency palette.
Window > Transparency.
Lower the Opacity to create a weave effect.

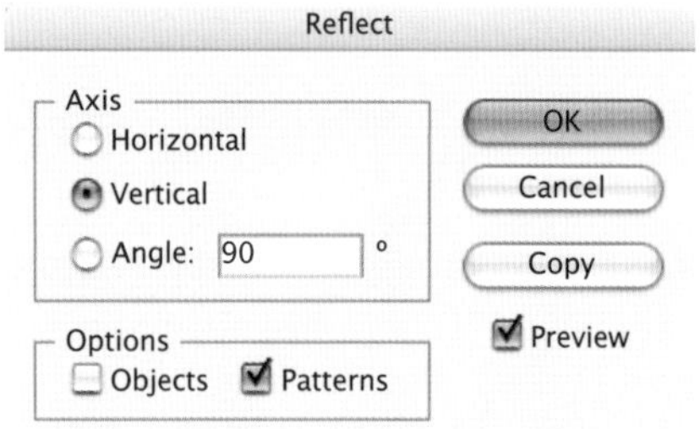

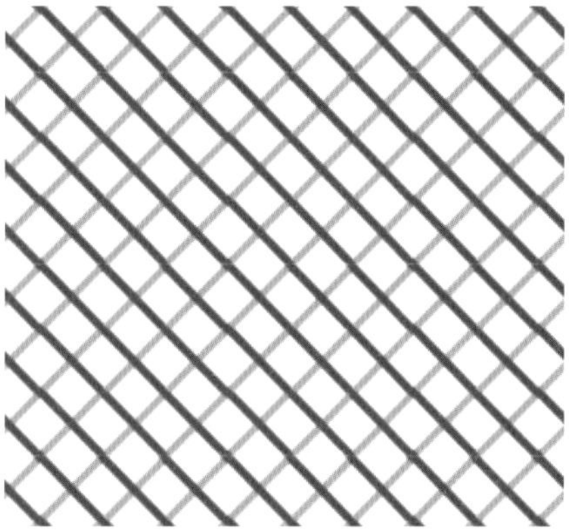

STEP 11

Create some different color variations and save your swatches to the Swatch Library.

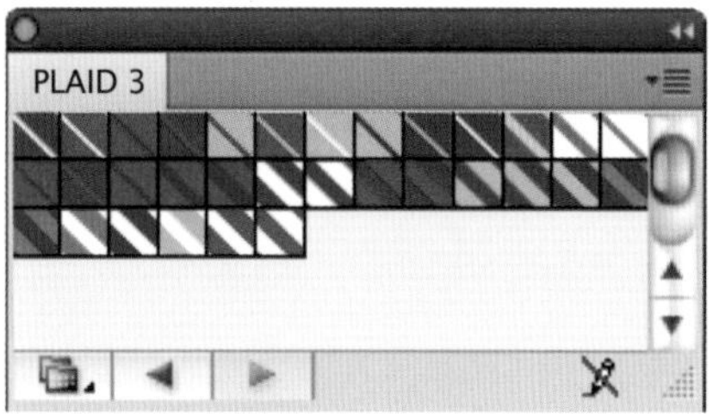

CREATING A PLAID WITH THE DIAGONAL PATTERN TILE

STEP 1
Open a new Letter-size (A4) document in Illustrator. Double-click on the Rectangle tool, and the Rectangle dialog box will open. Enter a Width of 0.4 in (1 cm) and a Height of 11.4 in (29 cm). Fill your rectangle with the new diagonal pattern fill.

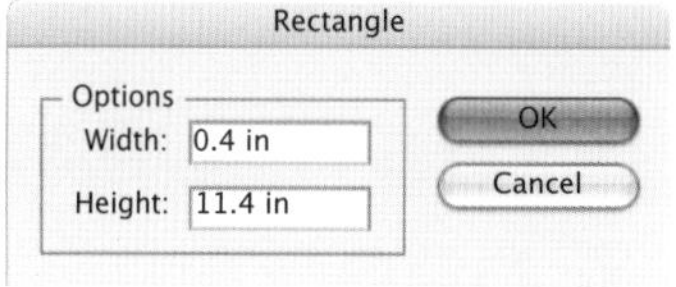

STEP 2
Select the new rectangle. Press Return and the Move dialog box will appear.
Enter a Horizontal Position of 0.8 in (2 cm).
Select the Objects option and press Copy.
Press Command + D repeatedly to complete the row.

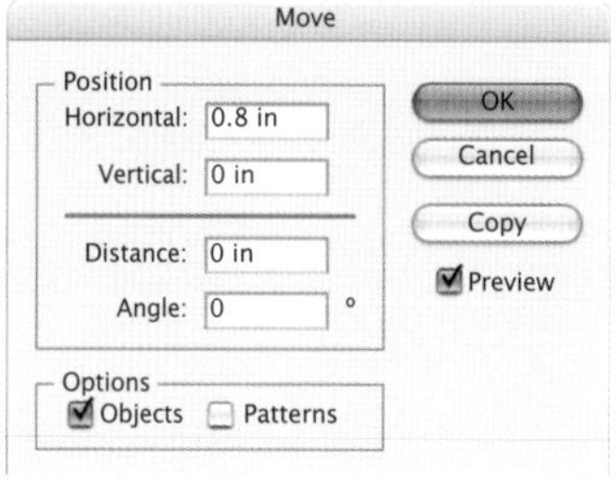

STEP 3
Fill alternate rows with a different color.

STEP 4
Complete the horizontal rows using the same method. Create a rectangle with a Width of 8.3 in (21 cm) and a Height of 0.4 in (1 cm). Enter a Vertical Position of 0.8 in (2 cm) in the Move dialog box.

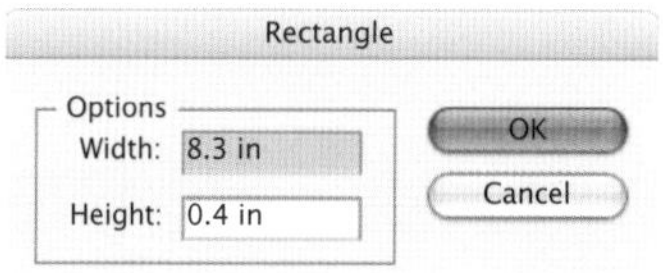

STEP 5
Select alternate rows and change the Opacity in the Transparency palette to achieve a woven effect.

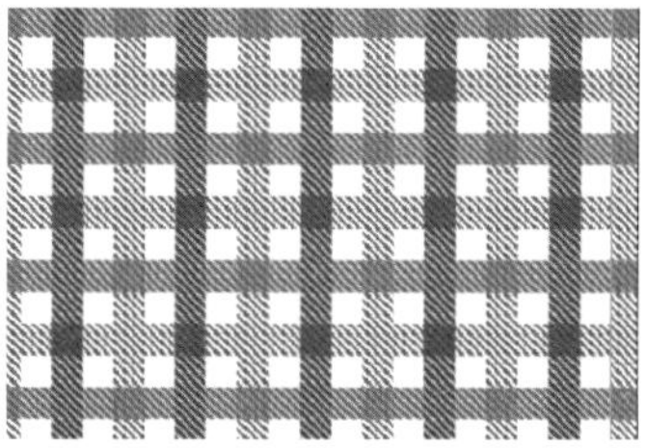

STEP 6
Create a new layer. On this, create a new grid with a fill color 0.2 in (0.5 cm) in width.

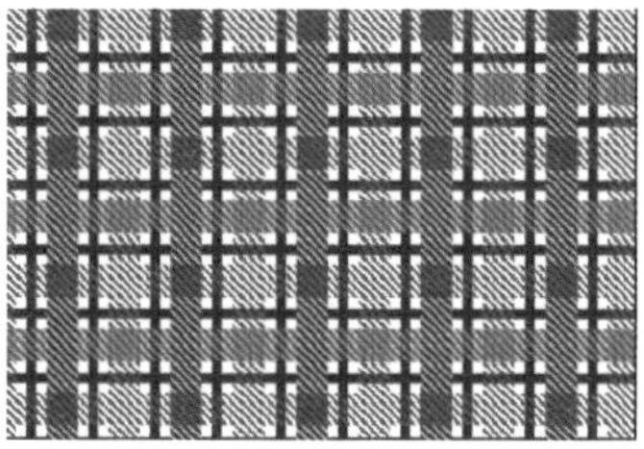

STEP 7
Turn off the top layer to reveal your new check. Select all and open the Pathfinder palette.
Window > Pathfinder.
Select the Exclude icon, which excludes the overlaps and cuts them away.

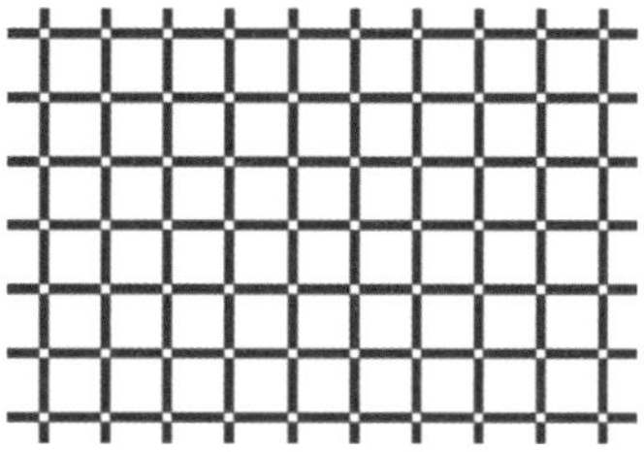

STEP 8
Now turn the top layer back on and begin to experiment with colorways by adding a background and changing the color of the block grid. Try creating other tiles in different colorways for more options.

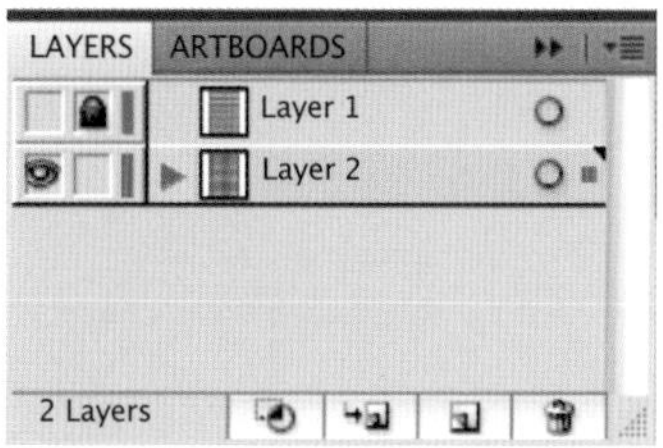

TUTORIAL 20

ILLUSTRATOR PATTERN: HALF-DROP

This floral design, created in Illustrator using various shapes and drawn with a Pen tool, is set inside a square box, which is useful if you wish to make a half-drop repeat.

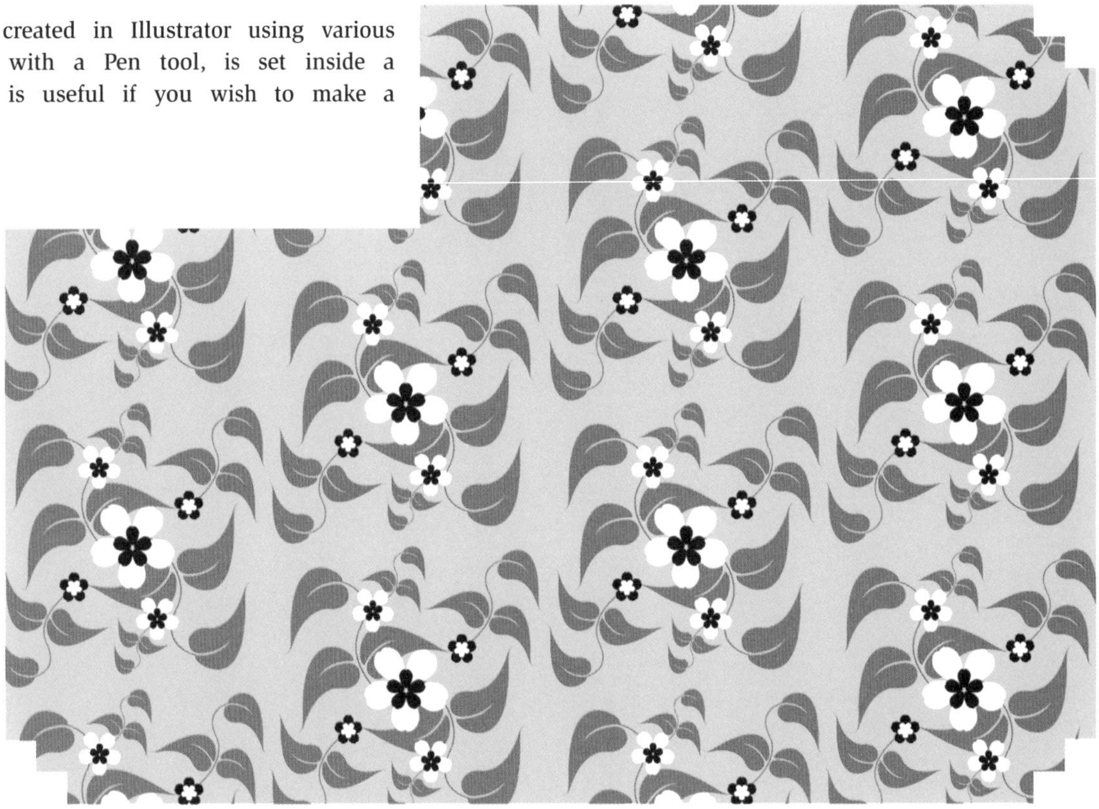

STEP 1

In the View menu, click on Smart Guides and on Snap to Point; a tick should appear next to each. Also show rulers.
View > Rulers > Show Rulers.

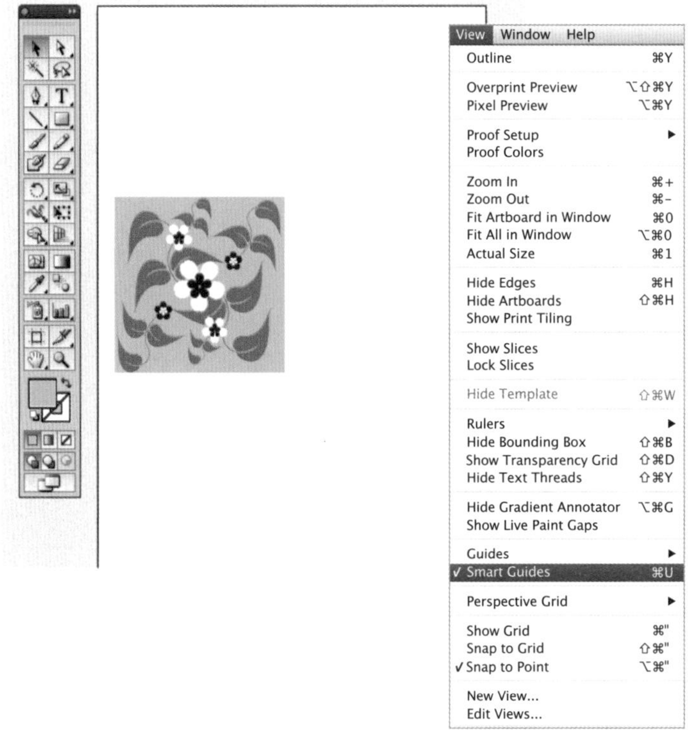

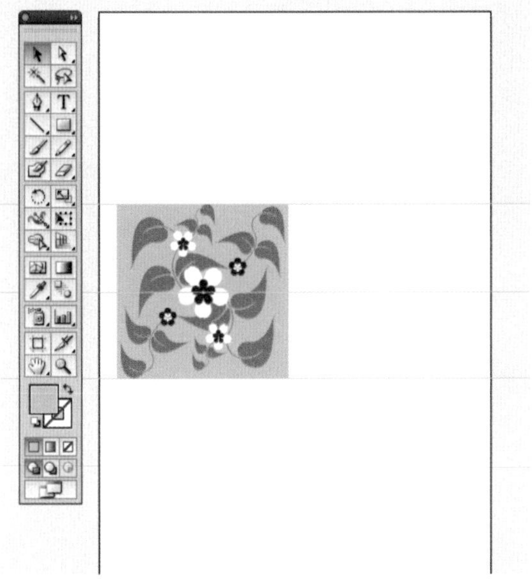

STEP 2

Drag some guides from the rulers until they snap into place on the top and bottom of the square design. It is important to find the center of the design using the Smart Guides.

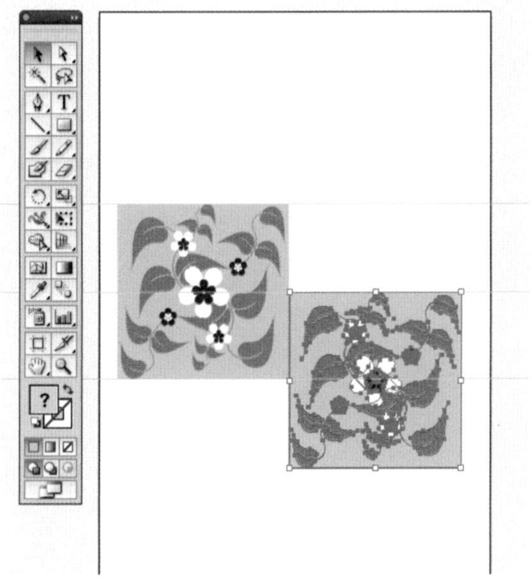

STEP 3

To create a half-drop repeat, duplicate the design and align it next to the original so that the box edges are touching and the vertical alignment is on the center guide.

You can duplicate using the Copy and Paste commands found in the Edit menu, and use the Align palette found in the Windows menu.

Alternatively, select and hold the object with the mouse, then press Option/Alt+Shift and drag the object away to automatically duplicate it.

If you drag from the corner edge of the box, the Smart Guides will snap to the edge of the original.

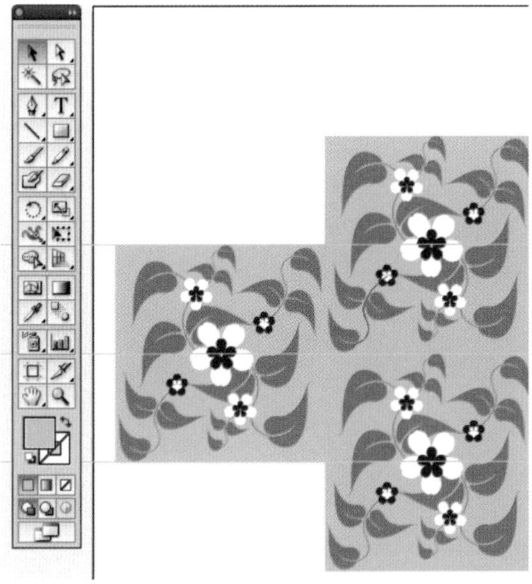

STEP 4

Duplicate and align the design again, with the bottom of the new box aligned with the center guide.

STEP 5

Drag some vertical guide lines to snap to the left and right sides of the design. Use the Ungroup command in the Object menu as many times as possible to ungroup all the objects.
Object > Ungroup.
Delete all the color boxes and make another box to fit the guide edges.
Edit > Copy.

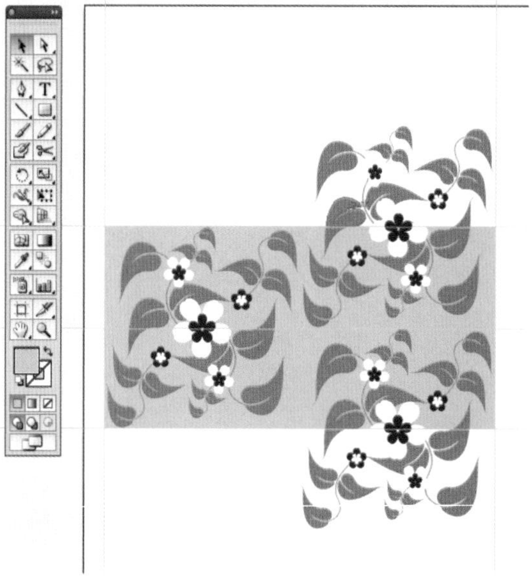

STEP 6

Select the new box.
Object > Arrange > Send to Back.
Object > Lock > Selection.
Make sure the box is still selected.
Edit > Paste in Front.

STEP 7

The top box should still be selected.
Object > Path > Divide Objects Below.
This will cut the excess design outside of the boxed area. Select and delete the excess design.

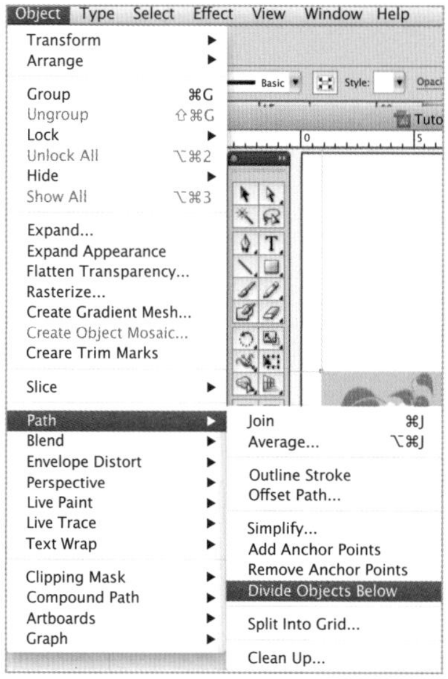

STEP 8

You should be left with something similar to this example.

Object > Unlock All.

Group all the objects together. At this point you can scale your repeat unit.

Object > Transform > Scale.

Then drag the entire design into the Swatches panel. You will see your floral design appear in the panel.

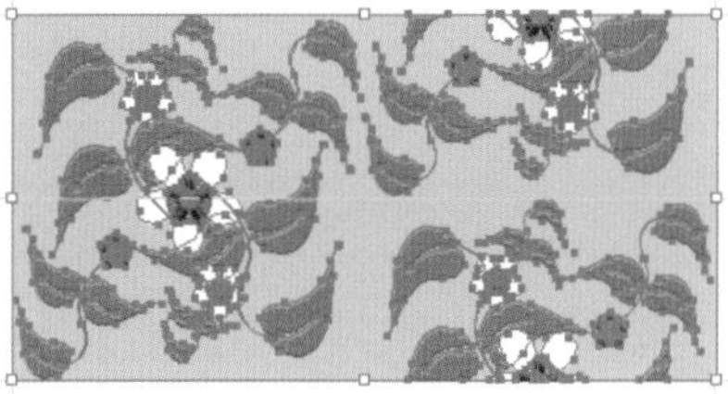

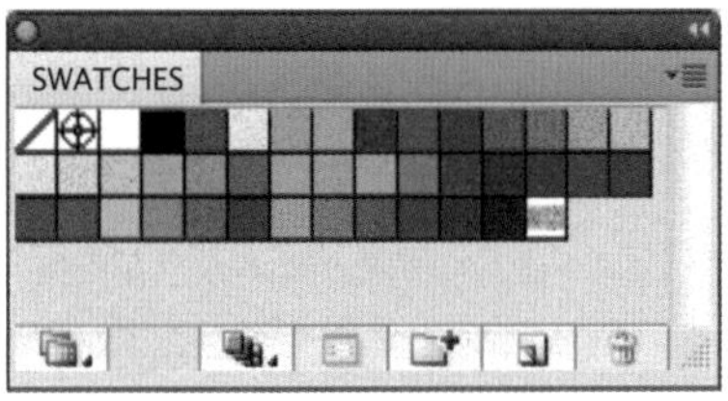

STEP 9

Test your design by creating a larger box and filling it with your new swatch.

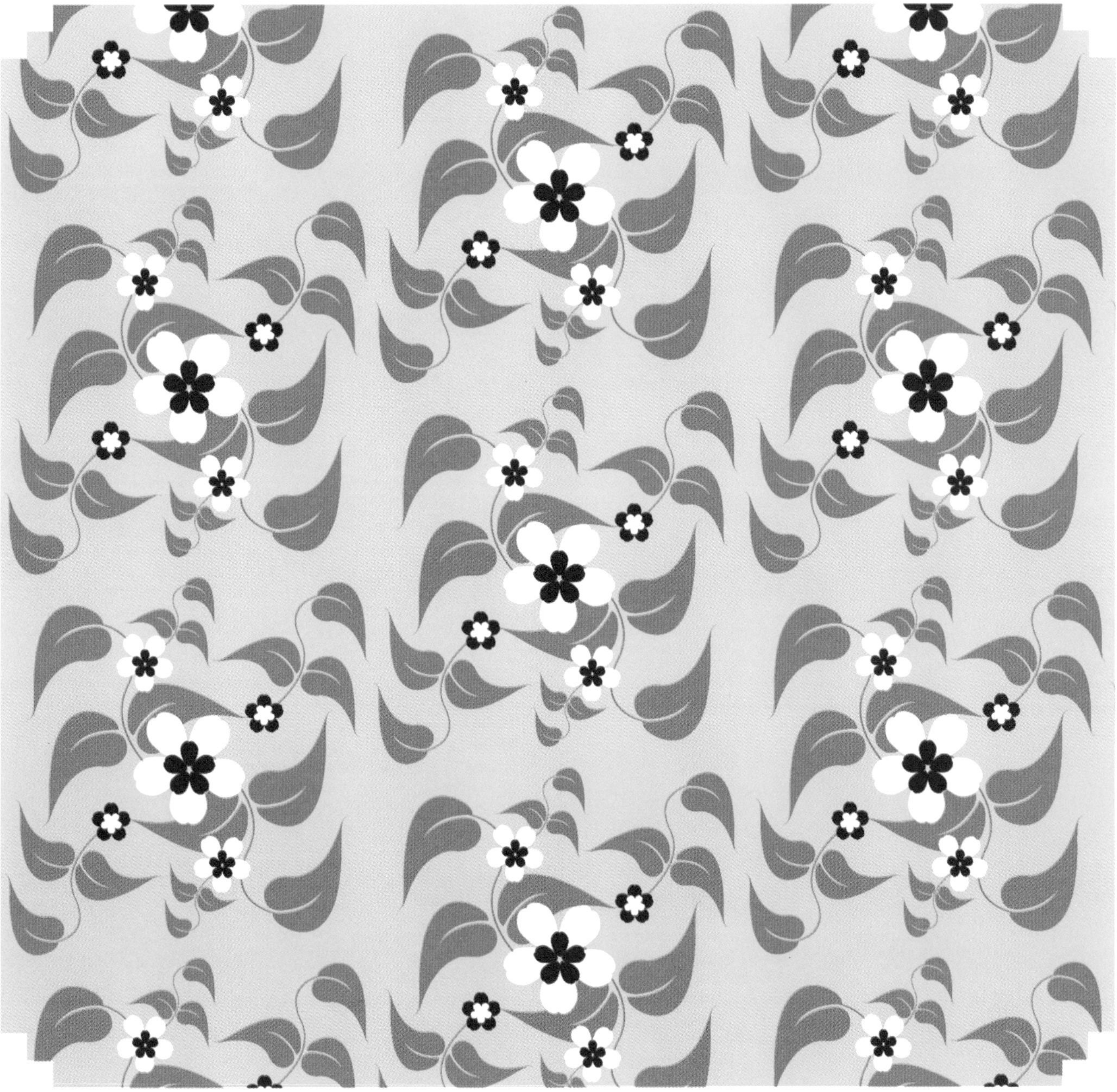

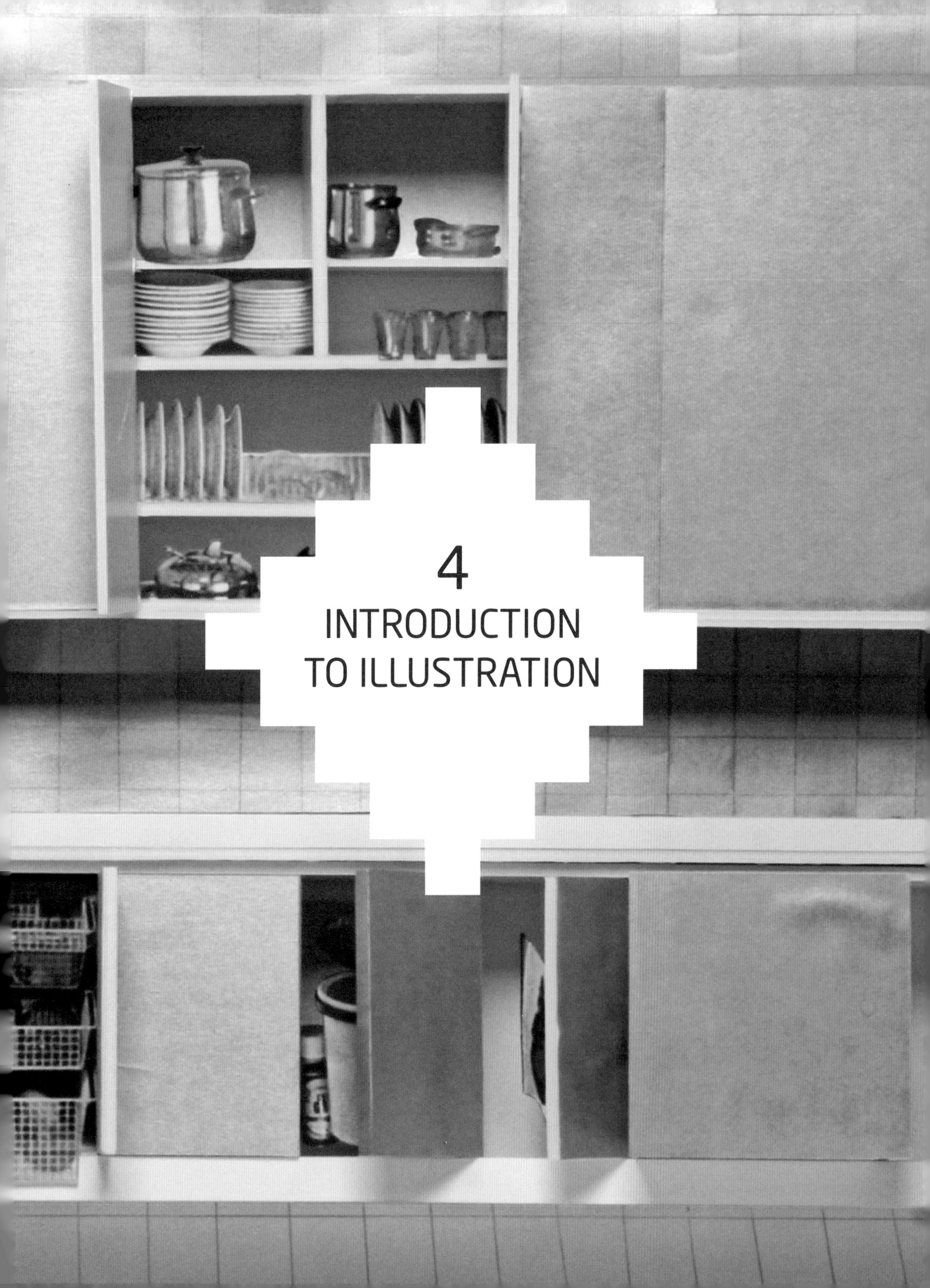

4
INTRODUCTION TO ILLUSTRATION

INTRODUCTION TO ILLUSTRATION

Textile designers need to present their collections, once designed, in a context that enables others to understand them. This usually means depicting the designs on a garment or an interior. This takes the designs to another level by putting them into a realistic environment and giving the collection a sense of place. Lately the industry has seen the arrival of a wealth of exciting new fashion illustration techniques, due partly to advances in digital technology. This has opened up not just a whole new medium, but also a fresh way to approach the subject.

Illustration is no longer a literal interpretation of textile designs. Instead, illustrators are playing with a world of fantasy and illusion, creating a mood and ambience in which viewers can lose themselves. The sensual and decorative approach that a textile designer has to offer is an excellent starting point. By combining drawing, painting, collage, and photography, designers can produce exciting and energetic work that can explore a narrative, giving their design work another dimension.

More often than not the computer is used only as a medium to assemble drawings and design work before collaging them together. The most successful illustrators include some form of personal "handwriting" in their work. The best starting point is often a sketch, painting, or drawing in which the designer experiments with mood and artistic style. Books and magazines can be a great source of inspiration and it is also important for the designer to keep up with trends—not only in fashion but also in graphic styles. Most of your inspiration will tend to come from your original textile collection though, and from this you will probably have established a theme and have already developed an idea of how you want to portray your designs.

Your style of illustration and the media you choose to use will also be influenced by the style of garment for which your designs are intended, as well as the weight of the fabric. If your designs are for heavy wools and knits, for example, then you might consider a collage medium to give a sense of weight. Alternatively, if your designs are intended for lightweight silks or chiffons then you could consider working with transparent paint effects to suggest movement and fluidity.

Finally, if you are designing textiles intended for fashion, you will need to develop a style of figure drawing. Most textile designers who are not fashion designers tend to panic at the thought of figure drawing. But, equipped with their sensual and sensitive drawing skills, they can soon find a confident approach to fashion drawing. A good way to overcome any barriers is through life drawing; developing sketches and line drawings of the figure in various media that can then be drawn upon at a later date. Photography is also a useful medium with which to experiment. Photographs can be traced by hand or digitally and are a helpful way to start an illustration. Tracing should not be considered as cheating, especially for textile designers who are not used to working with the figure. Once you have traced an outline you can apply your own illustrative style as you develop the artwork.

At what stage you apply digital techniques to your illustration is up to you. It may be that you use the computer simply to manipulate and assemble your drawings using Photoshop, or you may wish to give your work the kind of very computerized style that Illustrator can offer.

This chapter includes basic tutorials showing techniques in both Photoshop and Illustrator that you can adapt and develop in your own work to create an individual and personal illustrative style.

Previous page:
This illustration was created by Chae Young Kim for her "Camouflage Kitchen" dress, the concept being to create a "future vintage" by giving objects from the 1960s and 1970s a modern expression. After photographing her garment on a mannequin, she superimposed it onto a background created in Photoshop. The images were enhanced with lighting effects and filters.

Chae Young Kim used a complex mix of effects to create this stunning fashion illustration, "Kaleidoscope." The inspiration came from the reflection and distortion of color in glass. She used Photoshop filters to achieve the lighting effects and mood of her original design theme.

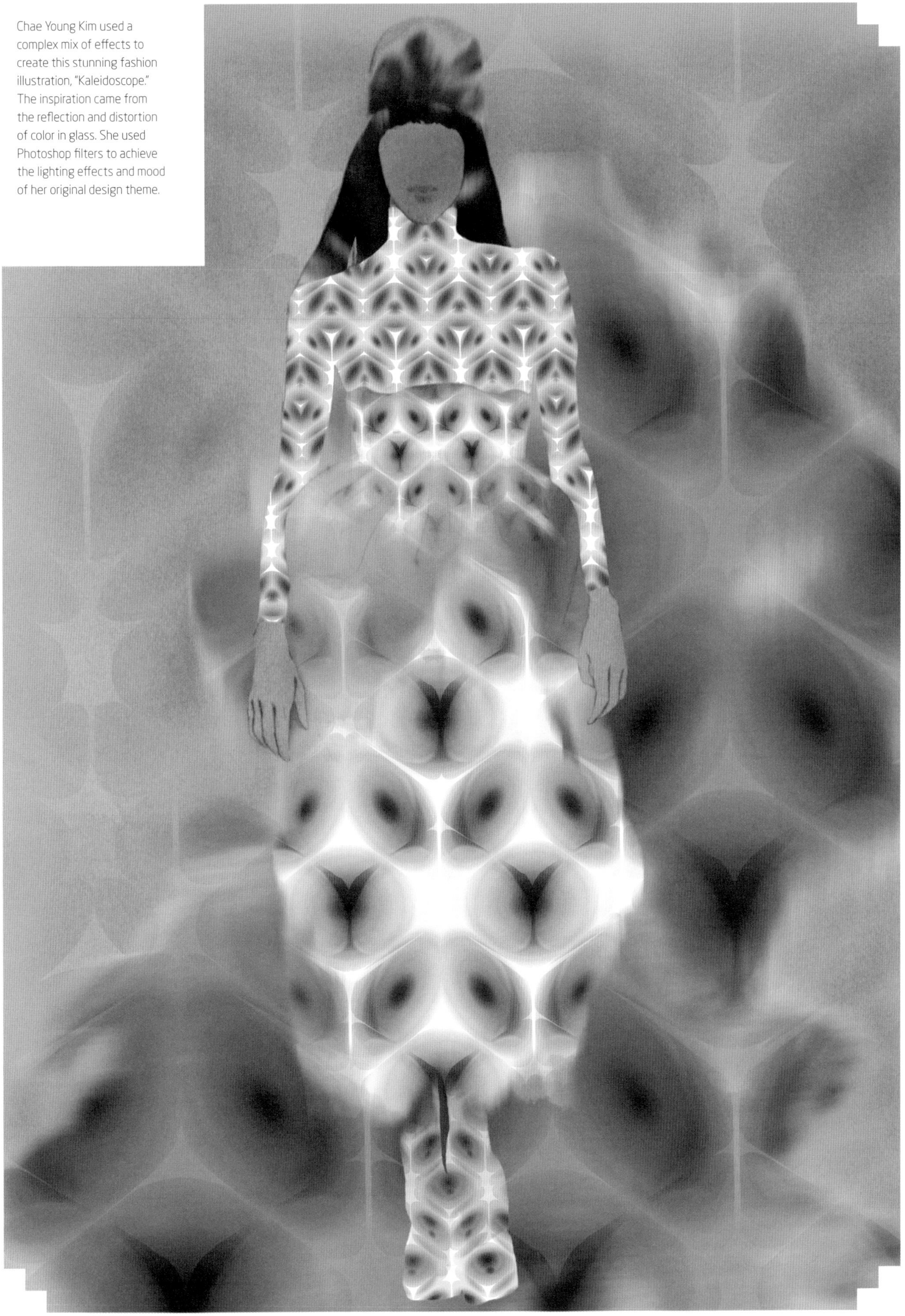

Amy Isla Breckon places her beautiful hand-rendered drawings in a realistic context. Photoshop allows her to mix drawings and photography to blend the real with the unreal. Here, the combination of an elegant hand-drawn figure with the rustic woodland setting of the photograph creates a dark but sophisticated mood and is perfect for showing off her animal-inspired prints.

Jennis Li Cheng Tien artistically manipulates and distorts photographs by overlapping filters in Photoshop to create digital paintings such as "es_cape."

Holly Holmes maps her designs on garment illustrations to coordinate her geometric collection "Repeaticities."

Pauline Fernandez's rich illustrations evoke the magical and playful mood that she wishes to convey in her designs. Working with a range of photographic imagery, Photoshop allows her to place her designs into a surreal and unusual context. She works with a complex mix of filters and lighting effects to build depth, luminosity, and atmosphere. Although her actual textile designs do not dominate here, it does not seem to matter, as the narrative of her illustration cleverly conjures up the mood of her work. This is perhaps more exciting than a literal interpretation.

TUTORIAL 21

DISPLACEMENT MAPS

In this tutorial, we texture map a design onto a garment using the Displacement filter in Photoshop. The Displacement filter will realistically place a design on an irregular surface. For example, a draped pattern can give the illusion of real fabric.

You will need two images: the image you wish to warp (the design) and the image you want to warp onto (in this case, a skirt).

STEP 1

To create the displacement map, duplicate your image.
Image > Duplicate.
Give your duplicate image a different name from your original image.

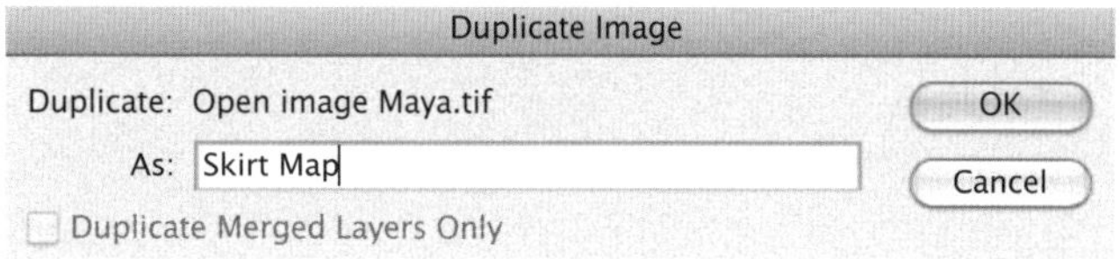

STEP 2

Convert the duplicate image to grayscale.
Image > Mode > Grayscale.
Save the grayscale image in Photoshop (PSD) or TIFF format so Photoshop can identify it and use it as a displacement map.
Return to your original color image.

STEP 3

Use the Pen tool to draw around the skirt and create a path.

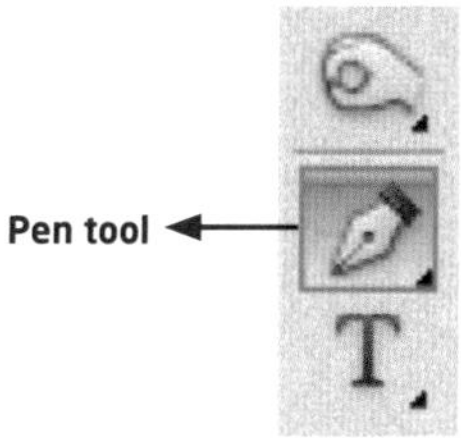

Once you have created the path, you can edit it with other Pen tools, found in the Tool panel. The Pen tool in Photoshop replicates the Pen tool in Illustrator. It can take a bit of getting used to, but it is worth getting to know as it can be an accurate selection tool.

There are also two useful Path tools located in the Selection tool menu: the Path Selection tool enables you to move the whole path; the Direct Selection tool will let you move a single anchor point.

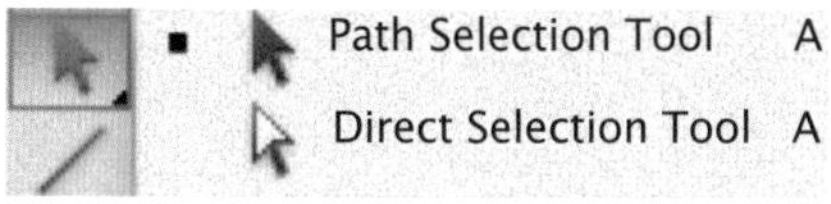

Your path will appear in the Paths panel. Save the path using the Paths panel drop-down menu, then click on the Path Selection icon at the bottom of the panel. This will make the path a live selection.

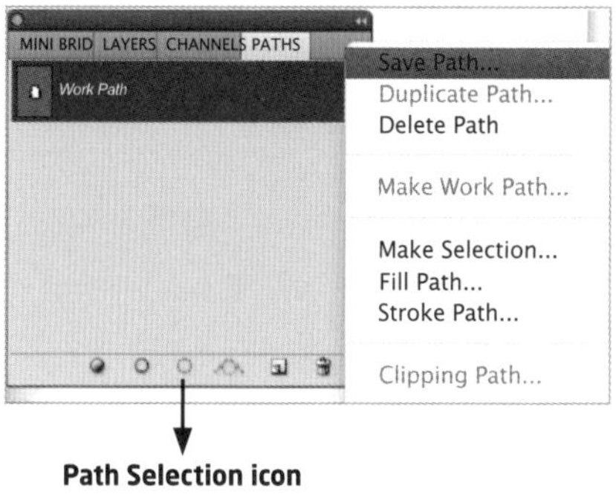

STEP 4

Open your design; in this case, it is a repeat unit. At this point you can rescale the pattern to the proportions of the image you wish to fill.
Image > Image Size.
Create a pattern with your unit.
Edit > Define Pattern.
Name your pattern and click OK.

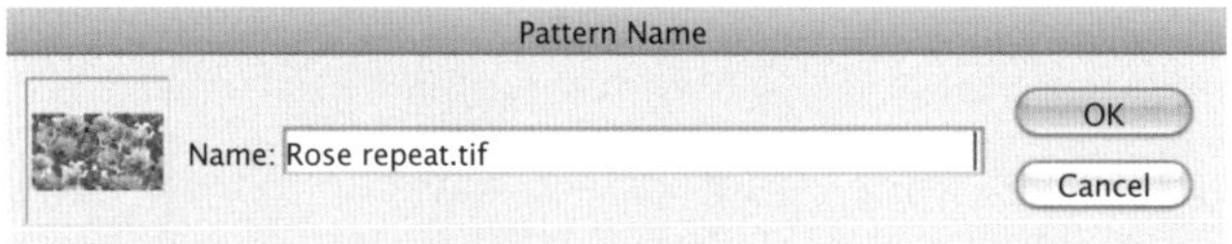

STEP 5

Open a new document and fill with your pattern.
Edit > Fill.
Select Pattern and find your design.
Select > All.
Edit > Copy.

STEP 6

Now go back to your original image and select your path.
Edit > Paste Special > Paste Into.

STEP 7

Your pattern is now pasted into your skirt selection. You can still rescale the pattern if you need to. With your new pasted layer selected, choose **Edit > Transform > Scale**.

STEP 8

Now it is time to use the displacement map. **Filter > Distort > Displace**.
The Displace dialog box will appear; accept the default options and click OK.
Photoshop will ask which image you wish to use as the Displacement Map.
Select your grayscale image.

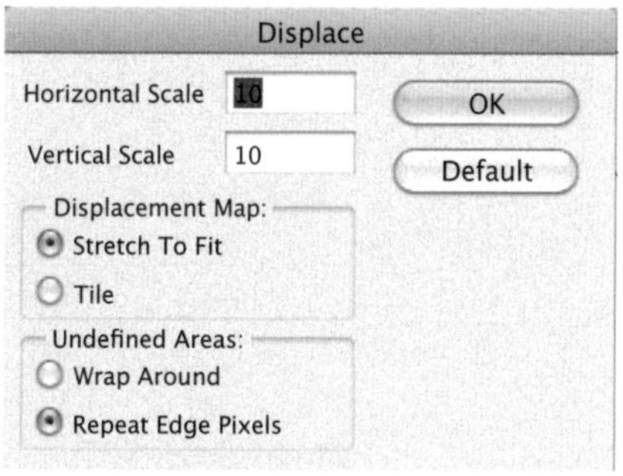

You will see the artwork bend slightly, but it will still look flat.

To reveal the folds of the skirt underneath the pattern, go to Multiply in the Layers palette.

TUTORIAL 22

TEXTURE MAP AND LINE DRAWING

This tutorial demonstrates how to texture map your design onto a fashion illustration using basic Photoshop tools. The key to fashion illustration is to have a strong vision and create an ambience. Here, Katie Hoppe's design work is inspired by folklore and romantic imagery. Her use of color is rich, evocative, and exotic. She demonstrates how important it is to have a body of original drawings and objects as a palette to work with.

Begin by selecting a fashion image featuring a simple garment that a more complex design can fit into, and create a black line drawing as a template. You can incorporate other drawings and scanned imagery to give the illustration depth and texture.

STEP 1

Scan your line drawing and open it up in Photoshop.

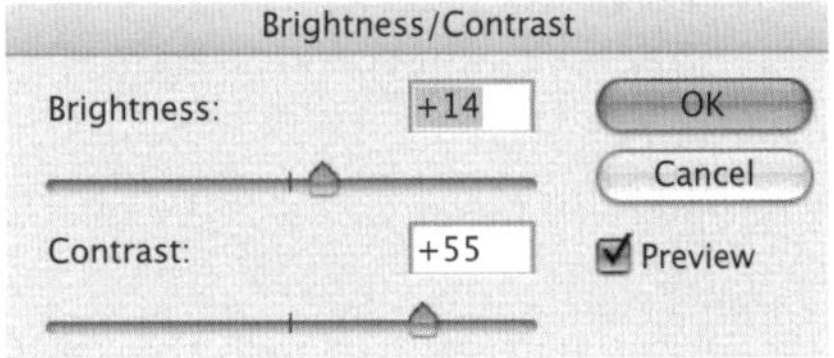

STEP 2

Image > Adjustments > Brightness/Contrast.
Move the sliders to achieve a good definition.

STEP 3

Clean up your image, using the Eraser tool to rub out any stray lines.
Join up any gaps between the outlines in order to make complete shapes to paste your design work into.

STEP 4

Use the Magic Wand tool (tolerance set to 50) to select a section of your black line.
Select > Similar.
Select all the black lines.

STEP 5

Edit > Copy.
Edit > Paste.
A new layer will appear.
Turn the background layer off to reveal your new layer.

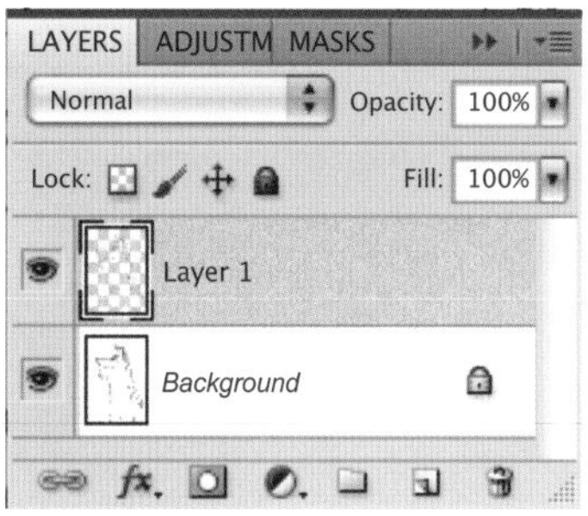

STEP 6

Open up your design work.
Select > All.
Edit > Copy.

STEP 7

Return to your fashion illustration. Use the Magic Wand tool to select the main part of the dress.
Edit > Paste Special > Paste Into.

STEP 8

A new layer will appear. Use the Move tool to move the design around.
Edit > Transform.
Scale or rotate the design to fit better within the garment.

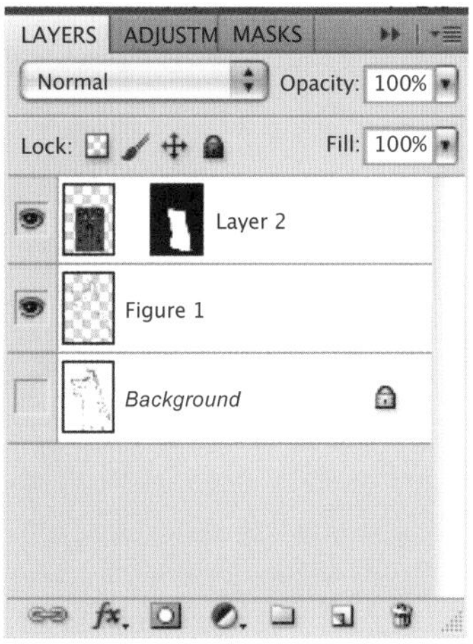

STEP 9

Go back to the original design and select a section to paste into the sleeves using the Paste Into command. It is important at this stage to manage your layers, as you can end up with too many. You should have five layers. Turn off the background layer and line-drawing layer. With one of the design layers highlighted, click on the menu button in the top right-hand corner of the Layers palette and a drop-down menu will appear. Select Merge Visible to flatten the layers.

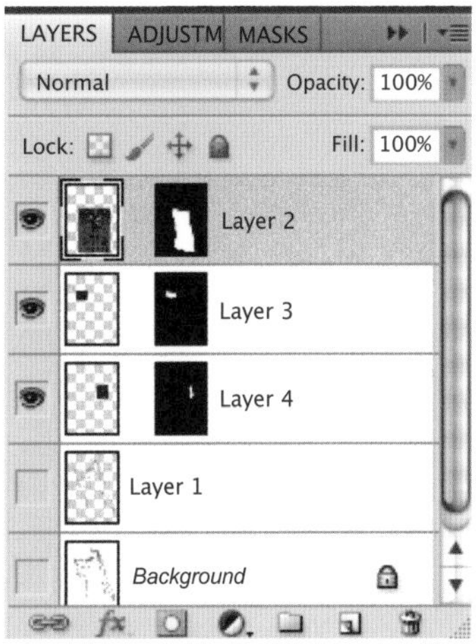

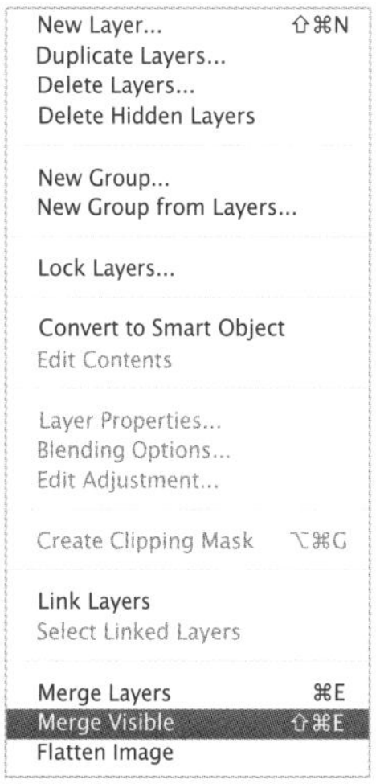

STEP 10

To incorporate added texture, scan in a sequin trim and open it up in Photoshop.
Select > All.
Edit > Copy.
Return to your fashion illustration with the figure drawing layer selected. Use the Magic Wand tool to select the sleeve.
Edit > Paste Special > Paste into.
A new layer will appear.
Use the Transform tools to fit your design to the shape of the sleeve. Repeat the process with the other sleeve.

STEP 11

Again, it is important to manage your layers. Turn off the background layer and the line drawing layer. With one of the design layers highlighted, click on the menu button in the top right-hand corner of the Layers palette and select Merge Visible from the drop-down menu to flatten the layers.

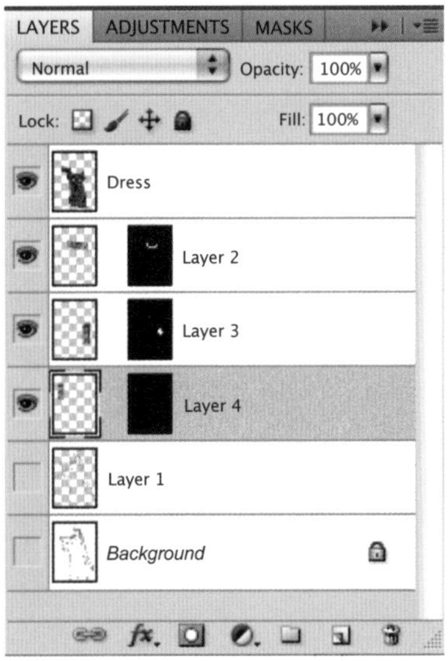

STEP 12

You should now have three layers. With the figure drawing layer selected, paint in the figure by making selections with the Magic Wand tool and filling them with color.

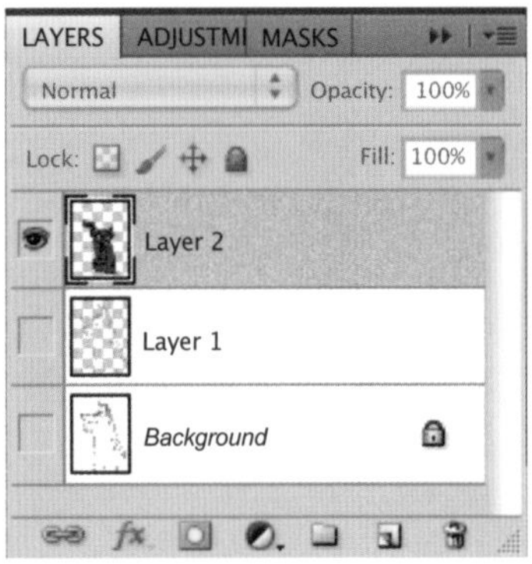

STEP 13

Now the figure is complete. Think about adding a background.

STEP 14

Create a new layer and shift it behind all the other layers.

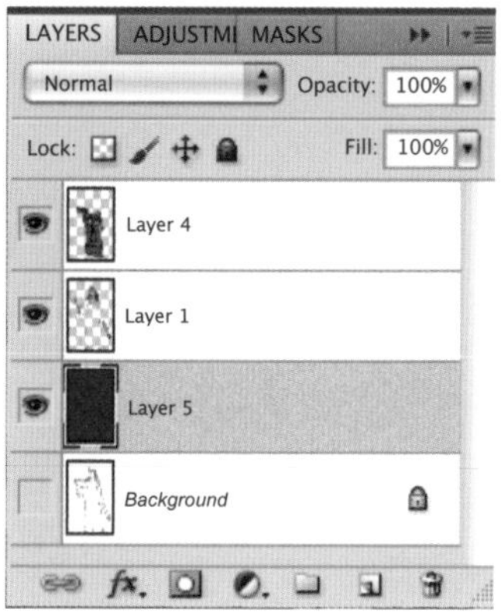

STEP 15

Edit > Fill > Foreground Color.
Fill with your chosen color.

STEP 16

Open up some drawings that you can paste into the background. Here, the bird was selected with the Magic Wand tool and copied and pasted onto the illustration, then colored in.

STEP 17

To create the button tree, scan in a tree-trunk silhouette, select it with the Magic Wand tool and paste it into the background.

STEP 18

Scan in some buttons. Use the Pen tool to carefully draw around the buttons, creating curves around the edges.

STEP 19

Go into the Paths palette, and make sure the path you have just created is active by clicking on it to highlight it.
Click on the Path Selection icon to make the path into a live selection.
Select > Inverse.

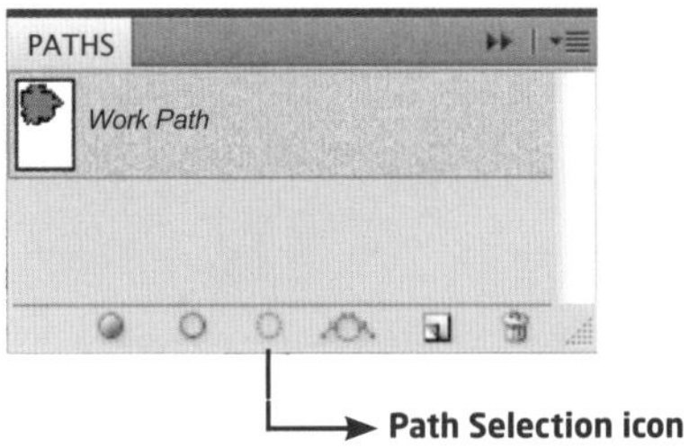

STEP 20

Copy > Paste.
Use the Move tool to arrange the buttons.
Duplicate the button layer to build up the button tree.
Merge the button-tree layers to create one layer, as before.

STEP 21

Select and copy some line drawings and paste them into the background. Color them white and lower the Opacity in the Layer palette to add decoration and ornamentation to the fashion illustration.

TUTORIAL 23

CREATING GRAPHIC SILHOUETTES

This tutorial demonstrates how to place a print design into context for display purposes. The example shows a simple stripe being placed into a basic fashion figure illustration.

The following sequence demonstrates how to create a figure template in Illustrator and then how to place a pattern into the template in Photoshop.

STEP 1

Create a new file in Illustrator.

File > Place.

Choose the photograph you wish to trace to create your figure template.

Once the photograph has been placed, open the Layers palette and lock the layer. The will prevent the photograph being moved during tracing.

Open the Layers menu by clicking on the menu icon in the top right-hand corner of the palette. Select New Layer to create a new layer.

STEP 2

Using the Pen tool, draw around the outline of the figure. You will need some knowledge of the Pen tool to create and control curves. You will also need to know how to cut paths using the Scissors tool and use the Direct Selection tool to join the paths together (this is to separate the drawing into different sections, ensuring that each section is closed so it can be filled with a color).

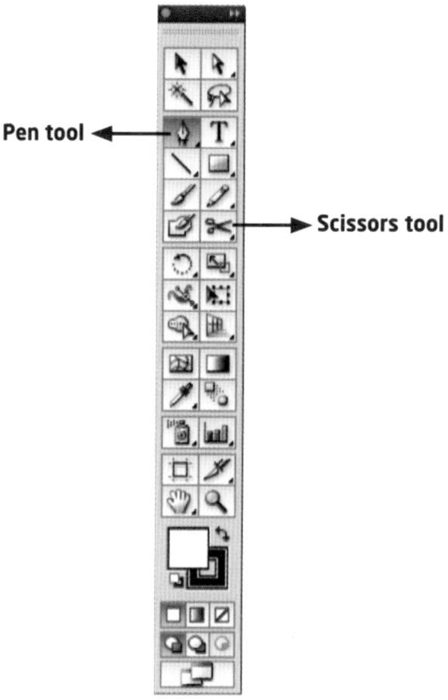

STEP 3

Now create a new layer below the illustration and place a rectangle, filled with a color, to emphasize the illustration.

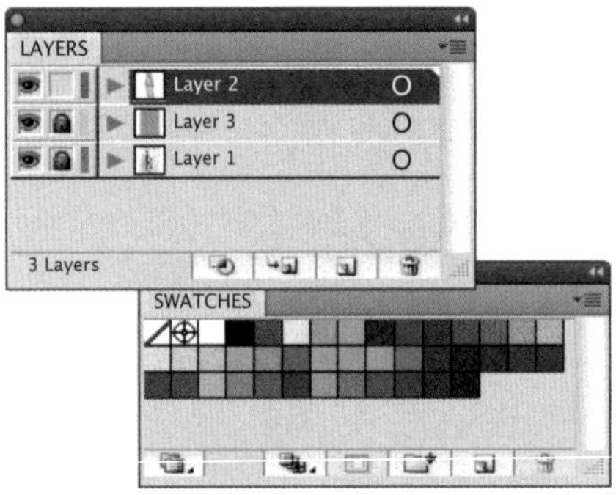

STEP 4

Now working on the figure layer, you can select parts of the garment and figure and fill with color.

STEP 5

Next, open a new Illustrator document and create a simple stripe for your pattern (see Tutorial 16, page 104).

STEP 6

Open Photoshop and create a new Letter-size (A4) document. From your Illustrator document, copy and paste each layer of your illustration into your Photoshop document, as well as your simple stripe pattern. Name your layers (you should have four).

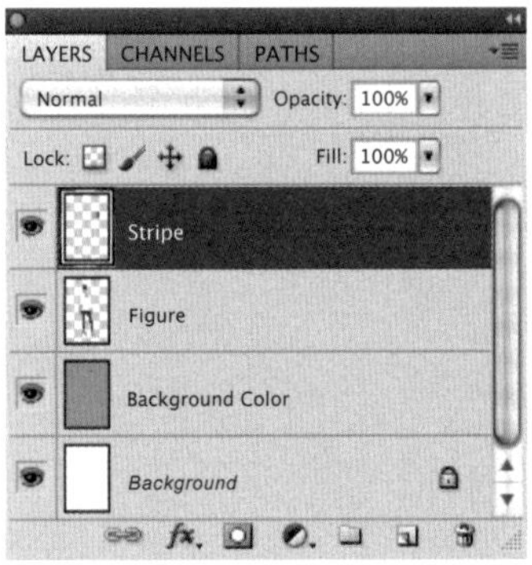

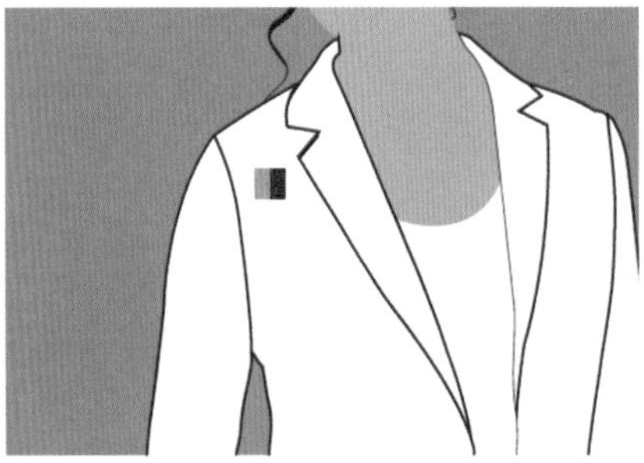

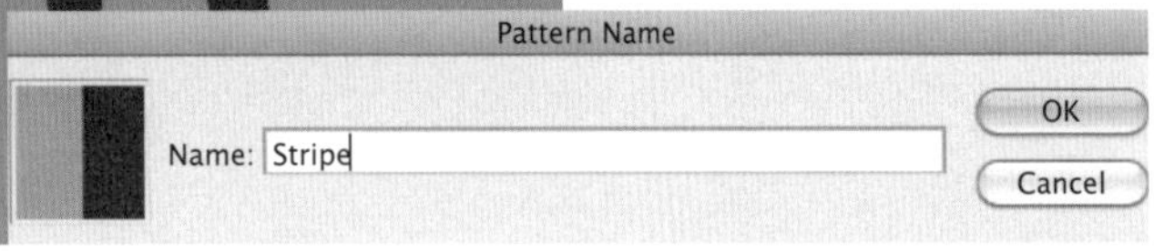

STEP 7

The stripe pattern may appear too large, in which case you can reduce it to the appropriate scale by selecting the stripe layer and choosing **Edit > Transform**.

STEP 8

To select the area you wish to apply the pattern to, select outside the pattern area with the Magic Wand tool.
Select > Inverse.
To create a pattern swatch, choose
Edit > Define Pattern.
Name your pattern and click OK.

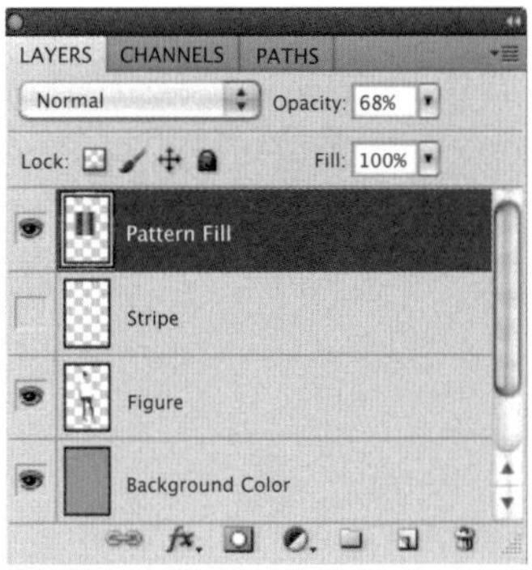

STEP 9

Create a new layer and draw a square marquee over the part of the garment you wish to fill with your stripe.
Edit > Fill > Pattern.
Find your stripe pattern. Reduce the Opacity of the layer to reveal the garment.

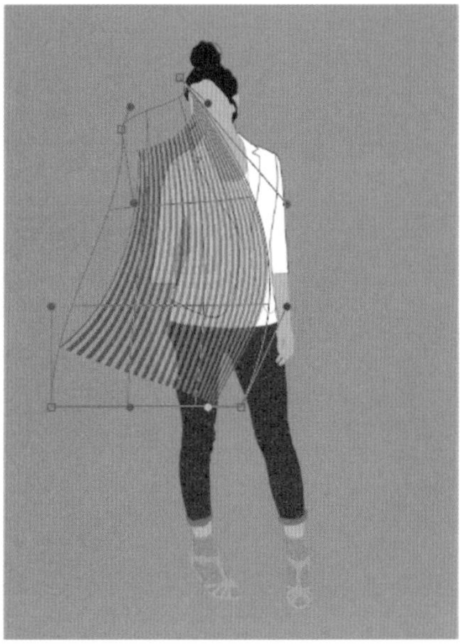

STEP 10

Now you need to make your stripe follow the contours of each section of the garment.
To do this, use the Free Transform tools. Choose **Edit > Transform > Rotate** to rotate your stripe to follow the direction of the garment section.
Choosing **Edit > Transform > Warp** will put a grid around the pattern. You can warp the grid so it bends with the contours of the garment.

STEP 11

Go to the illustration layer and with the Magic Wand select the part of the jacket you are working on. Now go to the pattern fill layer.
Edit > Copy.
Edit > Paste.
Turn off the pattern fill layer. Your pattern fill will be now in the jacket section. Repeat steps 8, 9, and 10 on each section of the garment.

5
DIGITAL CRAFT

DIGITAL CRAFT

The introduction of new technology in the 21st century is impacting on many different areas of our lives and is developing at such a rapid pace that it is sometimes difficult to keep up. For the "digital generation," technology has become second nature. For the designer rooted in traditional processes, technology is no longer possible to ignore. Some designers see it as a challenge to introduce new digital methods into their work, while others are fiercely protective of their tradition and craft.

This chapter looks at whether it is possible for a designer to maintain the "hand" quality of their work while using new technology. The first part of the chapter, "Combining old and new," looks at how designers are finding ways to reintroduce traditional handcrafting skills into their work. The second part, "Desktop digital textiles," examines how designers are taking advantage of the immediacy and hands-on approach of desktop printing to create a new craft tradition. Should the new skills that are being developed with digital design and print be recognized as a new craft skill, rather than just a mechanical process? This is for you to judge. But the potential for creativity using new technology is clear from the wealth of work shown in this chapter.

COMBINING OLD AND NEW

Working in a virtual environment with a mechanical output seems to make the creator keenly aware that the personal identity of the work is in danger of being lost. There is also a need for a textile designer to have a physical relationship with the cloth and this can become even more apparent when working in a digital environment.

Many designers are disappointed with the "flat" outcome of a digital print; the surface and tactile qualities created by traditional print methods are often lost. For some it seems too easy to print at the press of a button without physical effort, and the speed of the digital print process almost seems to compel the practitioner to work extensively on a fabric to slow down the process. The result is that some designers are now finding ways to put back these tactile qualities into the creation of fabric, and into the fabric itself by physical intervention such as over-printing and embellishment.

Above: Clara Vuletich scans vintage patchwork pieces and digitally prints them onto cotton/hemp, thereby preserving and enhancing heirloom textiles.

Right: Collaged digital prints integrated into a Burberry jacket by Claire Canning.

Digital printing can appear flat, but once the fabric is made into a garment, it can come to life again. Claire Canning experiments with a combination of traditional screen-printing and digital techniques, adding depth by layering, collaging, bonding, and cutting. The rich photographic qualities that can be achieved with digital print give a playful, storybook narrative to Claire's work.

Above: For her conceptual blouse "Found by the Sea" (2009), Shelly Goldsmith used dye sublimation to emboss pressed plant samples from London's Natural History Museum Herbarium on a reclaimed garment interior.

Left: Melanie Bowles and Sarah Dennis created "The Wallpaper Dress" by scanning and then digitally printing a sample of vintage wallpaper onto linen, which they then embellished with embroidery.

Dominique Devaux creates rich digital prints inspired by her love of jewelry and antiques. She adds metallic foiling to give them texture and light.

This chapter looks at a range of techniques that can be combined with digital print to re-engage the designer with the cloth, in order to create beautiful and innovative surfaces. These range from screen-print methods, such as devoré, discharge printing, flocking, foiling, and laminating, through dye techniques such as shibori, to fabric manipulation, embellishment, and embroidery. Many of these techniques have, until recently, only been explored by couturiers, fashion designers, and textile artists due to the cost of digital print.

However, now that many established art institutions have a digital textile print facility, there is a wealth of experimental textile work emerging from colleges and universities, and professional, small-scale designers are also taking up this newly emerging craft. Much of this work is very experimental and in its early stages of development, but the examples here show the rich effects that can be achieved.

HAND PAINTING AND DIGITAL PRINT

Hand painting or drawing onto fabric is the most immediate method of adding depth to a digital print. Because of its simplicity this technique is sometimes ignored, but its spontaneity can complement the mechanical process of digital printing and also make a design much more personal. There are many fabric pens available that can produce a very good effect, including glitter, pearlized, and puff pens.

Zoe Barker scans her beautiful floral paintings and then prints them digitally onto silk. She paints into the fabric by hand to add an extra layer to her work.

Dominique Devaux's collection "Exotic Paradise" is based on her love of exotic birds and florals and inspired by childhood memories of the Caribbean. Dominique has embellished the fabrics with hand-painted foil glitter, creating light and reflection and bringing the digital print to life. Bands of brightly colored silks give a contemporary and exotic appeal, and the juxtaposition of real jewelry, sewn over photographic images of the same jewelry, adds another layer. The result is a highly effective, sensitive, and sensual approach to digital design.

SCREEN PRINTING AND DIGITAL PRINT

Screen printing is a fast method of combining digital prints and traditional print techniques; color is positioned in a design using screens. There are several chemical recipes for silk screening, and the most suitable ones for combining with digital print are: pigment printing, devoré, discharge printing, and the application of adhesive for flocking and foiling. The screen print has to work not only in harmony with the design, but also within the limitations of the fabric and print quality. Achieving the desired results can require much testing, and you will need a good knowledge of print techniques and an awareness of the health and safety issues involved.

Here, Emamoke Ukeleghe digitally printed a design of text with a hand-drawn pattern onto cotton satin, and then used a screen-print method to overprint with peach pigment.

As a designer, Ukeleghe crosses between the textile traditions of Nigeria and East London, merging digital techniques with traditional techniques to create a fusion between old and modern, ethnic and Western. In the bag on the right, entitled "Purpose, Wisdom and Enlightenment," she digitally printed stripes onto cotton drill and then overprinted broken stripes in peach. In the bag on the left, "Laces," she made a large-scale drawing of shoelaces with black ballpoint pen, and then digitally printed the drawing onto cotton.

In her powerful textile collection "Belonging(s)," Ukeleghe uses digital print combined with pigment screen-printing. Her inspiration came from issues surrounding displacement, and each piece tells a personal story. Here, a circular pattern was digitally printed onto cotton satin then overprinted with blue and white pigments. By including a photograph of a family member, she integrates a personal memory into her work.

DEVORÉ AND DIGITAL PRINT

In devoré printing, a chemical paste is applied to a blended cellulose-protein fabric. When heat is applied, the paste burns away one of the fiber types to leave a transparent area. Many digital print bureaus supply pretreated fabric specifically for the devoré process, such as silk/viscose satin and silk/viscose velvet. The chemical paste is applied to the fabric, either by hand or by screen printing, in the areas that are to be burned away. This can be done after digital printing has taken place. A heat process is then used to burn away the pattern areas to reveal a sheer, translucent area of fabric. The devoré process is time consuming and labor intensive, but the results can be beautiful. It should be approached with caution, and health and safely guidelines followed, as strong chemicals are used in the process.

Once the fabric has been put through the devoré process, the base color of the fabric is revealed. This area can be cross-dyed to reintroduce color into the cloth. Cross-dyeing works well with the devoré process as it stands out on the fiber that has not been burned away. If you used a screen to apply the devoré paste, you can use the same screen to apply the cross-dye.

Louisa-Claire Fernandes's dramatic furnishings collection, "Simplexity," combines digital and screen-printing techniques. First she created a digital print that became a background on which she applied other techniques. A large-scale devoré print gave her work a luxurious quality, and the dip-dyed effect was created by scanning in hand-painted papers. Her work demonstrates the combining of mechanical and hand processes to create a "new fabric" couture-furnishing collection.

Devoré paste has been silk-screened onto the digital print. Once the paste is dry, heat can be applied with an iron or heat press to burn out the viscose and leave the silk.

Here, Louisa-Claire Fernandes digitally printed a large-scale design onto a silk/viscose mixed fabric. The devoré area was cross-dyed in turquoise.

FOILING AND FLOCKING WITH DIGITAL PRINT

Foiling and flocking onto a digital print are popular choices for highlighting and embellishing designs. They are not as risky as the more experimental processes such as devoré and discharge printing, which are time consuming and complicated. Foiling can give highlights and added sparkle to a fabric, especially when the fabric moves. Flocking gives a beautiful raised texture to the surface of a fabric, which is often lacking with digital printing.

Metallic foils come in a variety of jewel colors as well as metallic effects such as copper, gold, and silver, and can be bought in sheet form from craft suppliers. Iridescent and holographic foils are also available.

In foiling, water-based or solvent adhesive is either applied through a screen or hand-painted onto the fabric. A sheet of foil is then stuck onto the adhesive. Heat is applied with an iron or heat press and, once the foil has cooled, the sheet is peeled back to leave behind a foiled area.

Small areas of foiling can be added to a digital print to highlight areas and make them glitter. You can also use a clear "foil" to create matte and shiny areas on a fabric that catch the light when the fabric moves. Carefully consider where to apply the foil so that the design and the foiling effect work together.

The raised, "velvet" effect of flocking is traditionally associated with decorative wallpapers. However, it is also suitable for fashion fabrics and can add a luxurious surface to the cloth. Flock can be purchased on a roll, attached to a backing paper. It is usually supplied in white, but it may be hand-colored with dyes. Flocking paper can be digitally printed on a Mimaki digital printer and then applied to a fabric, but this is still an experimental process.

Similar to the foiling process, the flocking paper is placed (flock-side down) onto a glued area. Heat is applied using an iron or a heat press and, once cool, the backing paper is peeled back to reveal the flocked area.

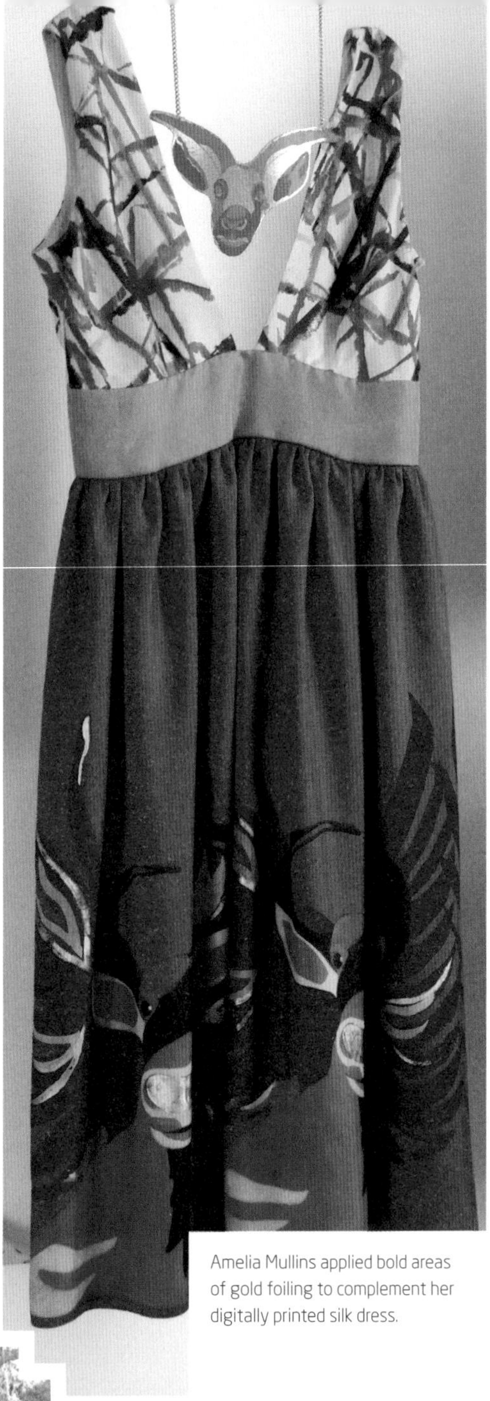

Amelia Mullins applied bold areas of gold foiling to complement her digitally printed silk dress.

Charlotte Arnold creates intriguing surface effects by applying digital flocking onto digitally printed silk. The result is a "new" looking fabric with a mixture of photographic imagery, light, and texture.

Emily House's "Plastic Maze" was digitally printed onto cotton poplin and then plastic-laminated and edged with a reflective trim.

Matthew Williamson's S/S 05 collection features this "Rainbow Dress" of digitally printed chiffon embellished with metallic foil.

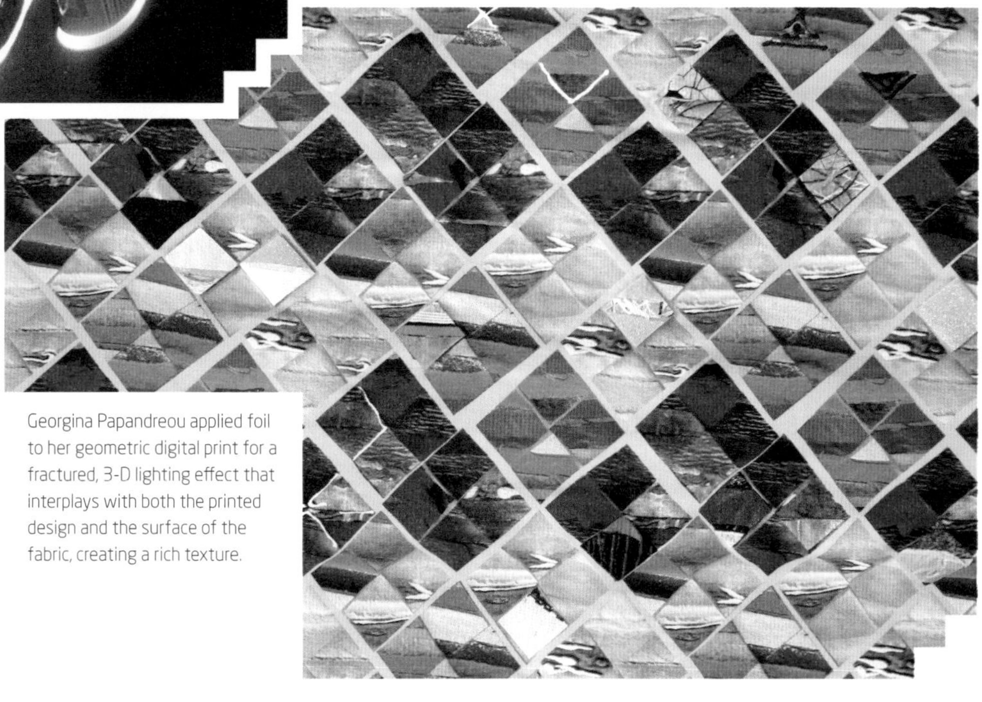

Georgina Papandreou applied foil to her geometric digital print for a fractured, 3-D lighting effect that interplays with both the printed design and the surface of the fabric, creating a rich texture.

DESIGNER PROFILE

RICHARD WESTON

The writer and architect Richard Weston, Professor of Architecture at Cardiff University, Wales, came to digital textile design through his passion for collecting beautiful precious stones, minerals, and fossils. Scanning in his mineral collection at high resolution, Weston was able to capture remarkable patterns and colors. "The way the color works in these minerals is partly pigment and partly optical effect, so the absorption and reflection patterns are very different. You can get two scans from the same stone and you wouldn't believe they were from the same mineral." Enlarging the scanned images and "cleaning them up" in Photoshop enhanced and magnified the original natural forms.

A friend told Weston it would be possible to digitally print his images onto fabrics. With this knowledge, Weston began his unexpected journey into the world of fashion through digital textile printing, turning his hobby into a range of luxurious scarves.

Weston took his digitally printed scarves to the biannual Best of British Open Call event at the world-famous London store Liberty. The Open Call invites the public to show their products to the top buyers in the world, giving them the chance of a lifetime to sell in the London store. Weston attended the Open Call on a cold February morning in 2010. His passion and enthusiasm for his product was quickly spotted by top New York buyer Ed Burstell, who had recently joined Liberty, and his journey from passionate amateur to top-selling designer began. Maverick Television, who also attended the Open Call, documented the fascinating journey of Weston's "Mineral Scarves" in an episode of the BBC2 reality series *Britain's Next Big Thing*.

Weston's designs are digitally printed onto the best silks by the finest digital silk printers in Como, Italy, maintaining the beauty of the original minerals; as a final touch, the edges of the silk are then "machine hand-rolled." After securing an order from Liberty, Weston launched his first designer collection in June 2010. His vibrant "Mineral Scarves" are now a best seller in the scarf department of the prestigious London department store Liberty, displayed alongside designs by Alexander McQueen, Christopher Kane, and Jonathan Saunders.

Weston's scarves demonstrate the rich possibilities that digital print offers and show how an amateur's passion and love of natural forms can be translated into a beautiful product.

Richard Weston discovered digital textile design through his passion for collecting precious minerals and fossils.

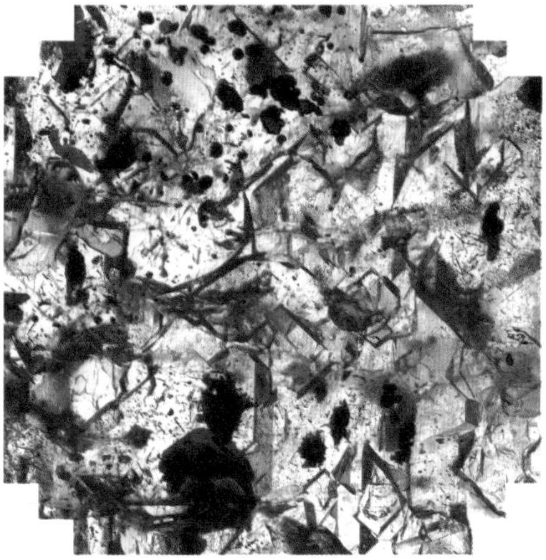

Weston begins his design process by making a high-quality scan of a mineral sample. He then spends hours "cleaning" the image in Photoshop to enhance each stone's remarkable qualities.

Using the very finest digital printing maintains the beautiful colors and details of the original minerals.

Weston translated the beauty of these natural forms into his "Mineral Scarves" collection, featured in the famous London store Liberty alongside scarves by other well-known designers.

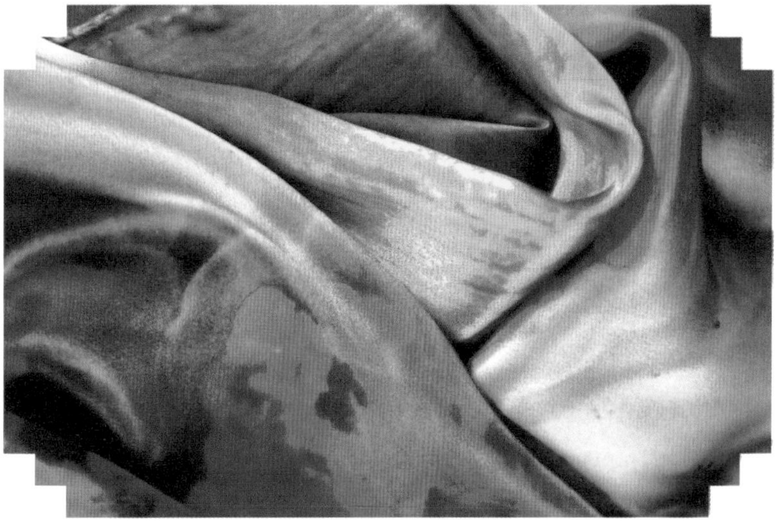

RESIST DYEING AND DIGITAL PRINT

Resist dyeing techniques—such as tie-dye, batik, and shibori—are among the oldest textile-dyeing techniques. They are used all around the world and are still a source of fascination to many artists and designers today.

Shibori is the collective Japanese term for tie-dye, stitch-dye, fold-dye, and pole-wrap-dye techniques, which have been used for centuries as a textile craft all over the world. Chinese in origin, it spread to Africa, the Middle East, and India, and is still used today. Shibori ranges from simple resist techniques to advanced methods in which complex layers of color are built up. With shibori, it is possible to create not only two-dimensional patterns, but also three-dimensional designs, where the folding and wrapping used to achieve the resist areas is left in the cloth.

An element of surprise is always present in the making of shibori cloth, which contributes to its special magic and popularity, and can be used to complement the mechanical processes of digital printing.

For her "Digital Shibori," Melanie Bowles translated traditional shibori effects into mathematical geometrics using Illustrator.

Joanna Fowles created this shibori piece in the traditional way—by hand—before manipulating it in Photoshop and then printing it digitally onto silk.

EMBROIDERY, EMBELLISHMENT, AND DIGITAL PRINT

In recent years there has been a revival of the traditional crafts of knitting, crochet, and embroidery. In a world dominated by technology, many people enjoy returning to traditional techniques and creating garments and accessories by hand. At the same time, there has been a resurgence in the popularity of vintage garments and embellishments, which has also encouraged designers to look back at traditional techniques of hand- or machine stitching to add interest, value, and individual style to their own designs.

Today, designers are combining the traditional techniques of embroidery and embellishment with digital print to add a "handcrafted" element to their textile designs. If carefully applied, the two skills can complement one another.

Emma Rampton's textile collection "Second Chance" consists of multifunctional garments that are designed to have a second life. The wearer is encouraged to customize and interact with the garment as time goes on. Working with contemporary and traditional imagery from domestic life, she combines new technology with traditional stitch techniques, worked back into the fabric.

Dominique Devaux sewed vintage embroidered sections onto digital prints to create her "Exotic Paradise" collection. The printed fabric echoes the real embroidered motifs, resulting in a look that successfully combines modern with antique.

Katie Irving Jones draws stitchwork patterns inspired by historic embroideries. She then scans and further manipulates them using imaging software. She prints her designs digitally onto a cotton/linen mix to give the effect of canvas work. Finally, she hand-stitches back into the motifs to give a personal, handcrafted touch to the fabric.

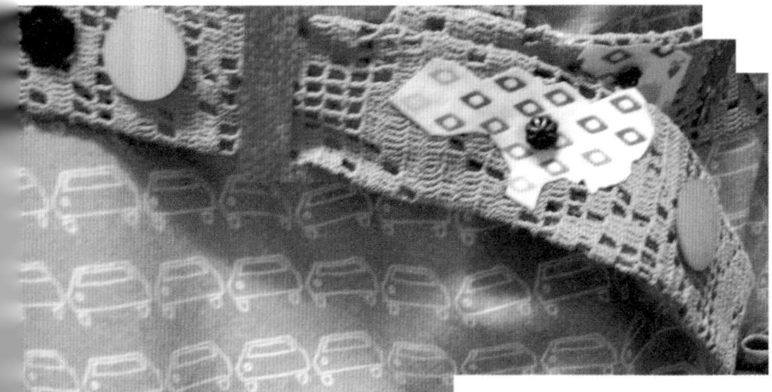

Andrea Patterson demonstrates her use of digital print and design techniques in combination with hand detailing to the fabric and garment, using appliqué, stitching, and trimmings such as lace, buttons, and ribbons.

Photini Anastasi's digital collection retains her beautiful and sensitive drawings and watercolor paintings of landscape scenes from her childhood. She prints digitally onto viscose satin and then hand embroiders back into the images, imitating the lines and marks of her drawings.

DESIGNER PROFILE

HELEN AMY MURRAY

British-born textile designer Helen Amy Murray is an emerging talent, creating beautiful, luxury one-of-a-kind textiles for interiors and wall coverings. Murray was educated at Chelsea College of Art and Design, London. In 2003 she won the prestigious Oxo Peugeot Design Award, as well as a prize for innovation from the National Endowment for Science, Technology and the Arts (NESTA). She then set up her own label, HelenAmyMurray, and has now exhibited her work internationally.

At Chelsea, Murray developed a passion for creating three-dimensional surface effects on various fabrics such as silk, leather, and suede. She has since developed a technique that has been recognized internationally for its unique handcrafted construction. She explains, "I'm excited about fabric manipulation and using innovative techniques, beautiful luxury materials, and design to create couture for the high end of the market."

Murray's inspiration comes from natural forms, from which she creates complex pattern structures using her unique technique. Her work achieves a strong graphic look, her innovative process creating sophisticated three-dimensional fabrics.

The designer's work originates from her love of working directly with the surface of fabrics, so when she decided to take the bold move of exploring digital design she discovered a completely new way of working. "At first I felt nervous working in a virtual medium. As I have a very physical and tactile relationship with fabric, I felt I was entering the unknown. But once I had completed the process of designing and digitally printing and had applied my technique, I could see the possibilities that it would give my work. I love the subtlety of color that digital print can achieve and the layers of pattern and form. It allows me to work with more complex and fantastical imagery, which gives my work a new narrative."

Murray's highly individual and sensual approach to textiles allows her work to develop without compromising her aesthetic values. She has merged digital print so well with her own cutting techniques that she has managed to create a truly "digitally crafted" textile.

For her "Art Deco Chair, Two-headed Bird with Sunrays" (2005), Murray integrated a digitally printed piece into her sculpted leather fabric, which was then upholstered onto a classic art deco chair. She scanned her hand-drawn image of an exotic crane, which she then adapted using imaging software. This was then digitally printed onto silk crêpe satin and carefully appliquéd onto the leather before she applied her cutting process. The digital print on silk satin allowed her to introduce an intricate gradient of color, adding both depth and movement.

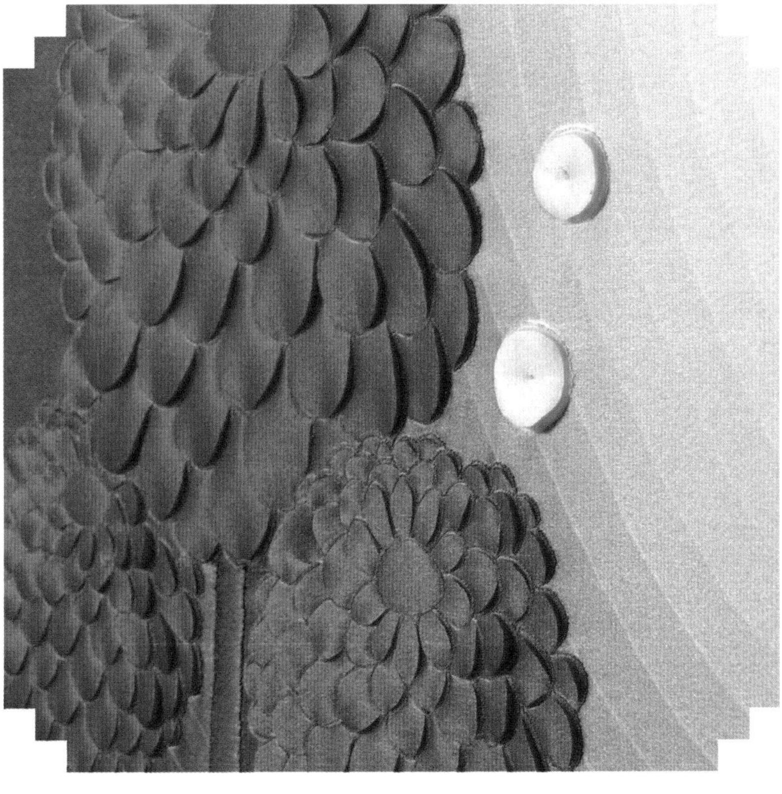

"Birds and Flowers" (2005) is an ambitious art piece. Initially working and adapting her design using imaging software, Murray dropped in color blends and gradients, then printed the artwork digitally. Drawing back into the design with her cutting tool to create a sculpted 3-D effect, she gave further detail, definition, shadow, movement, and depth to the piece. Finally, she framed it in wood covered with foiled leather.

PRETREATMENT OF DIGITAL FABRIC

All fabrics used for digital printing must be pretreated before use. The Textiles Environment Design (TED) project at the Chelsea College of Art and Design, London, looks at the role the designer can play in creating textiles that have a reduced impact on the environment, and provides a toolbox of designer-centered solutions. Part of the resource offered by TED investigates the coating of organic fabrics so that they are suitable for digital printing, such as organic cottons, linens, and hemp. These fabrics are specially coated by a digital print bureau. Melanie Bowles has created a collection, "Material Attachment," that is digitally printed onto a hemp/silk mix, proving that rich and vibrant colors can be achieved. The use of organic hemp/silk introduces a new fabric for digital print that has a beautiful surface and subtle sheen.

In her "Material Attachment" collection, Melanie Bowles drew inspiration from historical textiles. The collection was shown at *Ever & Again*, an exhibition at Chelsea College of Art and Design in 2007 which looked at recyling textiles. Melanie relined a favorite coat with digitally printed organic hemp/silk mix fabric to give it a new lease of life.

DIGITAL PRINT ONTO VINTAGE FABRICS

Nicky Gearing and Debbie Stack from the London College of Fashion experimented with the pretreatment process as part of an international research project with the Creative Industries Faculty at the Queensland University of Technology, Australia, in 2004. This was a design exercise featuring reworked vintage clothing dating from the 19th and 20th centuries donated by the National Trust of Queensland. Gearing and Stack screen printed the pretreatment paste—consisting of sodium carbonate, Manutex, and urea—onto an original Victorian damask. The vintage fabric took the inks successfully and withstood the after-treatment of steaming and washing well. They produced an interesting range of samples on various fabrics, integrating discharge and screen-printing techniques with digital print. Digital embroidery was applied to the fabric before the pretreatment, and also as a final embellishment after printing to create a rich surface quality. The project resulted in a collection of fabrics that show the potential of pretreatment on fabrics not normally used for digital print.

Digital print on vintage damask, appliquéd onto a traditional ticking cotton and combined with screen printing.

Digital floral print on dyed ticking fabric, combined with discharge printing.

DESKTOP DIGITAL TEXTILES

The rise of mass production and consumerism has led to a craft-focused backlash, and more people are now interested in DIY design-and-make. Amateurs are finding ingenious ways to personalize and customize their own products—and not just in the domestic arts, but in graphic design, journalism, and publishing, too.

You no longer have to be a trained graphic designer to create personal graphics such as business cards, logos, mouse mats, greetings cards, and simple websites. Imaging software is now available as a design tool for all to use and the desktop printer has developed into a key method of print production for all kinds of graphic materials. Craft enthusiasts are now embracing the hands-on digital technology that is available from the home, and this extends to textiles, primarily through inkjet transfers and sublimation printing.

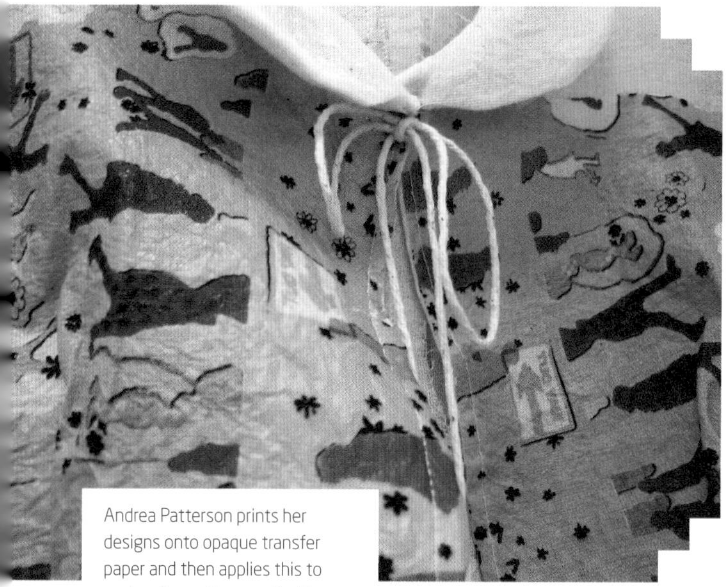

Andrea Patterson prints her designs onto opaque transfer paper and then applies this to contrasting cotton muslin. The "plastic" quality of the opaque transfer adds texture and contrasts with the coarseness of the natural cloth.

In her collection "The Old Farm House," Catherine Frere-Smith incorporates a fabric kit so her design can be made into a garment or a fabric house.

INKJET TRANSFERS

The simplest and most direct method of inkjet printing onto fabric is by running inkjet-transfer paper through a printer and then applying the pattern onto fabric using heat, either with an iron or, ideally, in a heat press. The paper is a special polymer-treated paper which is manufactured for use as a T-shirt transfer, and is available from stationery and computer suppliers. It is designed for use with water-based inks. In the past the paper left a "plastic" feel to the fabric, but now a softer result can be achieved. It works best on white or pale fabrics, but there is also an opaque paper available that can be used on darker fabrics, though this will leave a plastic feel.

This simple method of printing, which can be done using most desktop printers, has created a surge in DIY design and print for the amateur craft and hobby sector. Adults and children alike are enjoying this hands-on and immediate approach to transferring images onto mouse mats, jigsaws, coasters, and clothes.

Of the "craft" hobbyists, it is perhaps the quilter who can find the most creative potential in this method of printing. It is possible to apply a nontoxic chemical formula to a fabric to make the image permanent. This is applied by first soaking the fabric in the solution and, once dry, ironing it onto freezer paper. The fabric can then be fed through the printer. Quilters require small, sample-sized amounts of fabric to work with, and, using the inkjet transfer technique, they can create many individual designs to incorporate into their work. Added to this is the tradition of a quilt as a valued artifact that is passed down from one generation to the next. Using this new technology, they can include photographic imagery in their work, adding a highly personalized and powerful sentimental quality to the quilt, which is changing the aesthetic of the craft.

The bell-like dress used by textile artist Shelly Goldsmith in her "Fragmented Bell" (opposite page, bottom) was originally hand-stitched by the employees of the Children's Home of Cincinnati. The panoramic image of the piece references natural disasters–in this case a tornado. Goldsmith digitally manipulated the photograph in order to fragment the plane of the image to reference the actual fragmentation of the domestic landscape.

Goldsmith used reclaimed christening dresses to create "Baptism" (opposite page, top left). The dress references the use of water in the christening ceremony, while also commenting on how these garments are handed down and reused over many years. As in "Fragmented Bell," the dress shows the image of a natural disaster and raises the notion that cloth retains a type of memory that cannot be erased. The gown has been transfer-printed with digitally adjusted photography, carefully pieced together to create a panorama effect around the garment.

Zoe Barker uses the inkjet transfer method to build up complex fabrics for her children's collection, "Second Life." She encourages children to interact with the clothes and appreciate their worth with her "customizing kit," containing transfers, badges, buttons, and ribbons, which can be added to personalize the garments.

Alice Potter enjoys the immediacy of translating her designs from sketchbook to fabric via her desktop printer. She produces small fabric samples that she then pieces together to create patchworks such as this one, entitled "When I Sleep I Dream of Play."

The technique of transfer printing is used by aforest-design to present a limited edition of odori tabi socks designed by Sara Lamusias. The tabi is a traditional sock from Japan that is used in the home or is worn with sandals. These photo-collage designs were transfer-printed onto cotton socks.

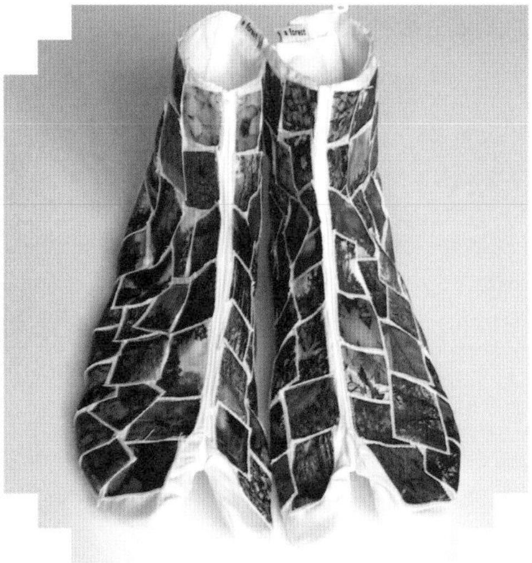

Textile artist Shelly Goldsmith creates her poignant textile pieces using a desktop printer to print digitally onto transfer paper. She meticulously jigsaws her images together by hand and irons them onto fragile, reclaimed garments. Collaging her images allows her to maintain a handcrafted quality to her work.

SUBLIMATION PRINTING

Dye-sublimation printing is a versatile method of printing using disperse dyes—available in cartridge form for large-format printers and for desktop printers—onto polyester fabrics. It is widely used in the promotional marketing industry for printing products such as jewelry, place mats, marble, ceramic tiles or mugs, skateboards, aprons, and other items of apparel. The majority of products printed using this process are somewhat crude in design, but there is huge potential to develop more sophisticated work. Many designers are now exploring this method of print, not least because the transfers yield stunning and beautiful photorealistic results, with vivid colors.

There is a wide range of polyesters available from fabric stores. These range from novelty fabrics to satin to metallic lamé and from stretch-knit jerseys to Lycra®. The affordability of these fabrics gives scope for the textile designer to experiment. Some fantastic results can be achieved with the vivid, clear colors of polyester.

In the textile industry, sublimation printing has mainly been used for printing on sportswear and swimwear. However, setting up a desktop print system is now proving to be an affordable option, and many textile designers, studios, and educational establishments are now exploring the possibilities of sublimation printing onto the large variety of polyester fabrics that are available. The choice of polyesters can range from Aertex, polymesh, lamé, satin, Lycra®, organza, and fleece to an array of novelty fabrics, but the higher the percentage of polyester they contain—preferably more than 60 percent—the better the results. It is always best to test fabrics as many do not state the proportion of polyester that they contain.

In the past, polyester has been uncomfortable to wear and has lacked the qualities of natural fabrics such as cotton. Recently, however, a number of manufacturers have come up with new processes that have resulted in soft, breathable, and comfortable fabrics. Polyester is also inexpensive, allowing designers the freedom to experiment with this hands-on method to create innovative print effects. Samples can be produced immediately, which is perfect for the ever-increasing pace of the fashion industry, where ideas need to be realized instantly.

Taina Lehtinen's handbag collection was created using sublimation printing onto faux suedette, showcasing the photographic qualities that can be achieved with this process.

Chetna Prajapati pushed the potential of sublimation printing in her edgy streetware collection "One Tribe, One Style." She printed on a range of polyesters, combining them to create her garments. The quality of the colors and the definition of the digital print is so strong that some colors look fluorescent; the metallic polyesters add sharpness to the graphic geometric designs.

Prajapati also used sublimation printing to create this beautiful pleated fabric. She printed a metallic polyester using the dye-sublimation technique, applied a pleating template, and then heat-pressed the fabric into shape.

Victoria Collins tests a wide range of polyesters, such as neoprene and Lycra®, before bonding them together to create new surfaces. Her sketchbook demonstrates the importance of testing different fabrics. She finds that most need to be heat-pressed for 60 seconds at 350°F, but care must be taken with nylon as it can melt quickly under a heat press.

Temitope Tijani used the sublimation technique to transfer her designs to plastics to create a stunning geometric accessories collection.

DESIGNER PROFILE

REBECCA EARLEY

Rebecca Earley is a lecturer in Textiles Environment Design at Chelsea College of Art and Design, London. She is an award-winning fashion textile designer who produces textiles for her own label, B.Earley, which she set up in 1995 with backing from the Crafts Council and the Prince's Trust. A practice-based design researcher, her work encompasses a wide range of design-related activities including producing digitally printed textiles for her own label, undertaking public art projects and commissions, and acting as an educator, facilitator, and curator.

Earley graduated from Central Saint Martins in 1994 and her graduate collection was widely recognized as groundbreaking. The heat-photogram print technique that she pioneered has since become an industry-standard process.

Earley's collections demonstrate how the designer can work fluently with digital technology and handcrafted techniques. She retains the original handcrafted look of the heat-photogram process, in which she paints disperse dyes directly onto transfer paper, places a real object directly onto the paper, and applies heat to transfer the image onto polyester. Now working digitally, she scans in the original photogram artwork and then rearranges it using imaging software. This gives her the scope to change the scale and composition of her artwork, and more freedom to experiment. Her designs are printed out on a desktop printer using sublimation printing.

In the collection featured here, shirts have been created and delicately embellished with stitched and pleated details inspired by research into traditional English gardening attire and images of old garden artifacts. Earley uses the digital process as another tool to integrate into her creative process.

In 1998, Earley's interest in the environment prompted her to analyze her own studio design and production practices. She subsequently developed an exhaust printing technique that produced hand-printed textiles with no water pollution and minimal chemical usage. She has continued to investigate new techniques and theoretical approaches to textile design, working on a variety of projects, including Natural Indigo at the Eden Project; *Well Fashioned*, an exhibition of eco-fashion at the Crafts Council Gallery; Ever & Again: Rethinking Recycled Textiles, a three-year project funded by the Arts and Humanities Research Council; and Top 100, a long-term polyester-shirt recycling project.

In 2002 Earley joined the Textiles Environment Design (TED) project–a research project where staff and students work collaboratively and on individual projects. This unique research cluster seeks to explore the role that the designer can play in producing more environmentally friendly textiles. TED places the designer, rather than the manufacturer or consumer, center stage, since "80–90 percent of total lifecycle costs of any product (environmental and economic) are determined by the product design before production ever begins" ("More for Less," Design Council Report, 1998).

TED has developed a series of environmentally friendly principles and strategies, including minimizing waste; using less harmful substances, energy, and water; utilizing new low-impact technologies; designing systems and services to support textile products; and creating long- or short-life textiles. Social and cultural awareness and concern for the environment have grown exponentially, and Earley and TED have played a key role both nationally and internationally in creating and promoting eco textile design.

Rebecca Earley's "Top 100" (2002–8), featuring a heat-photogram print.

Earley's "Digital Photogram Collage" was created using heat-photogram prints on fabric, which was then digitally scanned and manipulated and digitally printed.

Left: "Pin Print" (1995), heat photogram.

Center and right: "The Conscious Gardener" (2007) combines digital and sublimation printing with hand-painted transfer techniques.

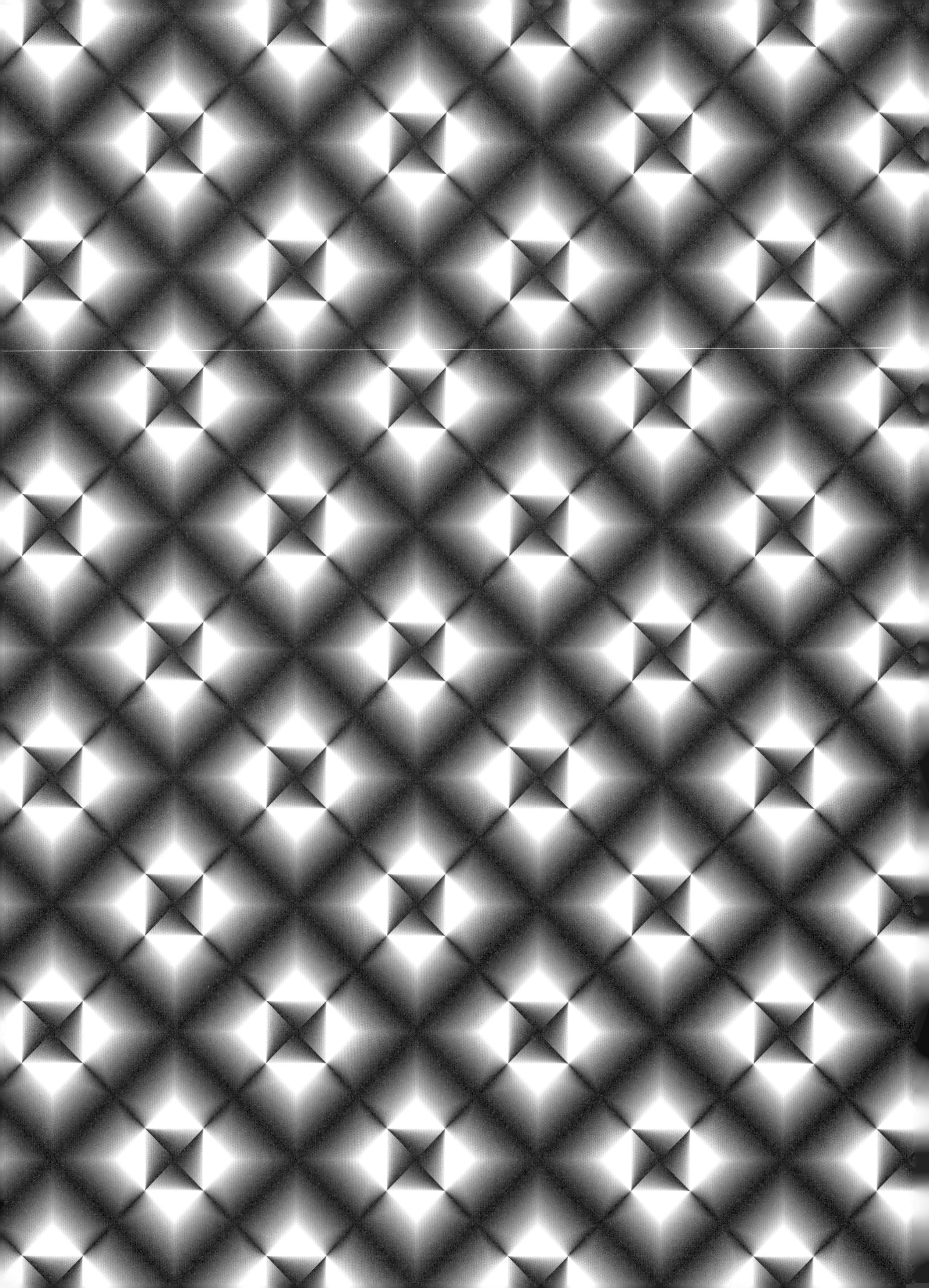

6
TECHNOLOGY FOR DIGITAL TEXTILE PRINTING

Digital inkjet printing is an increasingly important process within the industry, both as a mechanism for "sampling" printed designs and as a full production tool. Digital printing allows virtually any image quality to be printed but it does have its limitations, which are outlined within this chapter. However, it is important to recognize that it is printing processes themselves that have been responsible for many of the visual "languages" or styles that we see in textile design, and having an understanding of the technologies involved is key to appreciating this. This knowledge allows more control over the final result as well as the ability to create cutting-edge work. This chapter opens with a summary of the traditional technologies involved in textile printing, then examines digital textile printing in detail.

TRADITIONAL PRINT TECHNOLOGY

In order to understand the advantages of digital textile printing, it is important to comprehend the preceding technologies. Most traditional methods of printing textiles (as well as other media) are based on processes that use a template as a method for transferring a design onto the substrate. The techniques described here explain the basic categories of traditional textile printing techniques.

Relief Printing: a pattern is carved into wood or another material, as in woodblock printing.

Gravure or Intaglio: a process of incising marks into the surface, usually metal, as in copper plate printing.

Stenciling: a positive/negative process, as in rotary screen and hand silk-screen printing.

Heat Transfer: dye is transferred from paper to fabric using heat, as in sublimation printing.

Photoprinting: an image is broken down into four colors—cyan, magenta, yellow, and black (CMYK)—and printed out as a series of small dots, as in four-color process printing.

Woodblock prints on silk crêpe and linen (c. 1930–50) by Joyce Clissold, along with some of the original woodblocks used to make them.

WOODBLOCK PRINTING

Block printing is an ancient method for printing images onto fabric. It is generally associated with woodblock printing, but blocks have also been made from terracotta or metal. An image is carved into the wood to create a relief of the design and then pressed into colorant. The ink that remains on the surface of the block is then transferred to fabric by pressure. The blocks can range from a simple small motif using only one color to complex and large-scale blocks that require stamina and skill on behalf of the printer. The blocks are registered by pin marks that the printer lines up with each repeat of the block. This was the main process for printing textiles in 19th-century England.

GRAVURE PRINTING

Gravure printing is a method that first appeared in Europe in the mid-18th century. In this process, images are incised into a metal plate (usually copper) and dye is applied to the whole surface. The plate is then scraped, leaving the dye within the incised lines remaining. This allows the pattern to be transferred to the cloth by using pressure. Great skill in using linear marks and cross hatchings developed within the textile industry and the most famous examples became known as "toile de Jouy." A distinct visual language emerged with this print process and it is often referenced in contemporary textile design today.

A gravure-printed toile de Jouy textile from the collection of the Victoria & Albert Museum, London.

ENGRAVED ROLLER PRINTING

With increasing interest in mechanization in the 18th and 19th centuries, eventually the metal plate became a metal roller. This allowed the speed of printing to increase as well as new processes for transferring designs onto the metal, creating new design possibilities that allowed a fuller range of colors to be used. The ability to use halftone process or continuous tones or colors further enlarged the range of images that could be printed.

Examples of positive and negative paper stencils and their corresponding printed results.

STENCILING

All screen printing works on the principle of a stencil and the use of positive and negative imagery. Stenciling involves isolating each color found in an image as a positive or negative shape, defined by color boundaries. Holes defined by the area for each shape are cut into a thin substrate such as a metal sheet or waxed paper, through which the colorant is applied; the other colors are masked out. In Japan stencils are still used to create the intricate designs that are printed onto kimonos.

HAND SCREEN PRINTING

A silk screen is made by stretching a fine, porous mesh over a frame. The design is then delineated by masking out areas of the design that will not be printed, leaving areas open for each color, through which the ink is pushed using a rubber squeegee. The image that has been transferred onto the screen may also be laid out as a repeat.

The use of photochemical processes as a technique for exposing a template onto a silk screen that has been coated with a light-sensitive emulsion has increased the range of effects that can be accurately reproduced. This technique involves copying the artwork onto transparent film (one per color), so that each color is isolated as a grayscale containing gradated tones from black to light gray, allowing one colorant to be reproduced as a series of shades. This transparency is then placed against the emulsion and the image is transferred as the emulsion is hardened in the nonimage areas by exposure to UV light. The unhardened emulsion in the areas to be printed is then washed out, opening up the pores in the screen through which the ink will pass.

Most textile and fashion colleges provide students with studios equipped for silk-screen printing. The screen is moved systematically down the length of a piece of fabric to create a continuous design.

MECHANIZED FLATBED SILK-SCREEN PRINTING

The silk-screen printing process was first mechanized in 1954, when the flatbed process was introduced. Mechanized rollers feed the fabric under flat rectangular screens and the ink is applied using automated squeegees. More sophisticated flatbed printers are still used in print houses today, in the printing of luxury fabrics—the designs for which may contain up to 60 colors. Flatbed screen printing is much slower than rotary screen printing (see below). In the Lake Como region of Italy, famous for the superiority of its print houses, many companies use traditional printing technologies alongside digital techniques to produce some of the world's most luxurious fabrics.

A mechanized flatbed screen printer.

ROTARY SCREEN PRINTING

Rotary screen printing was also developed in the mid-1950s in order to speed up production and is currently the most widely used method of textile printing, now accounting for around 80 percent of printed textile production. Instead of a flat screen, this process uses a cylinder made from a very fine, reinforced metallic mesh. Initially the mesh is blocked, which entails coating the screen with a special emulsion and then burning out the areas to be printed using a computer-controlled laser. These cylindrical screens rotate as the cloth is moved under them at a high speed, and the ink is pushed through the mesh from the inside by a specially designed squeegee. In this way, single colors are laid down successively as the cloth passes under each cylindrical screen to build up the full-color image. The cost of rotary screen printing is significantly less than flatbed silk-screen printing.

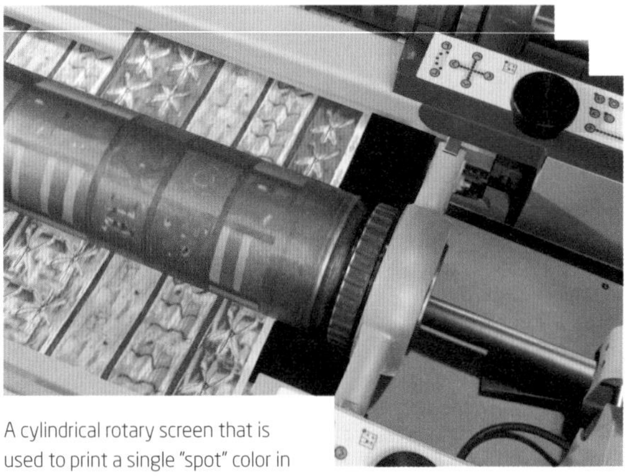

A cylindrical rotary screen that is used to print a single "spot" color in the mass-production process.

PHOTOGRAPHIC FULL-COLOR PRINTING

Four-color printing is the most common method used by the reprographic industries in the printing of books and magazines as well as in the heat-transfer method of textile printing. Unlike traditional textile printing technology, where the image is built up using premixed flat or "spot" colors, the photographic or full-color method of printing known as four-color or process printing involves the separation of the original image into the four colors (CMYK) used in the subtractive color model (see page 182). Additionally, in order to prepare the printing plates, a half-toning or screening process is also applied. This may be carried out digitally or by using photographic filters and results in a pattern of colored dots. The spacing of these dots is varied, with some overlapping in order to create the illusion of thousands of colors.

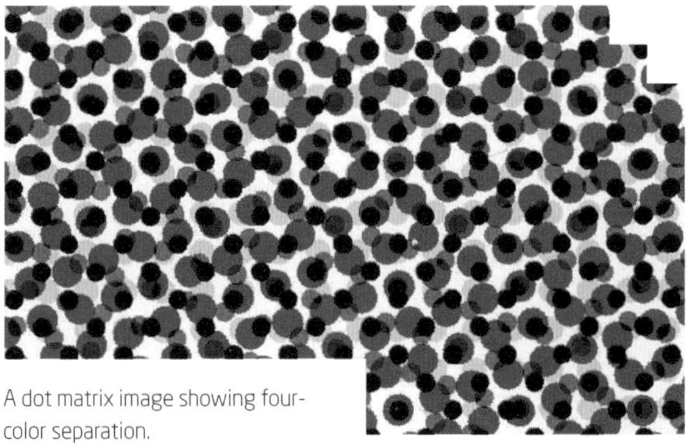

A dot matrix image showing four-color separation.

The print for this Paul Smith jacket has been separated using the four-color process, printed onto paper, then heat-transfer printed directly onto the fabric.

HEAT-TRANSFER PRINTING

While it was discovered in the late 1920s, the commercial development of transfer printing occurred during the 1960s. The process involves the printing or painting of transfer inks onto paper which will bond to certain fabrics upon heating. There are several methods of heat transfer but the most commercially viable is sublimation printing. The sublimation process turns a solid into a gas and back into a solid again. The paper can be printed by any paper-printing method, and this has increased the range of imagery that can be printed. It is possible to reproduce photographic images on textiles, though the process is mainly limited to synthetic fabrics.

As well as these industrial applications, transfer inks can be painted with an inklike substance directly onto paper and then heat-transferred onto fabric, allowing a spontaneous approach to be taken.

A highly detailed sublimation printing of photographic imagery onto a polyester shirt. This "Hobie" aloha shirt is typical of the 1970s.

COMMERCIAL VIABILITY OF TRADITIONAL VS DIGITAL PRINTING METHODS

Although digital printing is the fastest-growing method of textile printing, at the time of writing less than 1 percent of the world's textiles are digitally printed, with silk-screen printing still accounting for 80 percent of the global output of printed textiles. This is because rotary screen-printing technology is more financially viable for the mass-market sector of the industry.

Speed

The industry standard for digital printers at the time of writing is an average of over 220 yards (200 meters) per hour, giving traditional methods the advantage, achieving around 6560 linear yards (6000 linear meters) of fabric per hour. However, while the print time is fast with traditional methods, the lead time needed for a print to get into production is much slower. For example, it can take up to three weeks to get traditional textile prints into mass production, while digital production is almost instantaneous. This is because traditional printing plants require someone to color-separate the design, manage the repeat pattern, engrave screens, color-match and print a strike off (sample) for customer approval before proceeding to production. With digital printing the process requires only color matching and printing off for customer approval, reducing the lead time significantly.

Expense

Printing numerous colors has cost implications with rotary screen printing (as a separate screen must be prepared for each color), whereas with digital printing it makes no difference whether you have three or unlimited colors in your design. The cost of dyes and inks can vary significantly with traditional methods, and a lot of research is being carried out in this area. Pigments have many advantages over other dyes: they are more lightfast and retain color better after washing, can be cheaper, can be printed on a broader range of fabrics, and require less intervention in the fixation process.

Versatility

A clear advantage of traditional methods over digital printing is the ability to complete more than one process, such as discharge printing, resist techniques, devoré, flocking, relief techniques, and printing with metallic and pearlescent pigments. Research is being completed into these areas, but currently none are yet commercially available for use in digital printing.

DIGITAL TEXTILE PRINT TECHNOLOGY

"Digital printing" is a generic term used to describe all methods of printing where a digitized image is transferred onto the substrate. Currently there are two different types of digital print technology. The first of these, electrostatic (also known as laser printing), only works with paper and is the technology used in color copying machines and some office printers. The second method, known as inkjet printing, can be divided into two categories: continuous flow and drop on demand (DOD). In turn, DOD technology has two subcategories: thermal and piezoelectric. Piezoelectric DOD inkjet technology is currently the primary method for the digital printing of textiles and is used in printers such as the Mimaki.

Inkjet printing may be defined as a process by which the desired pattern is built up by projecting tiny drops of "ink" of different colors, in predetermined micro-arrays (pixels), onto the substrate surface. The ink is projected onto the surface as a controlled series of drops by using electromagnetic fields to guide electrically charged ink-streams onto the fabric. ("Ink" is the generic term primarily used in conjunction with digital printing and refers to both dyes and pigments.)

The mechanism that is responsible for this is the print head, which is an electromechanical device that contains ink, a feed system, a drop-formation mechanism, nozzles, and usually the ink supply in tanks or cartridges. The print head is moved across the fabric to deposit drops of ink in the correct positions.

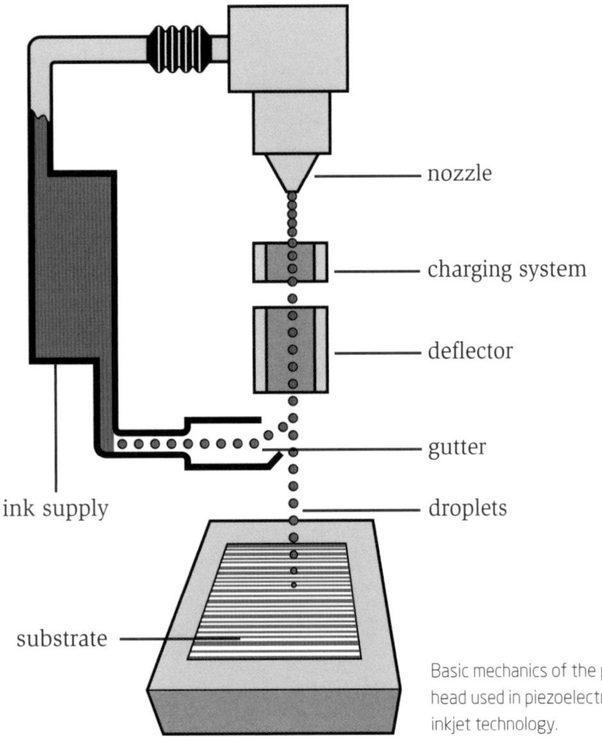

Basic mechanics of the print head used in piezoelectric DOD inkjet technology.

THE ADAPTATION OF DIGITAL PRINTING TECHNOLOGY FOR TEXTILES

Technology for the digital printing of textiles developed out of technology initially devised for printing on paper; large-format textile printers are essentially wider versions of smaller desktop printers that have been adapted to handle wide rolls of substrate instead of small sheets of paper. Digital printing is now used for printing onto a wide range of materials, including natural fiber-based substrates such as cotton, silk, and wool cloth as well as polyester-based fabrics, linoleum, and Formica.

There are two methods used for the inkjet printing of textiles: indirect inkjet heat-transfer printing and direct inkjet printing, both of which are examined on the following pages.

The digital printing process for textiles differs from that for paper because of the fixation process necessary to make the fabric washable and colorfast. This means that the printing process is less direct and involves more steps, due to the chemical reaction that must take place between the fabric, the dyes or pigments, and the fixing agents.

Short-run textile printers such as the Mimaki TX2 **(below)** became available for general use in 1998 and are widely used in large print houses as well as smaller studios. Mass-production printers such as the Robustelli Monna-Lisa **(above)** were first introduced in 2003.

INDIRECT INKJET/HEAT-TRANSFER PRINTING

As mentioned earlier in this chapter, the introduction of heat-transfer printing enabled images that could be printed onto paper by any traditional graphic printing method to be transferred onto fabric. This process was commercially exploited in the 1960s and 1970s, but, because the process could only work effectively with synthetic fabrics, its application was limited. The development of large-scale digital printers enabled the production of transfer papers, and the range of fabrics a print can be bonded to has expanded dramatically.

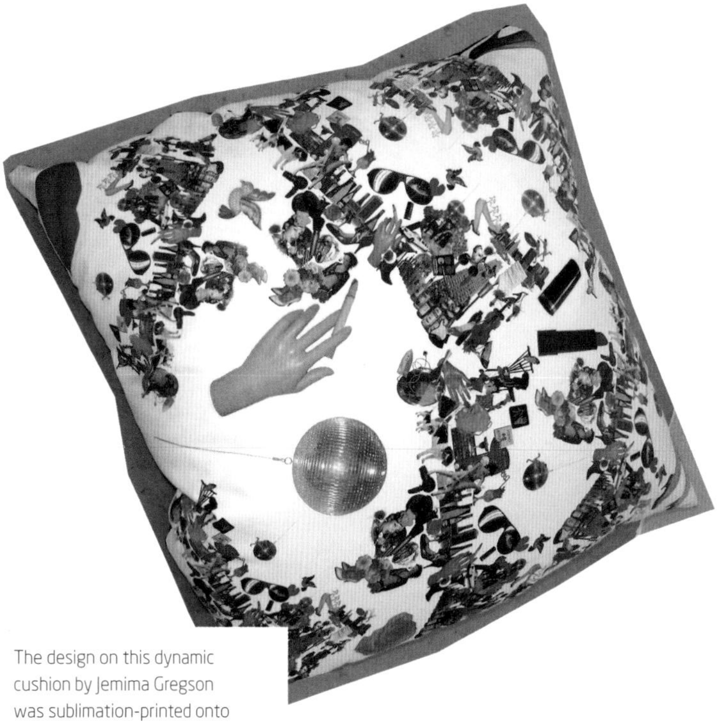

The design on this dynamic cushion by Jemima Gregson was sublimation-printed onto faux suede.

Another application of this process is in the growing arena of individual novelty products, where clients' photographs are printed onto bags, T-shirts, and even soft furnishings. This can be achieved by photocopying an image or printing it on your home inkjet printer onto specially finished papers.

Large-scale or mass-production heat-transfer printing is accomplished by first printing an image onto paper using a wide-format inkjet printer, and then transferring it onto fabric through the use of a heated roller machine (or calender). Heat transfer via inkjet-printed disperse dyes onto transfer paper is the primary method used in the printing of swimwear and sportswear today.

On a smaller scale in the home or studio, it is possible to buy heat-transfer paper which may be printed with a desktop inkjet printer; the image is then transferred onto cloth with an iron or a small heat press. DIY photographic T-shirt printing works by using the heat from an iron to adhere a digitally printed plastic layer onto the cotton of the shirt. This plastic layer is necessary because dye sublimation does not work with natural fibers.

Petra Boase's "Owl" children's T-shirt was digitally designed and printed on high-quality transfer paper and applied via heat press.

Photini Anastasi achieves soft and subtle photographic effects by sublimation-printing onto polyester chiffon.

DIRECT INKJET PRINTING PROCESS

The following sequence demonstrates the process of inkjet textile printing from start to finish, and shows how a detailed and colorful photographic design can be printed onto fabric.

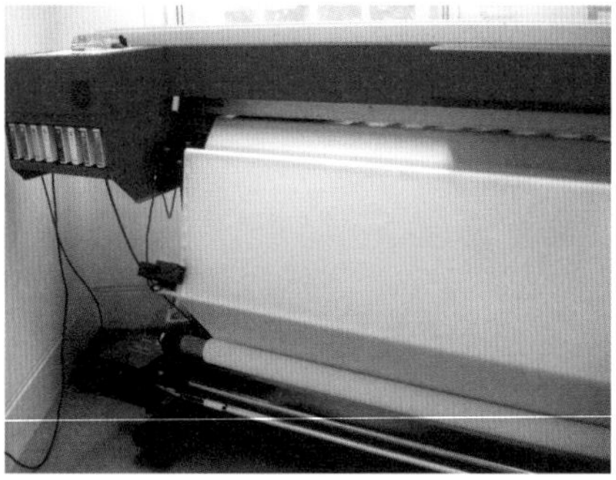

1. The roll of fabric is loaded onto the back of the printer. The fabric is then fed through to the front by passing it under a series of small rollers that run along the width of the printer, ensuring that the fabric will be fed smoothly as the print head runs across it.

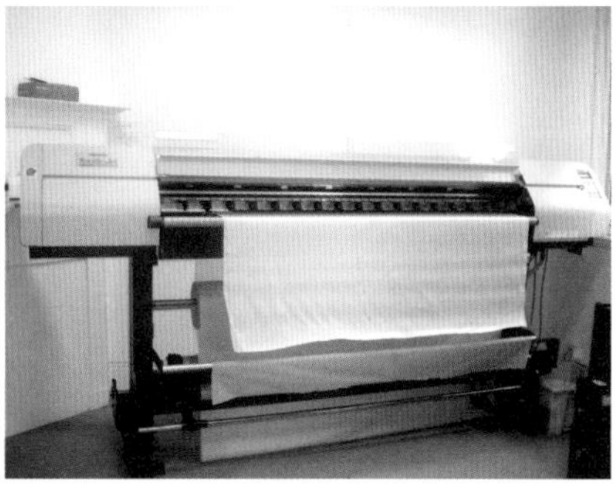

2. The fabric is attached to a motorized roller system that automatically winds the fabric forward under the moving print heads once the printer is in action. Careful attention must be paid to ensure that the tension of the length of fabric is correct and that the fabric is straight. In some cases the fabric is interleaved with tissue paper to blot any excess ink during the print run. A bar that runs across the width is clamped down to stop the fabric from crumpling as it passes under the rollers.

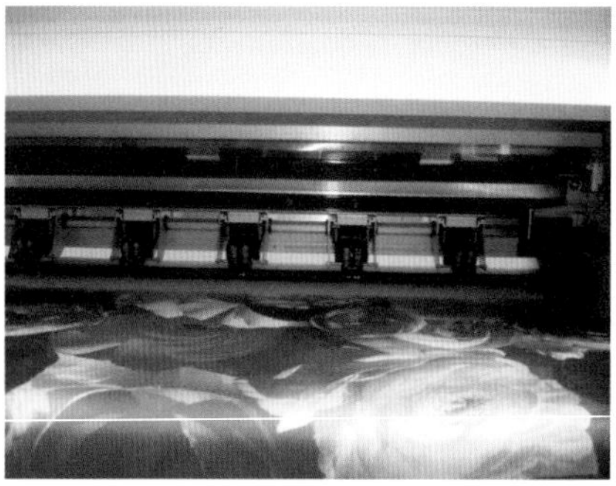

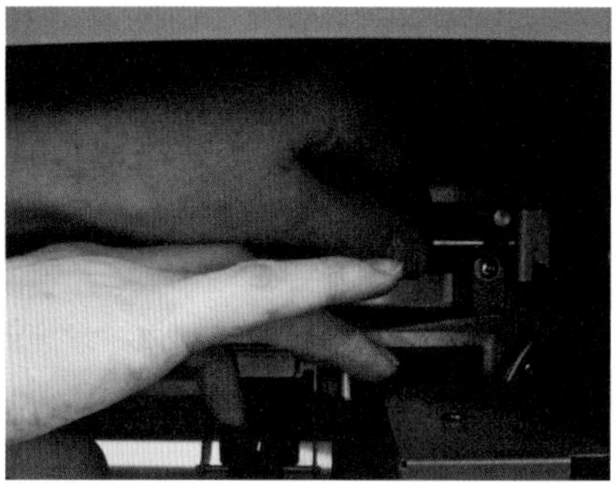

3. The height of the print head is then adjusted according to the thickness of the substrate.

4. A series of printer tests are carried out, including a "media compensation" and a nozzle check. The media compensation setting adjusts the speed of the printer according to how much stretch the fabric has and the nozzle test indicates whether all eight print heads are firing correctly.

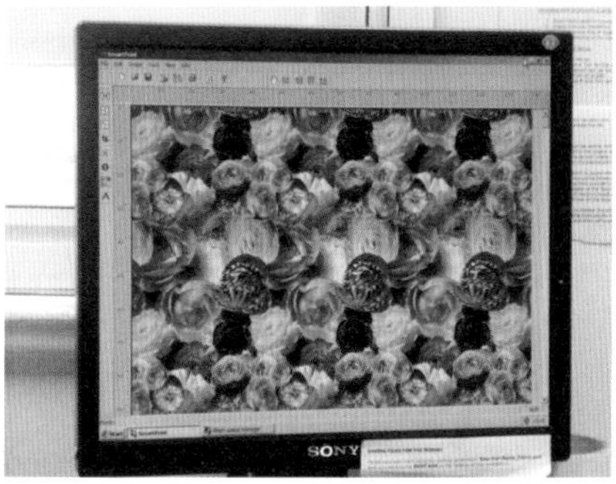

5. The design is opened into the RIP or print-driver software and parameters such as the number of repeats to be tiled out and the length of the print run are entered. The print-driver software is also used to set variables such as print speed, number of passes for the print head, and how much ink will be laid down.

6. The design file is then sent to the printer via the RIP to begin printing. Before proceeding to the final length, samples are printed, steamed, and washed to check color and image quality. Some fabrics require that the ink is left to dry before proceeding to the next step.

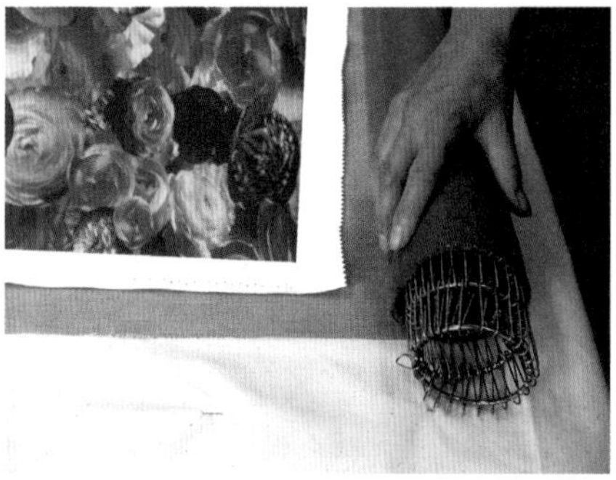

7. There are several ways of preparing cloth for steaming. Cheesecloth, steaming paper, or a fine plastic mesh may be used as a barrier to stop the ink from bleeding onto itself during steaming. In all cases, one of these porous materials is interleaved with the print, forming a protective layer through which the steam can pass.

8. The fabric is loaded into a steamer, to be steamed for a specific time to fix the color. If the design has been printed using pigments or disperse dyes, these colorants are fixed via heat rather than steam in a baking oven.

9. The fabric is washed to remove coating and excess colorant, and ironed. It is very important not to overload the washing machine as the image may bleed onto itself.

INKJET PRINTING TIPS

In ensuring the success of any inkjet printing it is important to remember the following:

Never underestimate the importance of sampling.

Remember that colors will brighten after printing (unless pigments have been used), and that the "hand" of the cloth will soften—in other words, if you feel that a fabric you are considering is too stiff, remember that once the coating has been washed out and it has been ironed this will change.

If you print a "sketch" of an initial idea, then in proceeding to a final print it is crucial that no aspects of the final file originating from the sample have changed at all.

Consider setting aside a roll with enough fabric for the final print as a new roll of the same fabric may produce slightly different results.

Protect unprinted fabrics from light.

Keep the printer scrupulously clean.

Don't allow any water near unsteamed fabric.

Keep the steamer in a separate, well-ventilated room.

A garment made from the finished fabric featuring a floral print designed by Daisy Butler and printed on the Mimaki TX2.

CHEMISTRY AND FIXATION OF COLORANTS

In order for cloth to retain its color for a reasonable period of time after repeated washing and exposure to sunlight, a chemical reaction must first take place between the fabric, the dye or pigment, and, in some cases, the fixation agent—a chemical that attaches to receptor sites on the surface of the fibers and makes a chemical bridge between the dyestuff and the fiber. This process is achieved by either steaming or heating the cloth after it has been printed.

PRETREATING FABRIC

Unlike traditional methods of printing, where the fixing agent is mixed into the dye or pigment, in digital textile printing the fixation agent is applied as a special coating onto the fabric before printing. This coating is also designed to ensure that when the droplets of ink hit the surface of the cloth they do not spread, so that the details of a design are maintained and are not blurred. This coating is basically comprised of an alginate thickener for reactive dyes and a carbohydrate-based or synthetic thickener for acid or disperse dyes. The fixing agent used for reactive dyes is alkaline soda ash, whereas a weak acid is used for acid dye. There is no need for a fixative in the case of disperse dyes.

It is possible to experiment with the inkjet printing of certain fabrics by silk screening the coating mixture onto the fabric yourself. However, in the printing of longer lengths it is more practical and will yield better results if you buy rolls of fabric that have been precoated by a specialist company. The chemicals in the coating are specific to the dye that will be used, so it is important to check.

TYPES OF INKJET COLORANT

In order to achieve consistent color and detail it is crucial that the coating has been applied evenly. If there is a significant variation either in the chemistry or the amount of coating that has been applied to two different rolls of the same type of fabric, it is probable that the printed colors will not match. In some cases, if the chemical formula for the coating is not correct then the ink may bleed or not dry properly. The coating may stiffen and in some cases will dull the sheen of certain cloths temporarily. Once it has been washed and steamed, however, it will regain its original sheen, softness, and drape.

There are two categories of colorant used: dyes and pigments. The chemistry of dyes and pigments used in inkjet printing of textiles is based on that used in the traditional dyeing or silk screening of fabrics, with the essential difference that only synthetic dyes and pigments may be used. The viscosity of pigments that have been designed for use in an inkjet textile printer has also been modified so that the print heads do not become blocked. Technological advances in digital printing have also led to improvements in the way that pigment-based inks adhere to the surface of the fabric.

Dyes Specific dyes must be used for different types of fabric. There are three categories of fiber used in the making of textiles: plant (cellulose) based, animal (protein) based, and synthetic based. Acid dyes work only with protein-based materials and nylon, while reactive dyes may be used with both plant-based and animal-based materials. Disperse dyes have been developed for the coloration of synthetic polymer-based materials. The colors that may be achieved vary according to the type of dye used. Acid dyes produce colors that are brighter than those created by reactive dyes. It is not possible, for example, to attain a "neon" green by using a reactive dye. However, disperse dyes also result in very bright colors.

Pigments In contrast to dyes, pigments may be used more universally. Unlike dyes, they do not directly associate with the textile fibers but are fixed to the surface of the cloth with a "binding agent." Pigments are bonded to the surface of the fabric by heat. The colors that result from printing with pigments are duller than those achieved with dyes.

As pigments sit on the surface of the cloth, fabrics such as silk satin will lose some of their shine after printing and will also become slightly stiffer than they would if printed with dye. Despite these disadvantages pigments are widely used in textile printing as they may be used on all types of fabric and are also intrinsically more colorfast than dyes. They are often less expensive, too. The most significant advantage of using pigments in an inkjet printer is that the fabric does not require pretreatment or coating.

DELIVERY OF INK INTO THE PRINTER

There are two methods of delivering dyes or pigments into a printer. Suppliers of inkjet printing materials sell cartridges that are similar to those used in a desktop photographic printer; however cartridges designed for use in a large-format textile printer contain a larger quantity of ink. "Bulk-feed" systems have also been developed where a separate device is connected to the printer and feeds ink into it from a bottle. Such bulk-feed systems are more economical, as the cost of textile ink cartridges can be prohibitive. It is also possible to use special cartridges designed to be refilled with ink from a bottle using a syringe. This method will also prove more economical than using disposable cartridges. When using either a bulk-feed system or cartridges it is very important to prevent air bubbles from entering the ink-feed lines as these cause the print heads to become blocked.

THE FIXATION PROCESS

Dyes After the fabric has been printed it is rolled up and sandwiched between a layer of special paper, plastic mesh, or hessian cloth, so that ink will not transfer from one side of the cloth to the other. This also facilitates the transfer of steam to the interior of the roll. There are several types of steamers used in the dye-fixation process. Small studios use a simple device consisting of an upright metal cylinder with a removable lid, in which water is heated to boiling point by an electrical element. These steamers are designed so that the fabric rests on a platform at the base of the steamer and the roll is held vertically by a device at the top, ensuring that it does not come in contact either with the water or the condensation that may form on the inside of the cylinder itself. If water does comes into contact with the roll it will cause the ink to bleed, resulting in a blurred image or one that—in severe cases—disappears entirely. Steaming time varies according to the type of steamer as well as the type of dye. If conditions vary within the steamer, or if the vapor is not evenly distributed, then colors will not be consistent. These upright steamers are only capable of steaming around 10 yards (9 meters) of fabric. It is also possible to fix fabric by hanging it in a steam chamber or cabinet.

In a factory setting, industrial-scale steamers are used for mass production. Mid-range equipment capable of accommodating up to 55 yards (50 meters) of fabric is also available, and priced at an affordable level for smaller studios. These devices are more sophisticated than the small steamer described above, making it easier to control temperature and pressure. Timing can be automated, as can the release of steam at the end of the cycle. Steam time is also shorter in an industrial steamer.

It is very important that all steamers are properly ventilated and that, upon release, the steam produced is filtered by an extraction device in order to remove any toxic fumes. Technicians should also wear gas masks.

Pigments Fabrics that have been printed with pigments are fixed by baking them in a special oven or heat press.

Disperse dyes These may be digitally printed directly onto the substrate and then fixed by heating. Alternatively, in the inkjet transfer process, the image may be printed onto special paper and then fixed and transferred simultaneously onto the fabric by passing the substrate through heated rollers or under a heat press. Synthetic fabrics and polyester-coated Formica and ceramics are all fixed in this way.

WASHING

After fixation, the fabric is washed to remove excess dye. Each batch of a longer run must be washed by machine under exactly the same conditions to maintain consistency. The washing machine should not be overloaded because if the cloth is packed too tightly it may become stained. Domestic washing machines usually accommodate around 10 yards (9 meters) of fabric. An industrial washing machine should be used for lengths above this amount. Fabrics should be washed until the water runs as clear of dye as is possible. Stickiness resulting from any residue of the coating may be removed by further washing. Temperature settings are the same as for nondigitally printed fabrics. Once washed, the fabric should not be left crumpled as staining may occur.

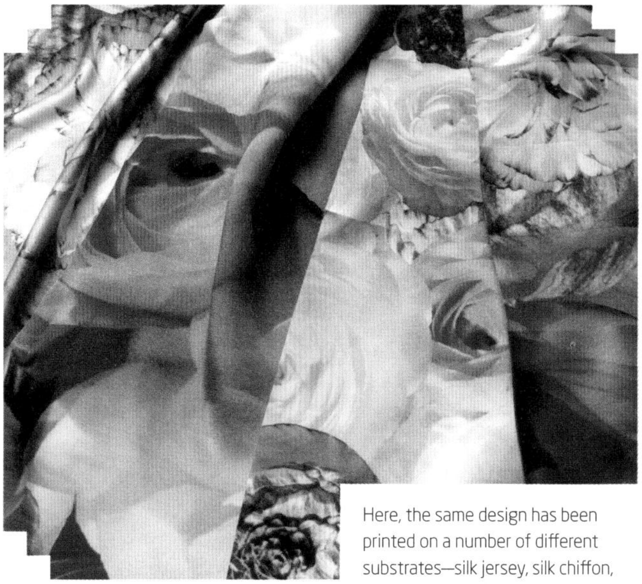

Here, the same design has been printed on a number of different substrates—silk jersey, silk chiffon, and silk satin (left to right)—to test how color and finish differ.

	ACID DYE (STEAM)	REACTIVE DYE (STEAM)	DISPERSE DYE (HEAT)	PIGMENTS (HEAT)
SILK	0	0		0
WOOL	0	0		0
LINEN		0		0
COTTON		0		0
NYLON	0			0
POLYESTER			0	0
RAYON		0		0

This chart shows the types of colorant, and their corresponding fixation processes, that can be used for different substrates.

ADVANTAGES OF DIGITAL PRINTING

Digital printing, as we outlined in the early section, can have many advantages over traditional printing methods, in speed and efficiency and costs at smaller manufacturing numbers. However, at present it cannot compete with costs at large yardage. With research being carried out into this area it will perhaps be able to compete more directly in time.

These cost and efficiency savings only demonstrate one half of the story: where inkjet printing makes a difference is in lessened environmental impact, and design advantages. From a design perspective, the ability to print full-color, detailed designs using any scale, repeat, or nonrepeating elements and engineered prints opens up a wealth of creative possibilities.

REDUCED ENVIRONMENTAL IMPACT

Inkjet printing has more environmental advantages than conventional printing methods, and a more sustainable future will be possible if this production method is adopted over others. This is primarily due to there being less wastage of dye, as the ink is printed on demand, and fabric can be printed as all-over fabric or to specific pattern placements, thereby reducing fabric wastage. Inkjet printing is reported to use 30 percent less water and 45 percent less electricity than conventional printing methods. These savings mean that the process has less impact on the environment than traditional print processes.

RAPID TURNAROUND

Once a design file has been finalized, the technical setup time for an inkjet printer is minimal. In comparison to most traditional print methods—which typically involve several preparatory steps before printing can begin—digital printing is direct, and turnaround time for short runs is fast. A Mimaki TX2 printer, for example, can produce between 3 and 30 linear yards (3 and 28 meters) per hour, depending on image quality, and uses 8 Epson-type print heads that may accommodate 16 channels. As the name implies, short-run printers are capable of producing a smaller quantity of printed goods to be used as prototypes, one-offs, or limited-edition products. However, such printers may also be set up as multiple installations in digital print production facilities in order to print larger volumes.

Printers capable of mass production were first released in 2003 and can typically print around 220 linear yards (200 meters) per hour. The best-known manufacturers are Dupont (Artistry), Reggiani (DReAM), and Robustelli (Monna-Lisa). Osiris has made a full production machine capable of printing 1970 yards (1800 meters) an hour—around 33 yards (30 meters) a minute.

The immediacy and minimal setup time for digital printing also means that fashion and textile houses no longer need to warehouse additional fabric stock in advance of manufacturing the final goods, resulting in less wastage. Print runs can be set up on demand to match orders from retailers as they come in.

This rapid turnaround time is also advantageous for the designer. For most artists and designers the successful realization of an idea usually involves a process of trial, re-evaluation, and adaptation. Digital printing is just one step behind the designer's imagination and facilitates the flow of ideas in design development.

UNLIMITED COLOR AND DETAIL

There's virtually no limit to the type of image that may be reproduced using digital inkjet fabric-printing technology as it is based on the CMYK or process-color method for photographic printing. Halftoning of primary CMYK colors means that millions of colors are perceived by the viewer, limited only by the color gamut of the dye in relation to the substrate. Extremely bright colors may be achieved using acid dyes, but neon colors are not yet attainable with the inks currently available. Due

The Dutch company Osiris has developed the Isis printer, which is set to rival the speeds of rotary screen-printing as it is capable of printing 33 linear yards (30 meters) per minute. The Isis uses continuous-flow inkjet technology as well as an unusual principle whereby a fixed row of print heads span the width of the printer.

to the photographic foundation of this technology, most of the subtleties and nuances of the original image may now be translated in detail onto fabric.

INCREASED SCALE

One of the first reactions from designers upon the introduction of digital print for textiles was excitement at the fact that repeat (of the design unit or croquis) was no longer necessary, as it was suddenly possible to print mural-sized images. Digital printing technology means that the only limit to the size of a design is the software's capacity to handle large files.

A bigger canvas and the ability to lay out extended placement prints is changing the way designers approach print, although there will always be aesthetic reasons for continuing to use repeated patterns. Facilitated by the possibility of developing software programming for longer design lengths, research has begun into the generation and printing of randomized, continuously changing structures such as those found in biological growth patterns.

ENGINEERING DESIGNS

In general, the mass market utilizes print to "fill in" garment outlines rather than to interact with the garment and body. Print is placed on top of garment shapes rather than being developed in unison. This often creates a clumsy and inappropriate use of print. Inkjet printing engenders a stronger relationship between the product and image. By printing the image to the exact specifications of a garment or product, print designers can more fully engage with the relationship between form and image.

"Branch" (2005), by Hitoshi Ujiie, makes use of two of the most significant advantages that digital design and printing has over traditional methods: the piece is nearly 4 yards (3.5 meters) high and, when viewed more closely, reveals an extraordinarily high level of detail.

DISADVANTAGES OF DIGITAL INKJET PRINTING

The most prohibitive factor in the adoption of digital inkjet technology is that it is still much more expensive than screen-printing and heat-transfer methods. While the costs are coming down, it will take a substantial period of development and integration to begin to compete with rotary printing. Commercially, many digital printers are currently used only for sampling and to create prototypes that will eventually be produced using traditional methods. At the time of writing, 1 percent of the world's textiles are printed digitally.

In design terms, the advantages of digital fabric printing far outweigh those of traditional methods, but digital printing is not yet capable of some of the decorative effects that are possible with silk screening, such as devoré and flocking. It is also not yet capable of printing metallic inks onto fabric. Research is currently underway into the development of these techniques.

DIGITAL TEXTILE DESIGN AND PRINTING SOFTWARE

Behind digital printing is a range of software that is used in the design process and also in the preparation of the design for print. This only came within the remit of textile designers once the technology for the digital printing of textiles became viable in 1998. The off-the-shelf package Adobe Illustrator was first released in 1987 as a font-development program for graphic designers, and Adobe Photoshop followed in 1990. Although textile designers would have been able to use these tools, they were initially the domain of photographers and graphic designers, as images created through their use could only be realized on paper. Therefore the advertising, publishing, and photographic industries led the way in the development of digital-imaging software and a true digital style for textiles would only emerge 10 years later.

Using a specialist CAD system to set up a design to print. On the right is a light box that is used to match colors within a calibrated system.

USING SPECIALIST CAD SYSTEMS

As well as off-the-shelf imaging software, there is a range of specialist CAD (computer-aided design) systems available to the printed textile industry. These programs are generally designed to be used by companies who will mass-produce their products. In most cases, although the programs are capable of taking in images that contain millions of colors, ultimately their purpose is to systematically reduce these colors down to the number of screens that will be engraved for rotary printing (a process known as color separation). Unlike Photoshop, which was designed primarily for the reprographic industries, specialist CAD programs contain tools that aid in the design-creation aspects that are unique to surface design, including the creation of colorways, the touching-up of a design ready for the engraver, and automatic live time-repeat function. Many also include sophisticated color-management systems. Although it is possible to carry out such operations using off-the-shelf software, specialist CAD programs streamline the process of preparing an image for print. Adobe Photoshop and Illustrator do, however, provide excellent tools for designers who intend to print shorter runs digitally and wish to retain the photographic quality of an image.

Color separation Within the context of the textile industry, color separation, also known as color reduction, is a process that reduces the number of colors in an image down to a finite number of flat or “spot” colors, usually shown as black and white shapes that represent the set of motifs that contain each color (typically less than 10 colors at the lower end of the market and many more for luxury goods). Tonal separations may also be created as grayscales in order to simulate images that contain thousands of colors, though in fact only a limited number of colors are used in the printing process.

These images show the four-color separations that have been creating using a CAD program in order to engrave the four screens required to print this flat color design using traditional methods. Color samples may be printed digitally to replicate final production.

This is an example of a design containing tonal effects. The eight color tonal separations have been created by reducing the millions of colors found in the original scan down to eight screens ready for rotary screen printing.

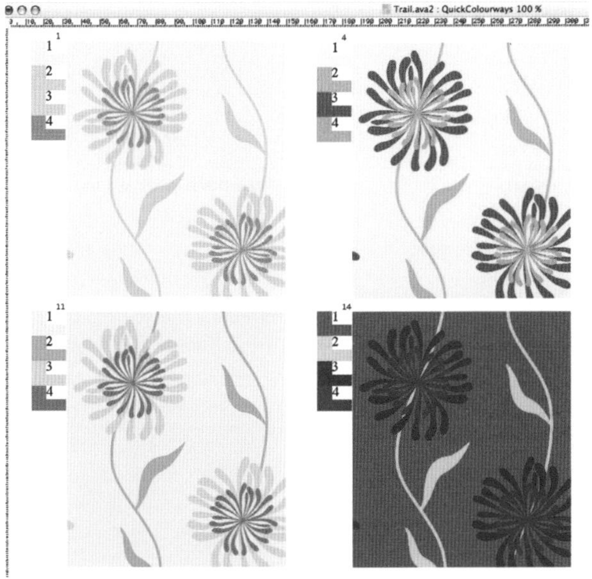

Alternative colorways for a design that are based on the same color-separation template.

Color separation serves two purposes. The first is to prepare an image for rotary screen printing; each separation is used to create one screen that will be printed in sequence in the mill. The second is that it makes color matching and the creation of colorways much easier. If a design is to be printed digitally then color separation will also mean that it will be easier to "plug in" matching colors across a range of coordinating designs such as borders or matching allover prints.

Color separation can be a highly skilled art, requiring much practice in an industry setting. Companies such as Hermès and Colefax and Fowler rely on separation artists who are masters of their craft. Most of the artwork used by high-end home-furnishing companies is painted by hand, and, although the final design may look deceptively simple, the scan of the original contains thousands of colors and a series of steps must be carried out before the screens can be engraved.

Colorways and color-palette databases "Colorway" is a term used in the textile industry to describe versions of the same design that have been colored differently. Usually, although the colors in each colorway will be different, they follow a set order from light to dark to help organize them for the printing process. Most specialist CAD textile systems also provide color-palette databases that can be organized by collection or season in order to facilitate the transfer of a set of colors automatically into an entire collection.

Live time-repeat Automatic live time-repeat functions work by creating almost instantaneous repeats, including half-drops, and can be extremely useful when preparing a print. As many repeat units as are desired may be viewed or "tiled" across large widths, and when a motif is moved or manipulated, all its copies in the repeat grid change at once. Automatic repeat systems may be more sophisticated in a specialist system; however, add-on software is available at prices aimed at individual designers.

WORKING WITH COLOR

Our perception of color is subjective and this, in part, makes our interpretation and translation of color from one technology to another difficult. Another factor in this difficulty is the difference between additive and subtractive color. Subtractive colors are those that are made from a combination of primaries cyan, magenta, and yellow: these colors absorb light and are the colors we see in printed inks and dyes. In theory, mixing them all together creates black. The colors that we see on a monitor are the result of emitted light and are made by mixing the primary colors red, green, and blue: these are described as additive colors. In the additive model, mixing all three RGB primaries results in white. Digital cameras, scanners, and monitors all use this additive RGB model as a basis for displaying or interpreting color, and prints on paper or textiles use the subtractive model.

THE SCREEN TO PRINT DILEMMA

In digital printing, achieving the colors we desire may be solved in two ways; either by carrying out manual adjustments and color tests or by incorporating separate color-management software into the setup of a digital print studio.

Newcomers to digital textile printing may encounter some difficulties in areas that relate to color and the workflow that is necessary to obtain the desired results. Many of the issues that arise around color and digital printing are often based on the mistaken assumption that the colors viewed on screen will automatically match those in the final print. This is not the case. When finalizing colors for a design that is to be digitally printed it is crucial to understand that what we see on screen is relative and it should not be taken for granted that the colors we have chosen will be reproduced exactly unless color-management software has been used.

There are two reasons for this: firstly, although all monitors and display devices use RGB technology, each individual type of device will display the same color differently unless they have been calibrated. Again, unless calibrated, printers of the same kind also have different "fingerprints" and it is likely they will display the same design differently. Additionally, it is the translation of RGB data into the CYMK data necessary to control a printer that will cause a discrepancy between displayed and printed colors.

Left: RGB additive color model of emitted light used to generate the colors displayed by monitors. **Right:** CMYK subtractive color model of absorbed light.

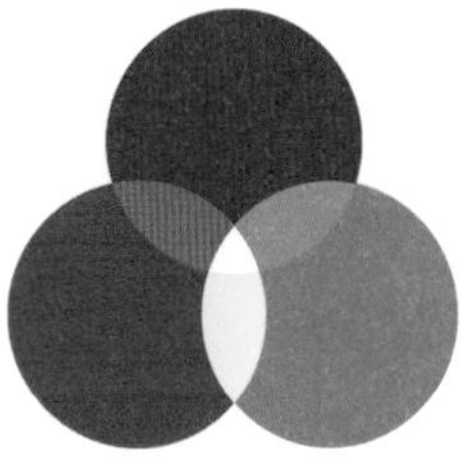

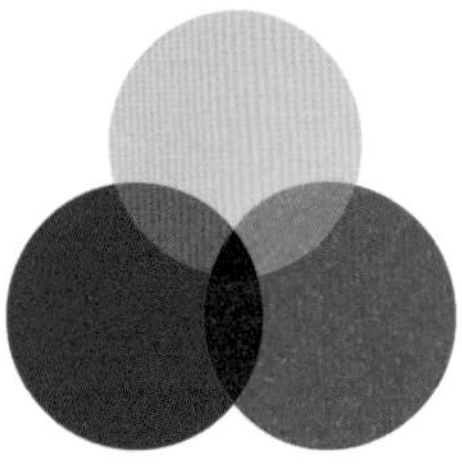

LINKING TO THE PRINTER, PRINT DRIVERS, AND RIP SOFTWARE

Most setups for desktop printing incorporate a program known as a print driver or Raster Image Processor—RIP—that is either supplied by the software company, such as Photoshop, or by a printer vendor such as Epson. However, drivers for large-format printers, like the Mimaki, are not built-in and so it is necessary to invest in a specialist print driver as the printer may not be operated without it. In digital textile printing the role that the driver plays in controlling print quality and the smooth running of a studio or "factory" can not be underestimated, and it is vital when setting up a new studio to research and choose the appropriate software carefully.

A RIP is software that rasterizes, or converts, the RGB data from the matrix of pixels (bitmap) in a displayed image into the CMYK information that will "drive" the printer. This software also dictates variables such as print speed and resolution as well as the number of print-head passes and the quantity of ink that will be laid down, thus affecting color. If color management has been incorporated then it is through the print driver that a technician will set the profiles described earlier in order to accommodate each type of fabric. Importantly, textile RIPs will also tile-out a design unit as a repeat as well as automatically incorporating half-drops. Such drivers are also designed specifically to accommodate very large designs as well as the extremely long-run print lengths necessary for mass production.

SPECIALIST COLOR-MANAGEMENT SYSTEMS

A range of specialist color-management technology has been developed for the photographic and reprographic businesses as well as for other industries where color accuracy is vital. The purpose of these systems is to streamline and facilitate the process of handling color as it is translated from one device to another through to the final production. A highly sophisticated textile system is, for example, able to send the color data necessary for dye formulation directly to a mill.

Most color-management systems work by mediating between and coordinating the various input and output devices used in a given workflow environment and managing the way that color data is used and transferred between them. Central to color management is a process known as calibration, which works as a loop and involves a feedback mechanism that begins by printing a set of files using the primary CMYK inks. These colors are analyzed by the technician in order to determine the best printer settings for each individual fabric type—such as how much ink a particular fabric may absorb before the color will bleed. These samples are then read in using a spectrophotometer (an instrument for measuring spectral transmittance or reflectance), and the data is used to generate a series of files—known as printer profiles—that will individualize print controls for each fabric type. Essentially, at this stage, the basic printer controls are being fine-tuned before a greater range of colors are analyzed.

Within a setup that has been calibrated, multiple printers, as well as monitors, may be included within a closed system. These profiles are then applied to a comprehensive set of color samples that have been generated systematically by the software in order to print, comparing them with the corresponding colors from the same file as they appear on the display. A spectrophotometer is again used to read in each color chip in the printed "target" sample for each fabric type once the colorant has been fixed and washed. Similarly, a series of color targets are also measured on screen by placing a spectrophotometer against the monitor. This data is then processed by the software and used to fine-tune the colors as displayed using RGB data in order to match those found in the final print. The spectral difference between the displayed and printed colors is compiled by the software in order to create profiles for each monitor and fabric type.

Tests carried out during printer calibration in order to implement ink settings, such as the quantity of ink to be laid down for each fabric type. The above image shows that too much ink has been laid down, causing the dye to bleed.

The advantage of this process is that, when a particular profile is applied to a displayed image, the designer will be able to judge more accurately what the final color results will be and see how they would change if a different dye or pigment were to be used in printing. If it is not possible to obtain, for example, a very bright red using pigments or a certain fabric type then some programs will show the closest match within the color space. Currently, however, there are certain colors that may be displayed on screen that are not possible to reproduce under any circumstances due to the limitations of the dyes and colorants used in textile printing. An achievable color is described as being "in gamut," whereas any color that may not be displayed or printed is described as being "out of gamut" (see right).

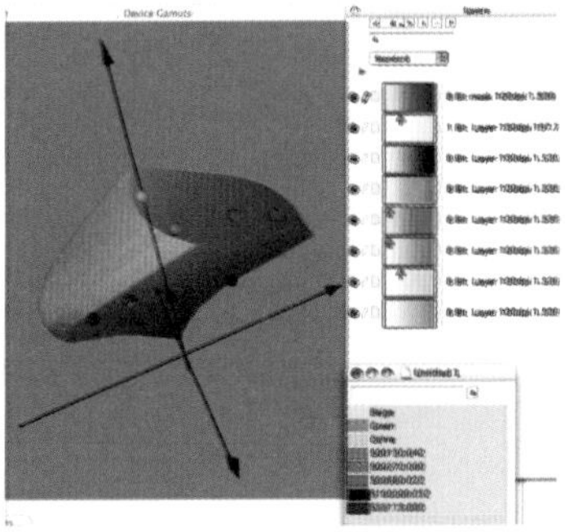

A set of achievable colors within a 3-D model of a specific color space. Unachievable colors are "out of gamut."

Colors taken from paper or fabric swatches may also be input into a design by using a spectrophotometer to measure them and so automatically generating a match once printed. It is important to take into consideration when using fabric or paper color samples for matching, that the same color will appear to be different depending on whether it is applied to a glossy, matte, or transparent substrate. Similarly, the colors in your print will appear to change if viewed under different conditions, such as daylight or fluorescent light. A specialist piece of equipment known as a light box will facilitate this.

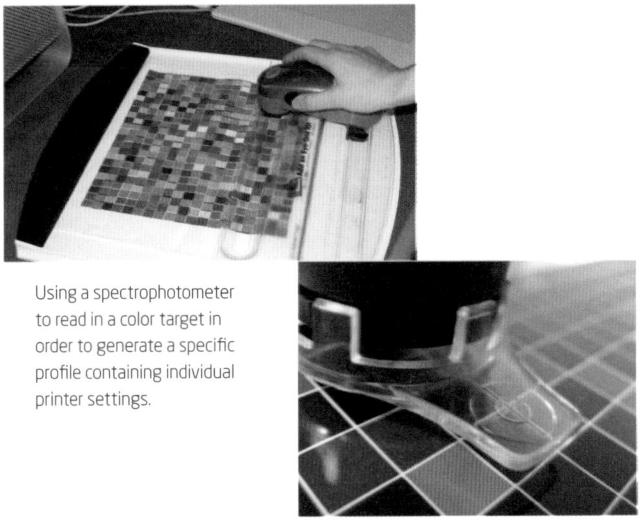

Using a spectrophotometer to read in a color target in order to generate a specific profile containing individual printer settings.

Color matching yarn and fabric swatches.

REVITALIZING THE TEXTILE INDUSTRY

Digital print is revitalizing the textile industry, not only in terms of design, but also production. Many established print companies in Italy and Japan are seeking to maintain their links with their couture clients—who are starting to explore digital design—by introducing digital print technology alongside traditional methods. Companies in China are also making a considerable investment in the new technology, while digital print bureaus are emerging in countries that have largely lost their fabric production to Asia. The relatively low cost of the equipment is also encouraging designers to set up their own print studios.

Using a CAD system to set up an image to print at the Ratti plant.

DIGITAL PRINT HOUSES

Many of the print houses in Como, Italy—such as Mantero and Ratti, who produce some of the world's most luxurious fabrics, and who are considered by many designers to be centers of excellence for printed textiles—have been using the latest technology alongside traditional methods ever since the first digital textile printers became available. The philosophy behind companies such as Ratti is that the quality of the prints they produce is far more important than quantity or cost. Investing in state-of-the-art technology is crucial to maintaining the competitive edge to the extent that some Como printers do not simply buy this equipment but work hand-in-hand with its developers to constantly improve the technology. Suffice to say, Como textile printing is considered an art.

The design studio, where traditional techniques such as hand painting are used alongside digital tools.

In Japan the company Seiren was also a pioneer of inkjet textile printing and began testing the viability of this technology as long ago as the early 1980s. By 1991, they had introduced inkjet printing alongside traditional methods; one of their primary markets being the market for custom car interiors. Companies in China such as Huang Wha have also begun to make considerable investments in inkjet textile-printing plants.

Large-scale digital printing in action.

The 50,000 square foot (4,600 square meter) Ratti print facility, situated on a plateau above Como in Italy.

DIGITAL PRINT BUREAUS

As the cost of a large-format inkjet printer is considerably less than the equipment necessary to set up a rotary screen-printing plant, many small digital print bureaus are emerging, specializing in the printing of textiles. Bureau printing services provide an invaluable resource for students, independent designers, and larger commercial companies alike. Some operate out of an artist's loft, while others are set up like small factories with multiple printers, catering to a growing demand for innovative and unusual products. These small businesses will support the growing demand for designer and customized goods in the future.

Small bureaus allow designers to produce prototype short runs of fabric and have access to face-to-face consultation. Sampling printed cloth in the traditional way can be extremely expensive and time consuming, and this can inhibit designers who want to see printed results fast. Using a bureau, it is possible to see and approve fabric at different stages in the sampling process and try out new ideas during the development process. Dan Locastro of First2Print, a digital bureau in New York, observes that "we can print in a fraction of the time it would take for a fabric manufacturer to get samples ready for showrooms, sales development and photoshoots."

Students are now using digital print bureaus to implement their designs. Learning to outsource in this way helps to smooth the transition from education to operating as an independent business in terms of gaining experience in budgeting, communication, and management, but it is important that students also maintain a hands-on approach to the digital printing process.

USING A BUREAU

Different digital bureaus use different hardware and software, so it is not really possible to give hard and fast rules as to preparation of files, etc., but J. A. Gilmartin, a London-based digital print bureau, recommends following these basic rules of thumb:

Always build in time for sampling. It cannot be stressed enough what an essential part of the process this is.

Check the shrinkage of the fabric you are printing onto: some fabrics shrink more than others and shrinkage will occur after printing so it's best to print a larger quantity initially.

Make sure your document is cropped to exactly the size you want, especially repeat units, as the printer will treat any white space as part of the design. If you are printing panels and want to include white space, include crop marks.

Remember that color matching can be time consuming and therefore expensive, as samples may have to be steamed and washed each time in order to properly check color.

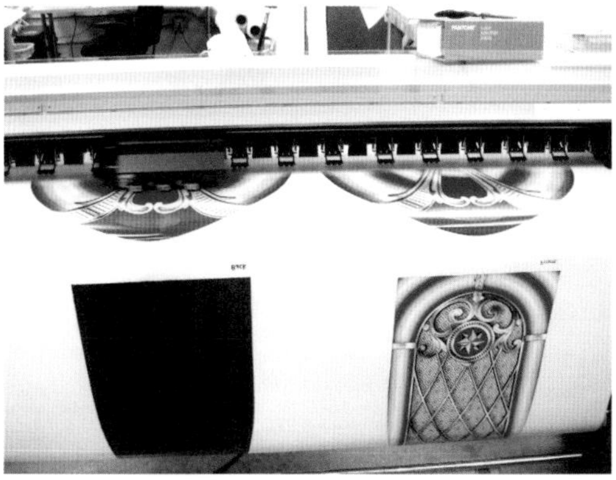

The print process at First2Print, a digital print bureau based in New York.

Left to right, top to bottom: Printer setup within the design studio; loading the printer; printing in progress; checking and approving the final print.

THE FUTURE OF TEXTILE PRINTING

The technology behind digital printing is advancing rapidly and research is taking place into many potential avenues for its use in textile design and print. Smart colorants, such as thermochromic inks that change color according to the temperature, are currently printed by silk screen but will undoubtedly be adapted for digital printing. Research is also currently underway into the inkjet printing of images onto flexible screens, using display technologies such as Organic Light-Emitting Polymers (OLEPs). It is likely that this will result in fabrics onto which changeable or moving images may be downloaded. As artists such as Maggie Orth (renowned for her work with interactive textiles) collaborate with scientists, the potential outcomes are beyond our imagination.

LED elements are being embedded into a variety of products. Hussein Chalayan used this technology to create a dress for his F/W 07/08 collection (right). Although LEDs are not digitally printed when applied to a garment, they provide a glimpse of what is to come.

Research is also underway into the digital printing of metallic inks—possible on other substrates, though currently not viable on cloth. Once developed, this will enable electric circuits that could double as decorative elements to be printed onto the surface of a garment.

The proportion of digital printing is clearly set to increase in the next decade as we see faster printers with a wider range of print possibilities develop. The range of inks and types of processes that may be possible could lead to new and exciting possibilities through digital mark-making qualities such as relief, burn out, density, and depth of mark. This will require the development of inks and dyes that lie on top of, burn into, or distort the fabric, and also fabric preparations to create effects such as resists and finishes using chemicals to distort or reveal layers of the textile.

Finally, the military, medical, and cosmetic industries are also funding research into the micro-encapsulation of nanoparticles into ink, which could lead to the digital printing of antimicrobial agents on fabrics, including insect repellents, vitamins, skin conditioners, and fragrances. As these technologies—and the means of applying them to substrates through digital design and print—advance, we can only speculate as to the exciting future of textile design.

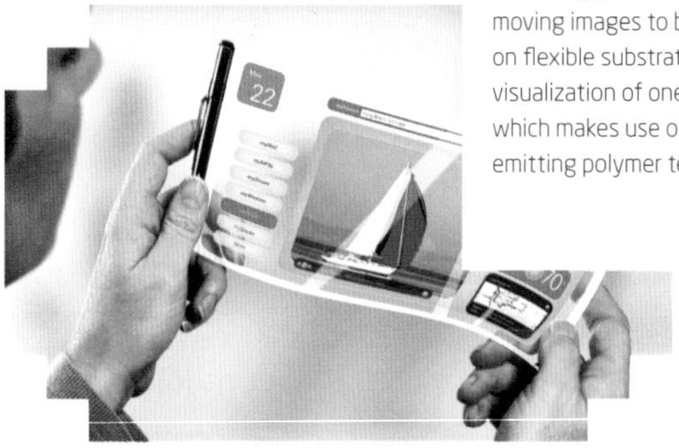

Companies such as the Universal Display Corporation have been carrying out research into the development of flexible screen technology, which will enable moving images to be displayed on flexible substrates. Here is a visualization of one such display, which makes use of organic light-emitting polymer technology.

Both Hussein Chalayan **(above)** and Lumalive by Philips **(below)** provide a glimpse of what the future may hold with the integration of LED technology into their designs.

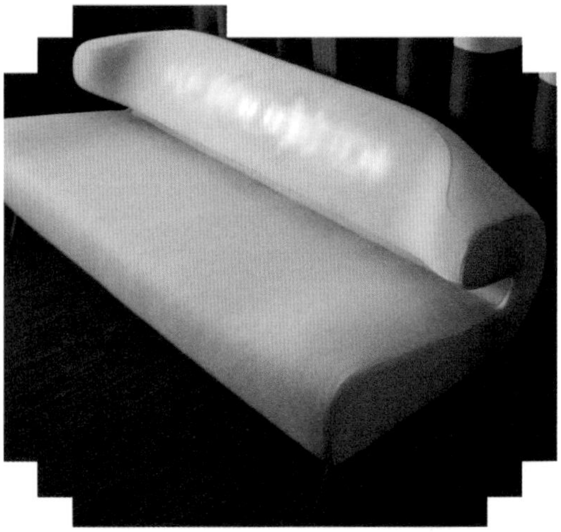

GLOSSARY

A

Alginate A substance extracted from seaweed that is used as a thickening agent.

Avatar A virtual depiction of a human figure, usually animated.

B

Batik A resist-based dyeing technique where wax is applied to a fabric in order to delineate the design by creating a mask before dyeing. (See also Shibori.)

Bespoke A one-of-a-kind customized product; made to order.

Body Scanner A device that is used to capture measurements digitally in order to create a highly accurate three-dimensional model of an individual's body.

C

CIE (Commission Internationale de l'Eclairage) This international commission on illumination was established to create objective standards for defining and communicating color.

CMYK Subtractive color model consisting of cyan, magenta, yellow, and key (black). In digital printing, these four basic ink colors are combined in a matrix of dots to create all the other colors that will be printed.

Color Calibration The management and adjustment of color data within a closed workflow environment for both input and output devices.

Color Gamut A complete subset of colors that can be accurately represented for a given device, such as a monitor or printer. Different devices have different gamuts.

Color Management A software system that controls the conversion of color data for both input and output devices. The goal of a printed-textile color management system is to aid the color matching process as data is converted from emitted RGB into printable CMYK values.

Color Profile Data characterizing the color output of an individual device.

Color Separation (also known as color reduction) A process where the millions of colors found in a photographic or scanned image are systematically reduced down to a finite number of flat colors in order to prepare the design for printing or engraving, or to aid in the creation of colorways.

Color Space A three-dimensional graphic model illustrating a set of colors in which the perceptual difference between colors is represented by points within the color space.

Colorways Versions of the same design that are composed of different color palettes.

Continuous Flow Inkjet Technology (CIJ) One of the two types of inkjet printing technology; in this process a high-pressure pump directs liquid ink from a reservoir through a microscopic nozzle, thus creating a continuous stream of ink. (See also DOD.)

Coordinated Prints A group of print designs based on the same concept and color palette, for use in conjunction with each other.

Croquis The original artwork of a design unit intended for a printed textile, before it is put into repeat.

D

Découpage A technique of decorating the surface of objects such as furniture or boxes by gluing paper cut-outs and illustrations from magazines; this is then sealed with varnish for durability.

Delta e The unit used to quantify the difference between two colors within the CIE color space.

Devoré (also known as burn-out) A method of printing onto fabric with more than one fiber type. The areas of the design are printed with a chemical that burns out one of the fabric's fiber types to leave a translucent area.

Digital Textile Printing A general term that includes all forms of digital printing, such as laser and inkjet technology.

Discharge Printing A method of printing using chlorine or other chemicals to remove areas of previously applied color and replace them with another color.

DOD (Drop on Demand) One of the two types of inkjet printing technology and the most commonly used in digital textile printing; the primary DOD method used to print on textiles is known as piezoelectric. (See also Continuous Flow Ink Technology.)

Dot Matrix In the case of inkjet printing, this is a two-dimensional pattern of CMYK dots that combine to generate the printed image.

dpi (dots per inch) Used to determine the resolution of a digital image, this is the number of dots per inch within a given image's dot matrix.

Dye-sublimation Printing There are two forms of this kind of printing: indirect and direct. In the indirect method, an image is first printed onto paper using disperse dyes. By means of a heat press, the dye particles are then changed into gas, and so transferred onto polyester-based fabric. In the direct method, the image is printed onto the fabric substrate, then fixed using heat.

E

Eco Design A method of designing a product that takes into account its impact on the environment at all stages of its life cycle.

Electrostatic Printing Also known as laser printing. A process where liquid toner is adhered to a light-sensitive print drum; static electricity is then used to transfer the toner onto the printing medium, to which it is fused via heat and pressure. This is the technology used in most photocopiers.

Emulsion A mixture of two unblendable substances; light-sensitive emulsions are often used in the preparation of hand silk screens.

Engraver In the textile industry this refers to a company that prepares silk screens for printing.

Engraving In the textile industry this term refers to the process of preparing a silk screen.

Engineered Print (also known as a placement print) A print where the design is laid out to fit the pattern pieces and structure of a garment.

F

Fixation The process of permanently bonding a dye or pigment to a substrate.

Fixation Agent (also known as a mordant) The chemicals used to aid the process of permanently bonding a pigment or dye to a substrate.

Flat Bed Silk Screen A silk screen that is stretched over a rectangular frame.

Flock Printing A method where areas of the fabric are first printed with glue, and then have flock fibers or paper applied to them. Once dried, the excess flock is removed to leave a raised velvet-like surface.

G

Gravure Printing A printing process where the image to be printed is engraved into a metal plate.

H

Halftone In the context of digital printing, the shade of a color as it gradates from dark to light in an image such as a watercolor.

Heat Photogram A method of printing where dyes are painted onto transfer paper, an object is then impressed directly onto the paper to create a design, and heat is used to transfer the image onto fabric.

I

ICC (International Color Consortium) An organization that creates objective standards for defining and communicating color.

ICC Profile A set of data defined by the ICC that characterizes a color input or output device, or a color space.

Inkjet Printing A specific form of digital printing that works by propelling variably sized droplets of liquid, or molten ink, onto the substrate. The two main types of inkjet printing technology are DOD (drop on demand) and continuous flow. (See also Continuous Flow Inkjet Technology and DOD.)

J

Jpeg (Joint Photographic Expert Group) A popular file format for compressing and saving digitized photographs and images.

L

Laminating A process of using heat or pressure to bond two or more materials, such as plastic and fabric, often used to make waterproof fabric.

Large-Format Printer Term used to describe all printers that are wider than desktop printers, and that are usually designed to accommodate rolls of material and print longer lengths.

Lay Plan A grouping of pattern pieces as they are laid out on a piece of cloth before cutting.

Light Box A specialist piece of equipment used in the color-matching process to view colors under a set of standardized light sources, such as simulated daylight or UV light.

M

Mass Customization A term used to describe the semi-customization of products where the customer is able to personalize an item by choosing from a preset number of features.

Micro-encapsulation A process in which tiny particles or droplets are surrounded by a coating.

Moiré Pattern A pattern where the design or texture of a fabric creates a wave-like effect.

Monochrome An image whose range of colors is made of shades of a single hue, usually black.

Muslin In the context of this book the term refers to a trial version or prototype of a garment.

P

Photochemical Process A process that involves the chemical action of light. Within the context of this book it refers to a technique where a light-sensitive substance is used to transfer an image or photograph onto a substrate.

Photomontage A technique of producing a composite image by combining a series of photographs.

Piezoelectricity (or electric polarity, produced by the piezoelectric effect) An electric potential generated by some materials, such as crystals and certain ceramics, in response to applied mechanical stress. As opposed to thermal DOD, this is the primary technology used to create the ink drops in piezoelectric DOD inkjet printing.

Pigment A substance that imparts color to other materials. Unlike dyes, pigments are not designed to permeate the fabric of the substrate, and bond only to its surface.

Pixel The smallest and most basic unit of visual information for a digitized image.

Polymer A large synthetic molecule composed of repeating structural units, usually of high molecular weight. An example of a polymer-based fabric is polyester.

Primary Colors Basic colors from which all other colors can be made. In the context of this book, the primary colors are those associated with the CMYK and RGB systems. (See also CMYK and RGB.)

Print Head The part of a printer that contains the print nozzles that are responsible for firing the ink droplets at the substrate during printing.

Prototype The original or model on which a product design is based or formed.

R

Raster A raster graphics image or bitmap is a data structure representing a generally rectangular grid of pixels, or points of color, as opposed to a vector-based image that is based on geometry.

Rasterize To convert an image into a matrix of pixels. (See also RIP.)

RGB An additive color model comprised of three basic colors—red, green, and blue—emitted as light and combined to create a broad array of colors. Digital cameras, computer monitors, and televisions all use the RGB system, as opposed to the CMYK system used in digital printing, in which the pigments are not emitted as light, but as ink to be absorbed by the substrate. (See also CMYK.)

Ready-to-wear (also known as prêt a porter) The garments in a fashion designer's collection that are produced in large enough quantities so that they may be marketed widely, as opposed to limited editions, couture, and show pieces.

Repeat A method of laying out/repeating an image unit to create a continuous pattern.

Reprographic The reproduction of text and images through mechanical or electrical means, such as photography and offset printing.

Resolution Term used to measure the level of detail in a digital image. Resolution is determined by the dpi (dots per inch) within a given digital image's dot matrix. (See also dpi.)

RIP (Raster Image Processor) Software used in printing that converts an RGB image into the pixel-based CMYK data needed to drive the printer.

Rotary Screen Printing A form of mechanized silk-screen printing where the screen is a cylinder.

S

Scan The process of capturing the two- or three-dimensional data of an image or object such as a fabric, photograph, or drawing into a digital image. (See also Body Scanner).

Shibori Collective term for the different resist-based techniques of tie-dye, stitch-dye, fold-dye, and pole-wrap-dye. (See also batik.)

Silk Screen A method of printing where a fabric with fine, porous mesh (often silk) is stretched over a frame. The design is then delineated by masking out the areas of the design that will not be printed, leaving areas open for each color, through which the ink is pushed using a squeegee.

Spectrophotometer A device for measuring light intensity as it relates to the color of the light.

Spot Color In printing, a term for any ink other than one of the four CMYK colors (cyan, magenta, yellow, and black).

Steamer In the context of this book, a device that generates steam at high temperatures and is used to fix dyes after printing.

Stencil A technique for printing where holes defining the shape to be printed are cut into a thin material, such as a metal sheet or waxed paper, through which the colorant is then pushed.

Substrate In the context of this book, any material which forms the printing surface.

Sublimation The transference of a substance from a solid to a gaseous state without passing through a liquid stage.

Strike-off An industry term used to describe a test sample meant to indicate what a design will look like once put into production.

T

Thermochromic A substance that changes color in relation to temperature.

Tiff (Tagged Image File Format) A popular format for saving digitized photographs and images.

U

Upcycling The practice of taking something that is disposable and transforming it into something of greater use and value.

V

Vector Graphic A digitized drawing that is based on lines and geometry rather than the individual pixels in raster-based programs, thus allowing it to be manipulated and scaled without affecting its image resolution.

W

Woodblock A carved block used to transfer a design onto fabric.

DIGITAL PRINT AND DESIGN RESOURCES

Digital print bureaus

UK

Artisan: tel. 0044 (0)1625 869859
CAD Works UK Ltd (pigment printing only): www.cadworksuk.co.uk
Centre for Advanced Textiles: www.catdigital.co.uk
Colplan Engineering Ltd: tel. 0044 (0)1706 655899
Digetex: www.digetex.com
Digital Fashion Print, London College of Fashion: www.fashion.arts.ac.uk
Direct Textile Imaging Ltd (heat-transfer printing): tel. 0044 (0)1706 656070
Elanbach: www.elanbach.com
FabPad: www.fabricprint.co.uk
Forest Digital: www.forestdigital.co.uk
J. A. Gillmartin: www.camerongilmartin.co.uk
RA Smart Ltd: www.rasmart.co.uk
The Silk Bureau: www.silkbureau.co.uk

USA

Advanced Digital Textiles: www.advdigitaltextiles.com
Carlisle Finishing LLC: www.itg-global.com
Custom Fabric Printing: www.customprintedfabrics.com
Dream Digital Fabric Printing Services www.dreamfabricprinting.com
Dye-Namix: www.dyenamix.com
Fabrics2Dye4, LLC: www.fabrics2dye4.com
First2Print: www.first2print.com
Karma Kraft: www. karmakraft.com LTS Design: www.ltsdesign.net
ROTHTEC Engraving Corporation: www.rothtec.com
Spoonflower: www.spoonflower.com
The Style Council: www.stylecouncil.com
Supersample: www.supersample.com

Digital printer suppliers

AVA: www.avacadcam.com (international)
Digifab: www.digifab.com (USA)
ITNH: www.itnh.com (USA)
Jacquard Inkjet Fabric Systems: www.inkjetfabrics.com (USA)
Sawgrass: www.sawgrassink.com (international)
Stork: www.storkprints.com (international)
RA Smart Ltd: www.rasmart.co.uk (UK)

Software manufacturers

Adobe software (design): www.adobe.com
Aleph (design, color management, RIP): www.alephteam.com
Artlandia Symmetry Works (design): www.artlandia.com
AVA (design, color management, RIP): www.avacadcam.com
Clickdesign (design): www.clicdesign.com
EAT (design): www.designscopecompany.com
Ergo Soft (color management, RIP):www.ergosoft.ch
Lectra (design, color management, RIP): www.lectra.com
NedGraphics (design, color management, RIP): www.nedgraphics.com
Pointcarré (design, color management, RIP): www.pointcarre.com
Scotweave (design): www.scotweave.com
Shiraz (color management): www.uscgp.com
Stork (color management, RIP): www.storktextile.com
Wasatch (color management): www.wasatch.com
Yxendis (design): www.yxendis.com

Color management hardware

X-Rite: www.usa.gretagmacbethstore.com

Fabric and ink suppliers

UK

AVA (ink): www.avacadcam.com
Colplan Engineering Ltd (ink): tel. 0044 (0)1706 655899
RA Smart Ltd (ink and fabric): www.rasmart.co.uk
Target Transfers (CAD/CUT materials): www.targettransfer.com
Whaleys of Bradford (fabric): www.whaleys.co.uk

USA

AVA (ink): www.avacadcam.com
Digifab (fabric): www.digifab.com
Fisher (fabric): www.fishertextiles.com
Jacquard Inkjet Fabric Systems (ink and fabric): www.inkjetfabrics.com
Stork (ink): www.storkprints.com

Further reading

Adobe Creative Team, *Adobe Illustrator CS5: Classroom in a Book*, Adobe, 2010

Adobe Creative Team, *Adobe Photoshop CS5: Classroom in a Book*, Adobe, 2010

Borrelli, Laird, *Fashion Illustration by Fashion Designers*, Thames & Hudson, 2008

Borrelli, Laird, *Fashion Illustration Next*, Thames & Hudson, 2004

Braddock Clarke, Sarah E., and Marie O'Mahony, *Techno Textiles 2: Revolutionary Fabrics for Fashion and Design*, Thames & Hudson, 2005

Brown, Claudia, and Jessie Whipple Vickery, *Repeat After Me: Creating Pattern Repeats in Illustrator and Photoshop*, www.patternpeople.com/ebook

Colchester, Chloë, *Textiles Today*, Thames & Hudson, 2009

Cole, Drusilla, *Patterns*, Laurence King Publishing, 2008

Colussy, Kathleen M., and Steve Greenberg, *Rendering Fashion, Fabric and Prints With Adobe Illustrator*, Prentice Hall, 2006

Da Cruz, Elyssa, and Sandy Black, *Fashioning Fabrics: Contemporary Textiles in Fashion*, Black Dog Publishing, 2006

Fogg, Marnie, *Print in Fashion*, Batsford, 2009

Jenkyn Jones, Sue, *Fashion Design*, 3rd edition, Laurence King Publishing, 2011

Knight, Kimberly, *A Field Guide to Fabric Design*, Stash Books, 2011

Tallon, Kevin, *Digital Fashion Print with Adobe Photoshop and Illustrator*, Batsford, 2011

Udale, Jenny, *Textiles and Fashion*, AVA, 2008

Ujiie, Hitoshi (ed.), *Digital Printing of Textiles*, Woodhead Publishing, 2006

Useful Information

American Association of Textile Chemists and Colorists: www.aatcc.org

Melanie Bowles, Senior Lecturer in Digital Textiles, Chelsea College of Art and Design: www.melaniebowles.co.uk

Computer Arts (monthly publication): www.computerarts.co.uk

Digital Arts (monthly publication): www.digitalartsonline.co.uk

Digital Stylist (news, software updates, and tutorials in digital design): www.thedigitalstylist.com

Digital Textile (textile industry news website): www.inteletex.com

The Dover Bookshop (copyright-free books and images): www.doverbooks.co.uk

Hitoshi Ujiie, Center for Excellence of Digital Inket Printing of Textiles: www.hitoshiujiie.com

Ceri Isaac, specialist in digital textile design and printing: ceriisaac.wordpress.com

Society of Dyers and Colourists: www.sdc.org.uk

TC2 (non-profit organization that provides information and undertakes research into emerging technologies within the industry): www.tc2.com

TECHEXCHANGE (online trade publication and sourcing portal for technology solutions for the textile industry): www.techexchange.com

Textiles Environment Design: www.tedresearch.net

Textile Futures Research Centre: www.tfrc.org.uk

Trade shows

CITDA (American Association of Textile Chemists and Colorists): www.aatcc.org

FESPA (Federation of European Screenprinters Associations, organizer of the world's leading screenprinting and digital-imaging exhibitions): www.fespa.com

ITMA (The worlds largest international exhibition of textile machinery): www.itma.com

Protextiledigital (European digital textile show): www.english.protextiledigital.com

INDEX

CREDITS

Photo Credits

The authors and publisher would like to thank the following for providing images for use in this book. In all cases, every effort has been made to credit the copyright holders, but should there be any omissions or errors the publisher would be pleased to insert the appropriate acknowledgment in any subsequent edition of this book.

(t = top, b = bottom, c = center, l = left, r = right)
Photography of student work throughout: Melanie Bowles, Rebecca Earley and Kenny Taylor; 4–5: Temitope Tijani; 6: Beatrice Moys; 8–9: Courtesy of Basso & Brooke; 10 t: Dorte Agergaard/Photo by Mathilde Schmidt, Denmark; 10 c: Designer/ Creator: Mark Van Gennip/MRRK/www.mrrk.nl / Photography: Cath Hermans/www.cathhermans.nl / Model – Annabel; 10 b: TRUST FUN! Money Bag, 2010/TRUST FUN! is Jonathan Zawada, Annie Zawada, and Shane Sakkeus; 11 t, b: Corbis/©WWD/Conde Nast; 11 r, l: Catwalking; 12 t: Corbis/©WWD/Conde Nast; 12 c, b: Catwalking; 13: Corbis/©WWD/Conde Nast; 14 tl: Paul Smith © firstVIEW; 14 tr: Nicolette Brunklaus; 14 b: Showroom Dummies courtesy of the designer; 15 l: Ceri Isaac; 15 r: Ceri Isaac and Hitoshi Ujiie; 16 tl, tr: Catwalking; 16 bl: Art Direction: Stefan Sagmeister. Design: Stefan Sagmeister, Joris Laarman, Paul Fung, Mark Pernice, Joe Shouldice, Ben Bryant. Photography: Johannes vam Assem for Droog; 16 br: Designer and Maker Lucinda Abell, Photography by Vivien Fettke, Make up by Immani, Model Rachael Sylvester (Fusion Models); 17 tl: Jula Reindell; 17 tr: Dorte Agergaard/Photo by Mathilde Schmidt, Denmark; 17 b: Imogen Houldsworth; 18 t: Joan Truckenbrod; 18 b: Dill Wallpaper by Michael Angove; 19 l: Hussein Chalayan © firstVIEW; 19 r: Corbis/©WWD/Conde Nast; 20 tl: Wexla; 20 bl: Cloth; 20 tr: Ceri Isaac; 20 br: Avatar software by Opitex; 21: Hussein Chalayan courtesy of the designer; 22–3: Nicola Scofield; 24 t: Jemima Gregson; 24 c: Shift Dress, Marie O'Connor. Moire digital print on cotton. In collaboration with Daniel Mair; 24 b: Rowenna Wilcox; 25: Claire Thorpe; 26 t: Kitty Joseph; 26 b: Beatrice Moys; 27 t: Anjali D'Souza; 27 b: Catherine Frere-Smith; 28: Melanie Bowles; 29: Kitty Joseph; 30: Hana Kitazaki. Photographer Hanako Whiteway; 31 tl, tr: Rosie MacCurrach; 31 b: Victoria Purver; 32 tl, tr: Deborah Vesey; 32 b: Rowenna Wilcox; 33 t: Brian Barrett; 33 b: Henry Muller; 34–35 c, 35 b: Melanie Bowles; 35 t: Melanie Bowles; 36 t: Melanie Bowles and Kathryn Round; 36 b: Alexa Ball; 37: Nada Herceg; 38: Emma Stone; 39 tl: Temitope Tijani; 39 bl: Jemima Gregson; 39 r: Deja Abati; 40: Melanie Bowles; 44: Emamoke Ukeleghe; 48: Melanie Bowles; 52: Claire Thorpe; 56: Jemima Gregson; 62; Katie Irving Jones; 66, 69: Daisy Butler; 70: Hong Yeon Yun; 76: Claire Turner; 80: Andrea Patterson; 81 t: Westside Story © Getty Images; 86–7: Rachel de Joode for Soon Salon; 89: Vicki Murdoch; 90, 94, 100, 104, 106 t, 112 t: Design by Melanie Bowles; 92, 96: Design based on Victoria Purver's *Ophilia*; 108 br: Daisy Butler; 116 t: Design by Kenny Taylor; 120–1, 123: Chae Young Kim; 124 t: Amy Isla Breckton; 124 b: Jennis Li Cheng Tien; 125 tl, tr: Holly Holmes; 125 b: Pauline Fernandez; 126 l: Melanie Bowles; 126 r: Photo: Melanie Bowles/Model: Maya Dolman-Bowles; 130 t: Katie Hoppe; 136 l: Melanie Bowles; 136 r: Photo: Melanie Bowles/Model: Ashleigh Lyon; 140–1: Melanie Bowles; 142 t, c: Clara Vuletich;142 b, 143 tl: Claire Canning; 143 tc: Melanie Bowles and Sarah Dennis; 143 tr: Shelly Goldsmith; 143 b; 144 bl, br: Dominique Devaux; 144 t: Zoe Barker; 145: Emamoke Ukeleghe; 146–7: Louisa-Claire Fernandes; 148 t: Amelia Mullins; 148 b: Charlotte Arnold; 149 tl: Emily House; 149 tr: Matthew Williamson © firstVIEW; 149 b: Georgina Papandreou; 150–1: Richard Weston; 152: Photo of Stacey Wickens by Melanie Bowles; 153 tr: Melanie Bowles; 153 l, br: Joanna Fowles; 154: Emma Rampton; 155 tl, tr: Dominique Devaux; 155 cl: Katie Irving Jones; 155 bl: Andrea Patterson; 155 br: Photini Anastasi; 156–7: Helen Amy Murray; 158 l: Melanie Bowles; 158 tl, bl: Nicky Gearing and Debbie Stack; 159 l: Andrea Patterson; 159 r, b: Catherine Frere-Smith; 160 t: Zoe Barker; 160 c, b: Alice Potter; 161 tl, bl: Shelly Goldsmith: 161 tr: Sara Lamusias; 162 t: Taina Lehtinen; 162 c, b: Chetna Prajapati; 163 t: Victoria Collins; 163 b: Temitope Tijani; 165: Rebecca Earley; 166–7: Melanie Bowles; 168: Joyce Clissold courtesy the Museum and Contemporary Collection, Central Saint Martins; 169 t: "Toile de Jouy" print courtesy V&A Museum; 169 bl, br: Melanie Bowles; 170 t: Flatbed screen printer courtesy Magnoprint; 170 ct: Rotary screen printer courtesy Stork Prints BV; 170 b: Paul Smith courtesy of the designer; 171: "Hobie" shirt courtesy Benny's Aloha Shirts, CA; 172 l: Illustration by Advanced Illustration Ltd; 172 tr: Courtesy Robustelli; 172 br: Courtesy RA Smart; 173 t: Jemima Gregson; 173 c: Petra Boase; 173 b: Photini Anastasi; 174–5 t, c: Melanie Bowles; 175 b: Daisy Butler; 178: ISIS printer courtesy OSIRIS Digital Prints BV; 179: Hitoshi Ujiie; 180–1, 183 c, 183 br: Images courtesy AVA; 183 t: Ceri Isaac; 183 bl: Courtesy Nick Cicconi at John Kaldor UK Ltd; 184: Images courtesy of Ratti SpA; 185: First2Print, New York; 186 t: Courtesy Universal Display Corporation; 186 c: Hussein Chalayan © catwalking.com; 186 b: Courtesy Philips.

Publisher's Acknowledgments

The publisher would like to thank the following: Anita Racine, Department of Textiles and Apparel, Cornell University; Edward J. Herczyk, School of Engineering and Textiles, Philadelphia University; Philippa Brock, School of Fashion and Textiles, CSM, University of the Arts, London; and Marcy L. Koontz, Department of Clothing, Textiles, and Interior Design, University of Alabama.

Authors' Acknowledgments

We would like to thank all the designers, students, organizations, and individuals whose contributions and support have made this book possible. Their shared enthusiasm for the subject matter has been a revelation. Special thanks are due to Hitoshi Ujiie, Amanda Briggs, Ashleigh Lyon, Betty Borthwick, AVA, and our editors at Laurence King Publishing. Thanks also to Eleanor Ridsdale for her wonderful book design. Invaluable support was given by the research departments, staff, and students at Chelsea College of Art and Design as well as the London College of Fashion. The project was aided by funding from the University of the Arts, London, and CLIP/CETL (Creative Learning in Practice Centre for Excellence in Teaching and Learning). We are also most grateful to Kenny Taylor, Kathryn Round, Jemima Gregson, Claire Thorpe, Andrea Patterson, Emamoke Ukeleghe, Katie Irving Jones, Hong Yeon Yun, Chae Young Kim, Daisy Butler, Katie Hoppe, Jane Walker, and Alex Madjitey, who generously assisted in the development of the design tutorials.

Last but not least, heartfelt thanks belong to Philip Dolman; Ben, Eve, and Maya Dolman-Bowles; Barbara Isaac; and all our friends and family who have lent their encouragement along the way.